TESTIMONIALS

As a man who's had his share of successes and setbacks, I can affirm that Carl is right on. Excellent book for the Man who needs a comeback.

David Lindemuth

Chief Strategist" at SouthlandAIM Investments.

Carl Logrecco is the real deal; the world is a better place, thanks to his capability and commitment to changing lives.

Chris Steely

Managing Director GPS Business Group

Carl Logrecco has created the ultimate man's manual on how to get back up, brush off the dirt, and reframe any challenge into sustainable new knowledge and direction for exciting new adventures to come.

Ray Doktor, Psy. D.

Carl is a catalyst for us all to stand up, live our dharma no matter what others think or believe.

David Sunwolf

Entrepreneurs & Business Owners will greatly benefit from Carl's abilities, experience and effectiveness in achieving goals.

Billionaire Bill Bartmann

(USA Today 23rd Wealthiest Man)

I cannot imagine someone more committed to helping me understand what I am about in life, finding my why, and staying aligned with my purpose. I have completely shifted my outlook on life.

Marc Rosenthal

President Mars World

His ideas are realistic and ones that I felt that I could do right away! This motivated me immediately. So I highly recommend this book--you won't be sorry!

Scott Dickerson

Capitol Growth Inc.

Carl hits it head on. He gets it. He gets how to touch the male psyche. No matter how you're wired, Carl will help you move forward faster!

Ken Stark

The Starks Team

SETBACK, NOW FORWARD

HOW TO ARCHITECT A MASTERFUL COMEBACK

CARL LOGRECCO

Motivational Press
LEADERS IN GLOBAL PUBLISHING

Published by Motivational Press, Inc.
1777 Aurora Road
Melbourne, Florida, 32935
www.MotivationalPress.com

Manufactured in the United States of America.

ISBN: 978-1-62865-431-8

CONTENTS

To my daughter Tristin,

It is because of you I fought so hard to become the man I am today. It is your love that sets me on fire.

I am forever grateful for who you are, and the lady you are becoming. I know that you will manifest everything you came to this planet for. I love you.

Love Dad.

ACKNOWLEDGMENTS

The greatest gift I have ever been given is my intuition, I give many thanks to this gift for guiding this book and its success. My intuition has also guided me to the love of my life, Jaime Gunn.

You, Jaime, are my best friend, my lover, my rock, and now my bride. The phrase "ask and you shall receive" is an understatement with you, I got more than I asked for with you. I am eternally grateful that I get to travel the rest of my life journey with you.

Thank you to my public relations dynamo, Matthew Dillon of MDPR. You are always setting me up to win and fighting the good fight so I can serve my purpose in life. Thank you!

Thank you to me publisher, Justin Sachs of Motivational Press for finding me on LinkedIn and his patience for the "endless" amounts of small changes during the editing of this book.

Amy Lipner, my editor. I found a gem in her, thank you Upwork. Amy help reshape and restructure how this book was presented and the impact of my words. Thank you Amy!

To my Mom and Dad, thank you for teaching me resilience, and that no matter how hard life knocks you down, just keep moving forward.

My sister Lisa, who wears her heart on her sleeve. You are a stand alone kind of gal, and I see how amazing you are. I love you.

To Dr. Ray, Chris Steely, Marc Rosenthal, David Lindemuth, Scott Dickerson, and Dick Lyles, each of you are truly amazing men who have supported me along the way. Your guidance and advice are part of the reason why this book exists. Thank you!

To Bill Bartmann who passed away before this book published, you are the most kind soul I have come to know. It was an honor to know you, and have you as a business partner. You are missed dearly my friend.

And to the rest of you that have touched me along my journey. I thank you. You have helped shape into the man I am today. I can only say, you do not go unnoticed in my life. I am grateful for you!

OVERVIEW

SO WHY DID YOU FAIL? In the pursuit of any success, there is a hidden fear that you might fail. While most try to educate themselves, create the best system, build a smart business plan, or gird themselves with relationships or life goals, you cannot BE free to fully GO FOR IT and put who you are on the line for what you want. For many, the fear of failure makes success a grinding experience, but it doesn't have to be this way.

Isn't it true, life doesn't always turn out the way you thought it would? No one taught us how to fail forward. Let alone re-create and reinvent our business life in a way that empowers us to move forward, become more powerful men, and anchor ourselves in purpose.

You know this story…a business that was destined for success is closing its doors. All it takes is an accident, a mistake, a divorce or even a small financial shift to set us on a path of confusion and pain.

Failure is hard to accept.

Disappointment hurts.

And trying to figure it all out rarely works.

So, ask yourself, what do you do when you have a SETBACK?

The truth may sting a bit. For most men they lose their raw masculine essence -- their spirit that makes them feel alive, that women love about men, and that our children respect. Far too many men give in, flat line or embark on another journey of struggle running into the same issues before. But there is a better what.

No one knows better than Coach Carl. Carl's journey has taken him to the highest highs and the lowest lows in life, until finding a way to balance it all. Like most men who dreamed of building an epic business-life, only to discover how overwhelming, burdensome and unfulfilling success can become. Often leading to some type of a crash.

This book is written to support men making an EPIC comeback after experiencing a setback, failure, or significant transition in life and business. This book answers the two most important questions that men ask themselves when they have failed, or experienced a major setback, "What do I do?" and "How do I do it?" Meanwhile, those questions will not set your soul on fire and manifest your purpose you are here to live out.

For businessmen and entrepreneurs to make a comeback they must learn a few things:

1. **Re-wire** how we approach success, money and achievement into a more powerful, complete and authentic mindset. One that sets us up to win, not having to grind and suffer our way to the top. For men, success has been a sacrifice, filled with pressure and burden. It consumes our life while trying to create a life. It's exhausting, and the masculine consciousness has fallen in far too many categories that women are now picking up where we have failed.
2. **Re-frame** the stories and events that led you to experience disappointment and regret can be reframed into a NEW perspective that frees up your passion, purpose and ability to create results.
3. **Re-set** your operating system, your identity, your brand, and your business into a richer, more satisfying experience, one that is no longer limited, but a complete "limitless edition" of what is possible for man.
4. **Re-ignite** your soul to feel on fire again. To do what you are here to do without living in doubt, fear of failure or questioning your journey.

This book is a blue print for your comeback. It only requires your courage and willingness to take on your journey again, reclaim what you think you lost, rebuild what you believe is your birthright and experience more freedom along the way.

Too often we lose pieces of ourselves in pursuit of a goal or dream. Success and failure often cause men to sell parts of themselves, even their souls.

Unfortunately, NOT everyone gets those pieces back.

Men are raised to get over stuff, to be tough, move on, and suck it up. We are taught to believe we have to sacrifice to get what we want. This simply isn't true, but these beliefs are deeply engrained in our biology and upbringing.

The roles for success, marriage, and fatherhood have expanded and frankly, don't work for all of us. Men and women have come to be interconnected. It is no longer seen as solely a man's job to make money outside of the home, while his wife stays home and raises the children. We have adopted these roles as couples and as single individuals.

The old-fashioned male-female role constraints, have made it hard for men, especially those who grew up believing there are specific ways to look like or feel like a man. It's nearly impossible to work hard in business, take care of your health, attend to kids, relate to the feminine who wants time and romance, especially if you are financially strapped or feel like a failure. Men limit themselves to feel they have more control, while starving for next level growth. If you strengthen your capacity, how you approach your life, business and success and operate from a higher ground, having it all becomes the norm. You're no longer a status quo seeker.

Many successful businessmen have problems – whether it is their marriage, kids or health -- that money alone won't fix. I will dig into this in greater depth later, but for now, it is enough to say that these men have an empire to disguise their tender masculinity. With an empire, they won't hurt as much when other areas of their life fail. Perhaps the biggest downfall of mankind is using success as a cover up.

The Future of EPIC MEN is not in pushing or pulling, but in HONORING and OWNING his soul, learning to keep it lit, on purpose and making progress.

And to do this, YOU must be as real as possible.

Let me be clear with you, I am nothing special or more valuable than you. Most of my success is a direct result of how spectacularly I've failed and just as dramatically rose again. Can you make a comeback? YES, you can and you can rise again.

I am sure you have experienced failure, but so what. You must not confuse a single failure with being conquered. No man can be defeated unless he has chosen to be defeated. Even then, you can reclaim your power. It is never too late. You must believe this is the beginning of you summoning the courage to be unshakable.

Two Types of Men

There are two types of men, there is the Lionheart, who is internally driven. He is motivated by peace, love, and joy and wants to make a difference. The Lionheart will sacrifice wealth, money, and success to keep love, connections, joy, and family unity. He is the nice guy who rarely hits the mark and makes it all happen. That's his primary way he feels he can support, protect, and provide. The Lionheart is more feminine or introverted – passive and empathic.

In contrast, the Alpha Man spends his time building an empire, controlling outcomes, and hoping to experience what the Lionheart has: to be loved regardless. The Alpha Man believes that once he is successful, he will have time to enjoy his kids, travel and perhaps focus on his health. He is driven by success, wealth, and achievement. He sacrifices what the Lionheart will not, and he is often more successful. He always wants more and nothing is ever enough. Despite other areas of his life that are on pause or out of balance.

But neither man has it all. There must be balance. The difficulty is you cannot have balance if you operate one way -- like a half man, all heart or all alpha. This comeback will require you to become more integrated in all aspects of your identity. You can be a great father, build a business, hit the gym, and have free time. That's what it looks like to be fully integrated. Integration, means thriving in each of these areas, not just going through the motions.

These two men live differently. The feminine Lionheart feels HURT and DISAPPOINTED during a setback, whereas the Alpha Male feels as if he FAILED or has been defeated. He will beat himself up and try harder the next go-around.

But, when you ask either man, "why did you fail?" Their responses are along these lines:

» I trusted the wrong people.

» I didn't have enough money or funding.

» Didn't have enough time to make it work.

» The system didn't work like it was supposed to.

» Some other company outperformed us.

» We missed the opportunity.

» I ran into obstacle after obstacle without a solution.

In other words, they blame a LACK of RESOURCES. *Time, energy, money, system efficiency, another company had more resources or performance abilities, missed opportunities are all resources.* Except men don't see it that way, men don't see it's a lack of resourcefulness on their part. Rarely is it their responsibility. "I'm the captain of my ship, I chose to create, and I will recreate," is a mantra of responsibility and provides potential to make a comeback. Blaming and pointing fingers at a problem you cannot change, leaves you stuck and disheartened. The fact is, YOU are resourceful enough to turn around any of those reasons, to believe otherwise does not support you, or your future.

You can make anything work no matter what! If it was your destiny, it will work. DESTINY always works, but people may NOT! Destiny rarely knocks; it only shows up if you're in the game and not sitting on the sidelines. You must knock first.

A powerful man says, "my team didn't show up because I relied on them, instead of empowering them." That would be responsible. If anything in your world is not working, your energy is always the common denominator. If it's your destiny, it's always within your power. Only YOU can be responsible that is how true power operates.

A POWERFUL MAN IS ALWAYS
RESPONSIBLE FOR HIS ENERGY.

It's rarely someone or something else that has caused you to fail. If you feel like a failure, YOU are the reason and the CURE for it. To BLAME anything else HOLDS you captive to remaining in your setback and stuck.

This book is the beginning in which, MEN can learn to make comebacks as a life journey, not a momentous one-time event.

It's a SHIFT in your operating system. By shifting your operating system, your come back can be filled with an unconquerable, undefeatable state of mind.

Chapter 1

JUST SAY IT

One of my first momentous failures was in baseball. By the age of 12 I was signing autographs for umpires who said, "Don't forget me when you make it, ok?" Once I had a group of parents who offered me money to let their kid get a hit. I knew my path early on, so I thought.

The more people wanted to see me succeed, the more I wanted to see myself succeed. As a pitcher, I was intense. I worked hard, I trained more and did all the pitching lessons I could fit in my schedule. I was obsessed.

Suddenly, for no apparent reason, everything became difficult. When I should have been getting better, I was getting worse. After having the best game of my life, someone said, "You're so much happier when you're catching and playing first, than when you pitch. I hate being around you when you pitch." It was a shock to hear this -- mainly because it was true.

This was a BIG red flag for me, inside I was not happy, unless I got what I wanted. I didn't like pitching. It wasn't for me, but I got to be in control, have others think I was amazing, and get attention. All of this made me feel like a powerful young man, which was exactly what I wanted.

Who watches the catcher during an entire game? No one stares at the first baseman either. The pitcher is the star, but that stardom did not last. After becoming well-known in San Diego for my pitching, suddenly my star fell, and I couldn't stop it.

After losing scholarships from a botched shoulder surgery, I went through an identity crisis at the ripe age of 18. This was exactly what men at all ages go through after a failure. I was unsure why I was on this planet. I had to accept my new life the way it was at that moment. It felt as if I had failed. I didn't know what to do about it, or what I was going to do with my life after my career dried up. It took a year before I could come to terms that my baseball path was over. I learned then that it is better just to say it, whatever it is for you. Just say what that failure is or was.

I BUILT UP A WORLD THAT CRASHED. I WAS PERFECTLY EQUIPPED TO SUCCEED IN A WORLD THAT NO LONGER EXISTED.

It was the biggest setback and utter failure; I began losing my baseball friends who went on to the next level. Suddenly, University aspirations were gone and replaced with Community College vibes. I was living at home, instead of a dorm room in a Division 1 College. Neither my family nor I knew how to relate this new life, one that none of us wanted. Even my father stopped talking to me, as baseball was the rock of our already inauthentic relationship.

All I knew myself to be was a baseball player, it defined my thoughts, feelings, and behaviors. Winning, losing, and grinding hard in practice was my life. It shaped me. Without it, I had no operating system. I was a hard drive without a program to run. I suddenly became clueless, half man without a purpose for existing. I felt being a baseball player was my identity.

MEN OFTEN MISTAKE WHAT THEY DO WITH WHO THEY ARE, THAT'S BACKWARDS!

I chose to have my life as a one-sided person. Baseball, although it was my purpose at the time, came to an end, but that does not mean my life came to an end. I couldn't help but wonder if I fooled myself, by believing I could turn pro. Despite feeling that way, it wasn't the end. Men fear giving their life to something and having it not work out, we don't want to be made out to be a fool. In retrospect, being fooled is easy if you're not following your purpose.

YOUR PURPOSE WILL NEVER FOOL YOU.

I set up my own setback, not by giving my life to the process, but rather by seeing myself only as a baseball player. The moment you think you are what you do, you're a slave to it. If I relate to myself as a man of instincts, intuition, motivated, disciplined, team oriented, loyal, and determined to do what it takes to win. If these qualities were my focus, I could carry on quite well, as they are applicable to life, not baseball exclusively. Little did I know these same skills, strengths, and characteristics led me to a far better life. Are you connecting the dots here?

YOU DO WHAT YOU DO BECAUSE IT'S WHO YOU ARE. NOT TO BECOME SOMEONE. YOUR PURPOSE PROCEEDS WHAT YOU DO.

A Failure or Setback May Feel Like This:

It is important to evaluate what you may be feeling about your failure, setback or recent experience. Depending on how recent your failure was or where you are in your comeback, take note of the following types of feelings.

Numb, *hard to feel excited or inspired by much.*

Disappointed, *shame or let down that things did not work the way you envisioned.*

Failure, *feeling down, dead or shut down.*

Hurt, *you want to hide or experience anger.*

Confused, *what do I do? And how?*

Spinning, *a mind going 100 MPH.*

Fatigue/Lethargy, *a heavy feeling about daily task, people or hobbies that used to excite you no longer do.*

When men feel hurt or emotionally suppressed, we also get blue balls. I say this bluntly. We lose the feeling of life. Our willpower, hormone, and desire zone all plummet. These are areas in a man's body that release dopamine and testosterone. They come to a halt when there is emotional suppression, it's a science as much as a feeling. Notice if you have an increased desire for external things to lift you up or you don't have a desire for anything at all.

This is also a time when drugs, alcohol, increased desire for sex or impotence, becoming overweight or lazy and the, "I don't care" attitudes begins to happen. Thinking that porn, prostitutes, sky diving and even doing things outside normal character, become saving graces.

It's a critical time. Men either AVOID things that could cause another failure, or they give in and give up. Do yourself a favor brother; don't let the world cause you to become guarded, disengaged, or cautious. It's how the masculine hides, once this happens, it's nearly impossible to create a new future.

Giving in sounds like, "I need to take care of responsibilities and put my destiny on the back burner." Giving up sounds like, "I don't care." In other words, you stopped feeling the pain associated with failure, disappointment and regret. Suppressing these feelings cuts you off from overcoming the past, letting it go and creating a new future. It can also give rise to anger.

What men really want is to be motivated or inspired to operate from LOVE. More on that later. Men really want to feel liberated and on fire with their life. The moment you stop feeling the pain, your setback becomes a several year challenge, instead of a progressive comeback.

POWERFUL MEN EMBRACE PAIN & FEAR. THIS ALLOWS THEM TO POWER UP, WHILE RESISTING LEADS TO A POWER LOSS.

Dig Deep

What is the truth about your current reality?

What is the actual failure? Is it the business closing? Is it a divorce? A story? A bankruptcy?

What?

What label have you given your failure? That label, whatever it is, is keeping you down. Feeling like you have failed, then labeling yourself a "loser" is gumming down your pain. If you numb the pain by avoiding it, you may never make a comeback. Hence the inside out game. What exists under that pain is what needs to be addressed. It's just a feeling and it's time to let it go. If you don't, masculinity will take action, trying to avoid those feelings and cause a struggle in the process. Think of it this way, one half of you is hurt, and feeling down, but the other half of you is motivated by some idea. Do you really think you can create an epic comeback with just one part of you? While hiding the other half of you? Isn't this why men refer to their wives as, "the better half?" In this simple analogy I want you to understand that the struggle is like a tug of war, every step forward, you take your shit with you. While trying desperately to ensure it does not manifest.

This is the time to be radically honest with yourself and speak the unspeakable. Those feelings you don't want to feel, don't want to admit are present, albeit hidden. If there is withheld communication on your part, you won't feel FREE from the story, it will weigh you down. Let's get real, you need to unveil the pain. Look at it because the pain is NOT who you are. But rather, a part of you that is relating to things so personally that you cannot see it -- yet! This is not the time to blind yourself. There is nothing more powerful and sexy about a man who has nothing to hide. In fact, it makes you untouchable and unfuckable.

Man's conditioning

Feeling NUMB or shut down is part of a man's conditioning; it's what we do and how we are wired. That means ignoring feelings, in fact, you have done it so many times growing up, it has become an automatic pattern. The challenge is that the mind does not know how to shut down a part of you; it's all or nothing. Your mind cannot stop a part of it from working, contrary to man thinking he can compartmentalize his challenges; the mind cannot block a part of it without blocking all of it. Therefore, the more we block or suppress, the more we vibrate at a lower frequency. It's your job to come out from underneath that trap.

While you're trying to make your comeback with a mind that has shut you down, your potential exists under that shutdown. Which is why we often feel the "odds are against us or struggle for what we want." You know you are better than this, but you're unable to access the potential you have.

YOUR POTENTIAL IS AVAILABLE IF YOU TAP INTO WHAT IS UNDERNEATH YOUR SHUTDOWN.

Men are conditioned to fight for what they want. While fighting for what you want may be required at times, you're only fighting with yourself. During his stardom, Tiger Woods said on CNN with Larry King, "There are only two competitors in golf, you and the course. I am not competing with anyone else." He was very wise at a young age, in his mind there was no one else on the course but him. The news covered him, and he owned the course and the game each time.

Then things changed, Tiger hit rock bottom. His wife, his marriage, his career and his relationships with himself, all came crashing down. Nearly 10 years later now and he still has not made a comeback. His behavior is all an inside out job. If you listen to him talk he has no emotions, he is emotionally void and numb. He cannot figure out how to comeback, and so he does what many men do, fix their mechanics, "how too" and get physically better and more focused. Once his swing is better, he will think everything else is also, despite being loaded with pain. Once his body has healed from injuries, he will assume his comeback is complete. This is a prime example of, ***"if you don't confront your demons, the world will confront them for you, and you will NOT like it when that happens."*** This single truth can change your life. If you doubt what is happening in the media, one man after another getting confronted and losing their families, jobs, and endorsements for past issues like harassment, assault, sexism, etc.

Fighting has become the stigma of man, and frankly, it's not the easier route. You are no more a man for carrying the bricks of your past, than you are for letting go and creating a new path. It's just life, stop evaluating your manhood based on the "fight" instead of the journey of your own evolution.

Your damn belief about FAILURE is the failure or setback you feel. Nothing more! If all the men we admire, from Edison to Facebook and Google, had your belief about failure, would they have made their vision a reality?

MAN'S LIFE IS A SERIES OF CREATING AND RECREATING EVENTS, THAT INCLUDES RECREATING FAILURES AND SETBACK.

I am not an astronaut, an accountant, a plumber or a mechanic. I never will be. Do I understand some of these skills? Yes, but that does not make me less worthy as a man. I may in one sense NOT be worthy, but the truth is, IT IS NOT my path. Therefore, my worth in comparison to something that is NOT my path is NOT relevant. Do you see and understand?

Unworthiness is the comparison to something that may not be on your path anyway. When I lived the way the world wanted me to, I rarely felt worthy of success. I wouldn't compare your worst day to someone else's highlight reel. That is a formula to feel worse about yourself and your accomplishments. What is more important is that you see the path other men are on and why, not that they have succeeded, and you have not. You cannot and do not have to *be it all*. And women don't necessarily believe you have to be either.

The masculine in you, that is constantly pushing the envelope. Telling you to stand on the edge of a cliff and move towards your vision, all the while embracing your fear. You have to RISK failure to fully experience your masculine energy, it's how the masculine works. But failure on PURPOSE does not exists. Do not confuse the two. Failing on purpose is a lesson or opportunity, but failing when you are not on purpose is suffering and painful.

Is My Divorce a Failure?

Have you been married before? Would you call your divorce a failure?

Until my coach made it clear that I was a failure, I had never seen my divorce in that way. Naturally, who would want to accept it as a failure? It's easier to avoid experiencing failure. Since I cannot change what happened, why admit it? Except that the most powerful thing to do is accept it and rise up again, without acceptance, I would defeat myself from future opportunities before they even arrived.

For men, getting married to the woman you love, building a family, paying the bills, and handling the responsibilities, as odd as it sounds, is somehow a success. Is it an American dream? Some men have been sucked into this dream, some consider it an accomplishment. The world does not decide your path or purpose unless you choose to subscribe to it.

Yet, it's one that none of us learned how to build or maintain. Or one we were prepared for in advance. Very few men can say they were ready for marriage, emotions, parenting, and business. We learned through the job training or the hard way, that is risky!

Surviving through life and making it all work is no epic accomplishment. Some view it as an accomplishment if they survived it. However, succumbing to conditioning is not the accomplishment men are looking for. There is no accomplishment in struggle because the struggle does not impact or create transformation. Usually, after the struggle, you find another thing to struggle with and around the rat race you go.

WHEN MAN INVENTS AN EXTERNAL OPPONENT, HE UNKNOWINGLY KEEPS HIMSELF LOCKED IN SURVIVAL "FIGHT AND GRIND" MODE AND MAKES THE CONDITIONS AND CIRCUMSTANCES BIGGER THAN HIMSELF.

Eric was a big-time stockbroker, family man, and multimillionaire in the UK. For whatever reason, every 7 years he went broke, hired strippers, and started drinking again. Literally every 7 years. He realized that every time he made millions of dollars he was less happy. He began seeing patterns that made his life harder and time was scarce. His family missed him and the love and connection with his family dwindled. Although, they were able to take more vacations and do more things than without money, he spent more time working and worrying. Eric was the perfect half man, yet in the eyes of many (mainly other half-men) he appeared to have it all.

Eric never shifted how he was showing up; he covered it up well. He would drive a huge amount of success, fail, and then redeem himself again a year later. He was a machine. Imagine that, 7 years of success, massive failure for one-year, then epic success and redemption and the cycle would repeat again. It's exhausting just to type it! Almost like he was punishing himself or was it a form of unnecessary sabotage.

Eric wants and struggles with the same thing most men do. To feel loved and appreciated. He was also terrified of turning out as a nobody. The male mind equates that to being alone. At the core of who we are, even the biggest and badass businessmen want love and appreciation for what they have done. The last 30 years of Eric's life, he admitted he wasn't sure if he had ever felt either, let alone if it was real.

A POWERFUL MAN IS NEVER FOOLED BY WHAT HE REALLY WANTS AND IT IS ALMOST ALWAYS TO FEEL VALUED AS A WAY TO BE LOVED!

It's easy to overrate the HAVING of something as a huge success and undervalue the reality of WHO WE BECOME to have it all. Who we become cannot be taken, no matter how many times we fail. No matter how much money you lose, your heart and character cannot be taken, except by you. There is a sad need for men to have evidence to validate their existence. Material possessions, in a man's mind, are evidence he has succeeded. But an amazing heart and character is NOT evidence of man's success? What is ultimately missing is "integration." When a man integrates who he is and his place in the world he can have it all, he can have both and not be defined by anything other than his character and purpose.

That is where man is defined; his character. His decisions to live fully and his overcoming of challenges along the path. Epic men want to be defined here, other men by external means. You are NOT your results. You are not your behavior. You are not the car, boat or house you have. However, most men define themselves by such, it's the ultimate mantrap set up for failure.

Men in business often live for the illusion that one day, when the business takes off, they will have time for family, kids, wife, and vacations. The truth is you can have all that right now, but your capacity is so compartmentalized that you think you can only have a small number of choices now.

3 Valuable Lessons Here

First, I created my divorce, I am 100% responsible and my ex is 100% responsible. There is no blame, shame or fault here. I chose to spend more time blaming than being responsible. The fact is I was afraid of being alone. I get to own that.

Second, I was stressed, overwhelmed, and easily shaken. I could not manage my own emotions. I shut down and lost my balls on a daily basis. The moment I shut down, the marriage was over. My wife at the time became more masculine and controlling. In other words, she did not feel safe and she ran me over. So, I stopped showing up because I was overwhelmed with the stress of trying to figure it all out and change things. Then I stopped showing up all together.

Third, I bailed out because I could not handle it anymore. I couldn't find a way to create enough space for me to SEE the truth, so I ran. And by doing so, I suffered intense consequences for it. The fact is that if I followed my intuition from the start, I never would have started dating her.

That is how you own your failure. As a result, I made a comeback that was better than anything I had felt before and frankly, more sustainable than ever.

Chapter 1 Notes: Just Say It

» Men often mistake what they do with who they are.

» Trust your purpose, it will not fool you into believing something that is not true. But your ego will.

» Do what you do because it is who you are.

» Powerful men embrace fear and pain. Avoiding it causes shutdown, pain and hurt.

» Just say it, what really happened? What is the pain you feel? Stop holding on to the past.

- » Massive potential is on the other side of those feelings you have been avoiding. Dig deeper.
- » Powerful men confront their demons. If you don't they will confront you anyways and you won't like it when its NOT your choice to have to face them. Chose to face them before they chose.
- » A man's life is about creating and re-creating, most men get stuck on how to re-create.
- » There is no situation, circumstance or problem that is bigger than you.
- » YES, a comeback is possible, you can recover, rebuild and redefine your life, business and family as you chose to.

END OF CHAPTER 1 NOTES.

I am with you brother. You got this. You can and will succeed at anything you chose to.

Let's move on to chapter 2.

Chapter 2

DEFINE AND REDEFINE SETBACK

Everyone fails at least once, but that does not mean you have been conquered. It is important to make the distinction between the two. Failing at something does not mean you've been beaten or something or someone has triumphed over you. Although, it might feel that way, avoid collapsing what happened with your feelings about it.

One of my favorite things to do is watch interviews of sports coaches after an important game. Listening to a coach after his team loses an important game when they were favored to win, reveals a lot about the coach. One of my favorite coaches is Geno Auriemma, the girls' basketball coach of UConn. He keeps things in perspective. In 2017 his team was 36-0 and 111-0 overall the past few years. They lost to Mississippi in the semifinals, his girls were crushed and most of the fans were stunned.

When I listened to him, he had made it clear that this day was coming. "It's inevitable," he said. "At some point we have to lose, this one game does not take away from our legacy. It does not take way from who we have become, or our future." They got beat and fell short, but they did not get conquered. They did not lose their identity, passion or purpose, at all!

It's rare to become so conquered that you cannot make a comeback. Even men who have lost limbs have made comebacks. To be conquered, you must completely believe you have no identity left as a man. That who you are is gone and not coming back. Unless you have no choice or say so in the matter, you cannot authentically claim you've been conquered. I have found that men *feel* they have been conquered, but when that focus on choices, there perspective opens.

There are many ways to view setbacks and to view failure. The important question is "how do you view it?" "How are you viewing it?"

A setback is defined as an event or occurrence in which you have to stop progress or a success. A baseball team has their top two players get hurt a week before the world series. That is a setback. They have not failed because they have not started yet. But it is a setback to the team to have their top two players on the bench.

A failure would be, the team losing the world series, at least in their mind they have failed. A defeat, a loss usually followed with disappointment, regret and some level of hurt.

Chronic Setback Syndrome

Years ago, a company called me from Nevada, they were in marketing, like me, and we were competing for the same clients. At that time, I was focused on working with doctors.

This company called RNS asked me to be a consultant with them. Unfortunately, we faced a grave setback, they didn't get the funding they had hoped and could not pay me. The deal as worth about $12 million once the funding went through and my cut was 10%.

Ouch!

This was early on in my career and I really needed a home run. On so many levels I needed this to come through. This was a big setback and if it had gone through it would have knocked out all my dreams that year, and in many ways opened a retirement like future.

Why is it that setbacks seem to happen one after the other? I've never been able to figure that out! But, the very next day I received another call about a similar opportunity, offering me $75,000 just to consult on the phone every monthly.

That also fell through the day before the contract was to be signed. All of this happened in a week and I was pissed. I was so close, yet now I found myself back at square one, but feeling more like a negative 10. It all fell apart right before the finish line, this was definitely a setback, not a failure.

A dear friend of mine once said, “doors never close without others opening. Maybe there is something better?” The last thing I could conceive of was something better was coming. The expectation that it was all going to work out was tearing me apart on the inside. Everything seemed to line up perfectly, it didn’t make sense.

A POWERFUL MAN STAYS ENGAGED IN THE GAME AND ANOTHER DOOR OPENS, IF A DOOR DOES NOT OPEN THEN YOU CHECKED OUT OR GAVE IN.

After a week, I snapped out of my setback and feeling bummed out. I took my friends advice and began believing it was all for the best. l did let it go, I decided that if I could manifest those two opportunities, then I could manifest many more. Three months later I got a call from an attorney asking to speak with me. The company from Texas was facing a class action suit and they wanted my help in getting millions of dollars back for their clients.

And the other company offering me $75,000 to consult with them went belly up.

Suddenly, I felt healed. Sometimes the deals that do not workout are not setbacks after all, they are forwarding my success, but in disguise. Sometimes we set ourselves up for setbacks by convincing ourselves that we want this. We do this while losing higher perspective; *this deal may or may not be for me, even if I am excited about it.* Sometimes our wants overshadow our gut. The moment this happens you won't see the red flags or believe them when they appear. What you want is more important, so you think!

LEADERS FOCUS ON OPPORTUNITIES NOT PROBLEMS, SETBACKS OR FAILURES. THOSE ARE GOING TO HAPPEN AND ARE SUBJECT PERSPECTIVE.

7 Perspectives to Reshape Setbacks:

Rule #1: You cannot get back what you lost SHOWING UP AS the same person that created it. You must shift how you operate or risk repeating the pattern.

It's common for men to convince themselves things can change, that something will be different this time. Although we mean well, shifting things is another level of courage and discipline. Our motivation for achieving something is at its highest when we start out and when we fear losing it. Somewhere in the middle of the journey we lose excitement or passion and sometimes both.

If you head down comeback lane pretending to be different, trying to be different, or convincing yourself it will be different, chances are you're just deceiving yourself. Nothing will be different. You don't want to lose or feel pain again, that is the biggest motivation. Not love, passion, joy or achievement, which should be the main driver or purpose for your comeback.

IF YOU DON'T WANT THE PAST TO RESURRECT ITSELF AGAIN, SHIFT YOUR COMEBACK TO ONE OF PURPOSE.

I knew during each of my comebacks, things were different because things felt aligned. There was an ease to it. I had also learned specific things and had time to practice those new lessons, creating a new habit or way of showing up that was capable of accomplishing my goals.

If you place a mouse in a maze and place a piece of cheese at the end of the maze, the mouse will find it. In fact, if the MOUSE runs down tunnel A to no avail, it will RUN back and head down another tunnel. He will continue to change his approach each time until victory. The mouse won't have any ego about it. The mouse will not go back down the same tunnel twice, but a man will. Then he will get upset, frustrated or begin to think he is unworthy of the goal.

Epic men continue to change the direction and shift their approach and to do that successfully, you need to connect to a new way of being. If perhaps you were being too aggressive, then connect with patience this time. If you were hesitant or doubtful, apply confidence and clarity. If you were too laid back, connect with inspiration and passion. Shifting directions from this way of being, produces a different experience and a different result.

Rule #2: Expectations are a silent killer.

The more you expect the more you get hooked by expectations. So much so that you may not see any other reality. When man fixes his mind on something, he narrows his vision and mindset to only seeing his expectations and nothing else. It's a gift and a curse and it can rob you of flexibility and changing direction if needed. Think of it this way; masculinity is like a rock, its strong and solid, rather than adapt to expectations and change like water, the rock gets pounded repeatedly. The water simply adjusts, and often time moves the rock out of the way.

When a man with willpower and expectation convinces himself that a particular goal is "the one," he will fight to win even if it is NOT right for him.

Placing all your energy in one area also creates pressure for that area to succeed. If not having to force it to succeed or fail. Even if the goal is accomplished, it may not be as fulfilling as you expected. If you do this a few times, you will likely end up numbing yourself from getting excited about future possibilities because "*things just don't work out the way you thought they would.*"

Rarely do men say, "my expectations in the past didn't work out the way I had planned." That would be more accurate and honest.

Here is a quick exercise:

Clarification is powerful. Refrain from answering these questions but describe and write out your responses. If you try to just answer them, you will miss the entire exercise. It's not about being right or finding the answer so you feel better, it's about seeing the patterns that operate within you.

1. Describe all the feelings you have about failing or having a setback.
2. Why do you think this happened?
3. What meaning are you giving your failure or setback?

Don't just answer, describe your responses, it's the only way to get to the bottom of it.

Rule #3: When you are 100% IN--roadblocks get cleared out of the way.

Here is another view on setbacks.

Often, when men call me for coaching they say something like this, "*for some reason every time we make progress, another road block appears.*"

Sometimes success feels like driving a car with one foot on the gas and one foot on the break. As soon as something good happens, you fall back a few steps. It's easy to want to give up or doubt yourself. There is something underneath this men don't see. Inner-resistance keeps the tug of war alive. Let's be honest, when you are all-in there is no inner resistance. You have fully given yourself to this process because you believe in it.

Ignoring the resistance or fear causes us to work harder and make things happen. When men experience stress, they rarely acknowledge it is a code word for FEAR. Anxiety, worry, control, impatience, and an adrenaline high are all fear-based. God forbid we acknowledge these feelings, right?

Setbacks can be defined as resistance; these emotions are based on fear and mistrust. In other words, there is a part of you, that does NOT believe what you are doing will work and setbacks keep happening to you, and it leaves you wondering why!

This resistance causes you to hold back and NOT fully engage. When I share this with men they often want to argue about their feelings, and claim to, "*gave it their all.*" Only to find out that you cannot give your all if you have resistance to process.

The only roadblocks and setbacks are the ones you create. You cannot avoid roadblocks with inner-resistance, but you can play mental chess. You can manipulate your way around the resistance and pretend it's not present. These acts are mere attempts to outsmart yourself only to discover you will end up back where you started – with resistance and it's not worth it. Clear your resistance and you clear your blocks, giving you freedom to pursue your goals.

If you operate from resistance, the world will give it back to you by creating more road blocks. You will find it happening with others, with deals, with vendors, contractors, they stop calling you back or emailing you, and your deal starts to break down, simply because you were already operating from a place of resistance. Things become challenging for no obvious reason.

People suddenly stop showing up to make your dreams work because a part of YOU believes your dream will also NOT work.

IF THINGS ARE NOT WORKING OR BREAKING DOWN,
NOTICE WHERE YOU MAY HAVE RESISTANCE.

If your belief is authentic, you are good at what you do, and you have the right intention, you WILL WIN. It's NOT an if, it's a when.

A client of mine wanted to create a YouTube channel; he was uncomfortable making videos of himself. I've never seen anything like what I am about to tell you.

Art invented stick yoga, a powerful form of yoga using a bamboo stick that rehabilitates injuries. I asked him to talk to explain on camera for 1 minute, about what stick yoga was. He couldn't do it without stumbling. When I finally got him on a roll, the camera shut off. I got the camera to work again, then the audio was picking up static in the background and the quality was poor.

Finally, we fixed it all and when Art was 45 seconds into his 1-minute pitch and his wife walked in. CUT! 3 hours later he didn't get a single minute in and Art was ready to quit.

It was one roadblock after another. I told him to practice that night and then we would try again tomorrow and he agreed.

The next day, my team arrived, and Art didn't practice at all. He decided he didn't want to do the video anymore. Suddenly, the excuse monster came alive and he had a patient emergency. It was date night with his wife and later an old friend called. Isn't it interesting how he invited things to roadblock his work and then succumbed to it?

What are the odds a high school friend of 30 years ago, calls him the night before we film?

When you are in resistance, while trying to move forward, roadblocks keep coming up. Without knowing it you are creating these instances to come up. Conversely, when you are clear about what you want, you open up the elements to align with you. In other words, Art didn't want to deal with his resistance, which is why everything we did failed. Art was holding back, unwilling to feel uncomfortable and creating several inconvenient events.

Six months later I fired Art as a client, he still had not done a simple 1-minute video. Now he is thinking of quitting his business all together. His own invention down the drain.

It was all in his head, he could not move forward and backwards at the same time and find success.

WHEN YOU ARE CLEAR AND INTENTIONAL YOU MOVE OBSTACLES OUT OF YOUR WAY.

Fast-forward a year, Art called me wanting to know if Facebook Live was a good idea for him. Really? That is a video just like YouTube, it's the same thing. If you can't trust yourself and do a one-minute video then how is Facebook live going to be different? When men lose excitement for something due to a block, they keep searching for something else that feels better, usually selling themselves short, instead of taking on what really matters; in this case for Art, its going on camera and sharing his message. That is simple, and all that is required of him is to speak powerfully.

Art finally revealed he was terrified of disappointing people and to do it on video would be a constant reminder that no one was inspired by his work. Finally, we got to the truth! I walked Art through a process called Bio Masculine Engineering. I will discuss it in length later, but essentially, it's a re-wiring of the masculine into accessing the full masculine potential we all have. To feel vulnerable and inspired simultaneously and still move forward.

The ability to feel FREE in all that you do, so you are not operating for the need to prove, gain approval, avoid failure or to achieve success. You do what you do because YOU OWN IT and BECAUSE YOU SAID SO.

That is masculine power.

In the next few days, Art generated more videos than we had planned. He went on to create full courses and recorded all his seminars, causing a huge influx of new clients.

Rule #4: You are your only setback

Men unconsciously constrain themselves by holding back. Holding back comes in the form of not asking for what we want powerfully, hiding our truth or intentions, not fully showing up, all of which accompany some doubt or uncertainty. We do this unconsciously because if failure does happen it won't be as painful. It's an instant rationalization that "you were right" and you knew this would happen. Therefore, don't be all in. Frankly, I would rather fail 100 times giving it my all. Because when I do succeed it will be with a high level of intelligence, passion, commitment and a lot more ease to it. The guy who has never failed is a liability because it's not a matter of "if" he will, it's a "when." I want the guy who has failed and has risen again on my team.

Men have a belief that says, "if we keep the status quo alive, that success is a grind, then when things don't work out, we can claim that we at least tried." For some reason we take pride in failing if we work hard. People feel bad for us in a good way, yet, it's not useful or helpful. There is no pride or accolades in not getting what you want and feeling ok with just sweat and tears and nothing to show for it. That is a low standard and a great way to avoid fully experiencing failure or disappointment.

It's how we avoid FACING our own reality to avoid feeling bad or looking bad.

FACING REALITY IS HOW YOU GET TO OWN YOUR LIFE.

Setbacks are an opportunity to CHECK IN, to face your own reality about why you are doing what you are doing. The best course of action you can take during a setback is to do what most of us men fail to do, objectively face your own reality.

Checking in may sound like this, *"does this really resonate with me? What are my true intentions? Is this what I want? What about ME is causing this to not work effectively?"*

Setbacks are a part of our journey and everything is a test. Are you willing to do the work? To rise up when challenged? To take YOU on every step of the way? The reason people who win the lottery are broke a year later is because they didn't have to fail, face fear, or learn anything along the way to becoming a millionaire. 90% of lottery winners spend all their money a year later. They didn't do any work to create their wealth and then lose it quickly.

I have found numerous times, personally and professionally, that if I had check in with reality I would not have made decisions I did. For example, getting married or doing as much real-estate as I did. Humorously, I have clients who didn't even know they were millionaires until they faced their financial reality by writing down their finances and organizing them.

It costs men more to avoid looking at the reality than it does to look at it.

Rule #5: Let go of how it should look.

Part of our masculine wiring is to control things, especially the outcomes. Men love to create visions and try to do everything to see the vision through. Yet, we have to check ourselves. Sometimes the vision does not fit our plans and rarely, does it fit perfectly. It's more important that our "why" is fulfilled rather than, checking all the boxes off the original vision. If you don't, you may have to reset things in midflight.

When you acknowledge a setback and work to reset it, great things can happen. Once a client of mine, Eric, was set to marry the woman of his dreams. They had a perfect relationship, until he was left standing at the alter in front of hundreds of family members and friends.

He called me from the church in a panic, "what do I do? We cannot find her anywhere!"

I told him to thank everyone for attending and that what is most important, is finding out if Meredith is okay. I reminded him that although it may not feel like whatever was happening was for the best, it truly was. ***"if your fiancé is having doubts now, that is far better than after saying I do; because it won't be fully authentic," I said.***

Eric went on to confess his love for her and everything that she meant to him to all the wedding guests. He did a stand-up job during the WORST setback of his life.

I continued to talk to him on his way back to his hotel room, he was in tears and distraught, he could not feel anything but pain.

That night Meredith called, it turns out she had a breakdown of her own. She thought she might be gay. She met a woman a few months ago that started out as a friendship and this woman even helped her with the wedding arrangements.

Then something changed. They fell in love. They were both confused. They never had any interest in each other, or women at all, at least before they met.

So how could this be a blessing? How do you hit the reset button?

Would you want to be married to a woman who wants to be with someone else? The simple fact that Meredith and Eric committed to marriage is what caused her to face her own reality and sexuality. That is a blessing. Could it have happened a different way, YES, but it didn't, and we have to face this reality in order for anything else to be possible.

It is difficult to acknowledge anything as a blessing when you feel hurt. Eric and I spoke every day and uncovered the confusion, realizing there were times when Eric sensed something was off, and learned a lot about his decisions. Finally, he got to a place of peace and could acknowledge this was a game changing curve ball and it was for the best. Rather than fight to fix his vision and make it work, he chose to reset things. He can still have his vision, just not with Meredith.

Eric took back his balls, not from his fiancé, but from his story and his emotions. He faced the reality of what happened and realized **he could not change what happened or how.** He had no control at this moment, except what choice he made.

YOU ALWAYS HAVE CONTROL IF YOU REALIZE YOU HAVE A CHOICE.

Eric called Meredith and wished her well and said he is in full support of her discovering who she is, and it is still weird and hurtful to him, but his vision was always for the best of them both. Now some people say that, but the reality is they move on. Eric on the other hand chooses to be a friend and meet up with Meredith every once in a while, and that's rare.

Eric is the man! He took on reality and won big. Eighteen months later he married his soul mate and Meredith decided that having been raised to be a housewife, have kids and find a good man to marry was not her path. She wanted to explore her new-found love, she never expected a woman to be her lover. They are still together today!

Rule #6: Setbacks provide a 360-degree view.

Setbacks are a perfect time to see things from a new perspective. I have found in my own life that if I don't spend time alone to reflect, meditate or listen to my gut, things stop flowing for me. Men are notorious for letting things build up and dishing off emotions with the casual, "I'm fine" remark. Pay attention!

How often do men in relationships reach the point of overload? Overwhelm? And even frustration, all because we need space to get clear? I am not referring to the man cave. The man cave is checking out and ignoring reality. Checking in can be done anywhere; you can find silence or space. Often for men we see things clearly when we step away from them.

CREATING SPACE ALLOWS YOU TO BE FREE FROM YOUR MIND AND SEE THINGS CLEARLY.

Business is the same way and getting on top of things and staying on top of your path is key. In other words, don't get lost in the grind as to not see or feel. Or worse, lose your identity along the path.

You can absolutely comeback from anything. Taking a higher road is NOT necessarily taking two steps back in order to take one step forward. That is all made up. You really are never taking steps backward, it just seems like it. You are always on the path, there are no forwards or backwards. There is progress and results, which defy emotional interpretations. Only social conditioning thinks it's success or failure – they are not the measure of your life purpose!

Rule #7: Comebacks are not age dependent; it requires more energy than before.

Comebacks require you to reach back with more energy, more passion, and a renewed sense of empowerment. It has nothing to do with age, race, gender, or circumstances. It's available to you right now!

What kills your ability to create energy is holding onto the past. How it should and could have been kill your core energy. Add to it a heavy dose of unworthy feelings and suddenly one step forward feels like pushing a boulder. Your spirit is ageless and timeless.

Setbacks are NOTHING more than an energy loss.

ENERGY is the ONLY thing in LIFE that is replaceable and there is an INFINITE supply.

You can turn any failure or setback into a lifetime of achievement.

Learn to say, "I am grateful for this." Then you will be free from it.

Learn to experience PEACE and EASE and you will be free from suffering.

Realize, now or later, that it will be the perfect set up for what is next for you. Every time I've failed I learned how to make it RIGHT the next time. It's the ultimate education.

I will take a man with scars, who has experienced failure over a man who is woundless. When I searched for a flying instructor, I called 4 guys. The first question I asked was, "have you ever crash landed a plane? If so what happened? The first two guys said NO, so I ended the call right then. If they have not experienced a crash landing and neither have I, I certainly did not want to be their first.

The final two guys said YES. One said, the engine failed, and he landed on a narrow beach during a storm. The other guy was in engine failure and landed on water. The worse place to land and deadliest. I chose him.

He is who I want to be in a plane with. The man can handle the worst and I can trust him with my life at 30,000 feet.

Is he less worthy because of what happened?

Is he less worthy if he damaged his only plane in a crash landing and it put his company into bankruptcy?

It's all interpretation isn't it? Little did I know that the crash was recent, and he had to file bankruptcy. I was his first new client that got him back on his feet. Our first day together he walked me through what happened in the plane that day. What a perfect way to learn! Any fear I had about flying was gone at that point. Now, I knew how to handle the worst-case scenario, one that rarely happens. I had no fear of flying and could focus without worry. Samuel was an amazing teacher.

Chapter 2 Notes: Define and Redefine Setback

» A setback is defined as an event or occurrence in which you have to stop progress or a success.

» A failure would be, the team losing the world series, at least in their mind they have failed. A defeat, a loss usually followed with disappointment, regret and some level of hurt.

- A powerful man stays fully engaged in the game even if the doors slams shut.
- Leaders focus on opportunities not problems, setbacks or failures. Those things are going to happen and are subject to perspective.
- You cannot get back what you lost showing up as the same guy who created the loss.
- If you fear your past failures resurrecting themselves in the future, then discover why you failed and shift your purpose to a higher source.
- Let go of expectations, they are silent killers.
- Clarity can move roadblocks for you.
- You always have control when you realize you always have a choice.
- Making a comeback has nothing to do with age, it has everything to do with energy.

END OF CHAPTER 2 NOTES.

I am with you brother. You got this. You can and will succeed at anything you chose to.

Let's move on to chapter 3.

Chapter 3

CHASING A PHANTOM

Excitement is a red flag in disguise because it's from the mind and hormones, and not necessarily purpose. External devices causing men to feel excited stimulate dopamine and testosterone. If men allow that excitement to decide for them, they are not operating from purpose. Men often chase things because they feel excited about something, but that energy wears OFF. Then we question why we headed down a path to begin with. Operating without purpose is dangerous.

PURPOSE DOES NOT WEAR OFF, IT GENERATES MORE POWER.

Think of it this way, when a man is excited about a woman, he never says, "I am so excited for me and who I am that I met her?" He's just excited about her. That she is hot, fun, talks about interesting things and isn't drama. Then suddenly, she asks him deeper questions or challenges him, and his excitement wears off. He doesn't call her every day like he once did. The difference is his excitement is ABOUT her, something external and he makes up justification as to why, but rarely does he see that his purpose can be respected and honored having her along his side through life.

Excitement is a dopamine response and it comes and goes, it makes you high and will drop you low at some point. It's an addiction. You want more excitement and when you lose it you want it back. It traps men into a mental rat race of two extremes, excitement, shortly followed up with burnout or fatigue. You're operating from will power. Wake up brother, that is a clear sign you're not on purpose.

A MAN WITHOUT PURPOSE OPERATES FROM EXCITEMENT – EXCITEMENT – EXHAUSTED. A MAN WITH PURPOSE OPERATES FROM PASSION – PASSION – RELAXED. HE NEVER LOSES HIS SENSE OF CONNECTION, EMBODIMENT OR HIS COOL BY OVER STIMULATING HIMSELF SO MUCH THAT HE LOSES HIS PURPOSES WITH WOMEN OR EXTERNAL DEVICES.

A man's biology is very powerful. Testosterone drives much of our lives from a protect, provide and procreate stand point. But not everything in our lives need protecting, providing or our sperm.

My all-time favorite is when a man meets a beautiful woman and even though she is rude and bitchy, men say the sex is great, she is good to them and somehow, they are happy with that arrangement. Really? Notice your purpose, passion or mission in life is not considered in that equation. But, this is nothing more than intense and mutual stimulation of each other's hormones getting off on each other. It feels great, but you're just pushing each other's buttons like a game of cause and effect, avoiding the deeper reality that you are terrified of surrendering into love.

The reptile brain assumes man's excitement is TRUTH and convinces him how great it will BE when he achieves this goal; all of which is a fun way to seduce himself into believing that everything else will all come together once this happens, but it doesn't.

A good friend of mine, Jason, is making millions selling marijuana in Colorado, legally. He invited me to be a part of it with my sales and marketing skills.

I said no to a $150K contract to run his company. To his dismay he offered me a percentage of the profits from the company. All the bells and whistles to entice me. My mind loved the idea. My belly was filled with adrenaline thinking of the number of women I would meet, being in "happy" environments and working on something new. But I still said no. I recognized the difference between these biological responses and while it felt great, my heart space was actually heavy; almost like a brick had been quickly placed on it.

When he asked me why, I told him, "this was not my path". Although I love the money aspect of it and I never saw this coming on my path. My purpose is to see people come alive and do what they thought they could not, not sedate them into a temporary state of mind.

I am sure people come alive under the influence, but this is NOT my purpose. I would only be selling out to temptation, and it's not who I am. Jason reminds me each Christmas that I missed out. He even takes pictures of his bank account numbers. I send back pictures of the many men thanking me online for working with them. It's fun, but Jason still does not get it.

BE HIGHLY AWARE OF CONVINCING YOURSELF FOR SOMEONE OR SOMETHING.

Convincing yourself this is your goal is usually ego seduction. You want something because it makes you feel good, so you agree with it because it feels good. But are you really listening to your gut feeling? Which is underneath the sensory feelings. Convincing yourself is a MIND game. Be highly aware of having to convince yourself of anything. That is usually a sign your off purpose, or at the very least disconnected from it. As an example, "I do not have to get myself excited for my wife." I may have to get myself excited to go to church, but the reality is it's probably because I don't want to have to deal with something I should be dealing with. Or because it does not resonate with you in that moment.

Think of it this way, if you want to marry a woman by having to convince her, you may want to take a 360-degree look. You shouldn't have to, you should not need to convince her to love you and spend her life with you. Nor should she have to convince you.

Fooled by Illusions:

Achieving what you are supposed to, usually fails. Trying to become who you think you should be or what others want you to be creates disappointment. You are not here to impress anyone or gain their approval.

You may know this intellectually, but unconsciously I see it all the time in men's behaviors. Especially around women, relationships and money. The need for approval and validation. Even if you win, it is at the expense of yourself, not the betterment of who you are.

THE MAN WHO IS OUT FOR PURPOSE FULFILLS IT, THE MAN WHO IS OUT FOR APPROVAL FAILS OFTEN.

There are two types of motivation for men, the first is running away from what they don't want and don't want to experience emotionally. To do that you must focus on NOT failing. These are the guys that when someone says, "you cannot do it" they do it to prove others wrong and themselves capable.

Other men do it for the sheer adventure, thrill and passion for the goal. They move towards everything that makes them feel good and often don't care. They are just out for a good time. These men are often terrified of being alone or insignificant.

A comeback man does it because it's who he is and that's all that matters. He doesn't justify, defend or have a bunch of reasons to look good, he just is good. This man is dangerous to other men because he has nothing to hide. He allows people to see into him. When he walks into a room, others notice.

REAL MEN ARE RARE, THEY LET OTHERS SEE INTO THEM AND HIDE NOTHING. THE MOST POWERFUL MAN WALKS INTO A ROOM WITH NOTHING TO HIDE.

Most of us, unknowingly, are driven by fear and pain. We are afraid of failing more than we want to win. I used to hate losing more than I loved winning. It drove me; I went the extra mile, did the extra rep, ran the extra stair and obsessively thought about destroying any and every opponent. It scared me how intense I could be and that grind is not sustainable and wears us down faster than a bad marriage and financial debt. This fear made me a mad man on the baseball field. When I initially tried to play baseball for the joy and passion of it, I got bored. Not realizing I wasn't in warrior mode, angry or afraid, I was not as stimulated to play. Despite, my production and performance went up playing relaxed. It made no sense. It was easier this way, I was taking on challenges and winning. I was over dramatizing stuff to feel better, to feel like a winner, rather than just playing for the love of it. After a while, I noticed that the previous path was exhausting and not even necessary. I didn't have to grind it all the time, its required only sometimes. Until then, I played in my own zone of passion and intelligence, when the game got intense; I became more relaxed and fierce and could grind down even the most difficult opponents. I became unbeatable. By playing both relaxed and quickly accessing warrior mode, I was winning over my opponents. When they tried to score, I became even better. This is the perfect athlete, he wins no matter what or at least finds a way to win no matter what is happening in the game.

Men are after a very specific feeling. The feeling of being on top of your world. Winning. Being known. Remembered. Having it all. Balance. Happiness. Etc.

So, start there! Start your new comeback from this place.

STOP chasing the white rabbit. Your life does not exist outside of you. You are not successful because you have a wife, child or money.

Nor are you a failure because you don't have a wife, child or money. The love you want is not in a woman. The certainty you want is not in the accomplishment. That illusion keeps men running, chasing and pushing. It leads to burnout. I am suggesting to you that you already are everything you want to become. Start with the feeling of it and then act.

If you keep chasing the white rabbit, you will burn out. Making your epic comeback is about declaring what you've been chasing is already within you and you're only goal is to express and experience it by giving yourself fully to it. Just declare what you deeply own, that alone will create a momentous and sustainable comeback.

Always challenge your wants and your whys. The clarity places you on a new level and enters you into the realm of the "next best version of yourself."

Chapter 3 Notes: Chasing a Phantom

» Purpose down not wear out, it generates more power.

» A man without purpose operates from a state of mind that causes excitement, excitement, and then burnouts.

» A man with purpose operates from passion, passion and a relaxed state of consciousness.

» If you have to convince yourself of something, you may want to take a step back and have a reality check.

» A man who is on purpose wins, a man who is out to prove himself, fails often.

» The most powerful man in the room has nothing to hide.

» Always challenge your wants and your why's.

» Your comeback starts with a feeling, what is the feeling your are after?

» Don't chase the white rabbit, make declarations that you will have what you want right now.

END OF CHAPTER 3 NOTES.

I am with you brother. You got this. You can and will succeed at anything you chose to.

Let's move on to chapter 4.

Chapter 4

THE HIDDEN GOAL AND VISION

ONE OF THE MOST POWERFUL THINGS I have done with clients is the clarity generator process. On the first day we meet, I challenge every goal and why they set it.

Often, by the end of the day they are either 100% clear about their goals or 100% clear their goals were not in alignment. Once there is total clarity, the rest of the time is spent manifesting or in execution mode. As a side note, I suggest you spend more time in clarity mode rather than, perfecting the cart before the horse is clear and ready.

Clarity over ego, means you fully understand the difference between a goal, a vehicle, and why you want the goal. A goal is something to accomplish. Making $1,000,000 is a goal for many men. I don't believe that is the goal in its entirety. $1,000,000 is the vehicle for the goal. The goal is almost always a *feeling called an experience. It's something that you value and think you don't have or want more of because you got a taste of it before.*

Wanting to make money so you don't have to worry about money ever again is a why. Wanting to experience freedom or to provide for your family and self are often big why's for men. What is underneath that is the feeling of being valued and important -- and to have a sense of certainty. Most of what men want has a theme of freedom. **Freedom is the one**

true connection between our biology and our spiritual self. Both are designed perfectly for freedom, it's our natural state of consciousness.

If you approach each goal with the truth about what you want, and why, you are more likely to accomplish it. Why hide it? Why not just lead with the end in mind, knowing it is yours to have?

LEAD FROM THE BEGINNING WITH WHAT YOU WANT IN THE END. BRINING THOSE TWO TOGETHER NOW IS OPERATING FROM GROUDEDNESS.

There is always something underneath the goal; goals are often disguised as vehicles. $1,000,000 is the vehicle to travel more and experience freedom, among other things. The money allows you to experience what is underneath the goal. Money gives you more access to choices. What I am suggesting is that you make the goal and the vehicle equally important. You can do that by starting with the feeling you want to experience, and lock onto that feeling and you will manifest powerfully without any fear of failure or loss. I always create my goals from the realm of BEING. I am an accomplished, authentic, and wealthy man manifesting $1,000,000. I start with who I am, what I want to feel is congruent with how I feel about myself, then I pursue my goal relentlessly. I have set this goal four times in my life and achieved it all four times. Most men have it backwards, they want the goal to become someone, to feel something, or experience something. A perfect setup to either fail or succeed. Either way you are a slave to the process, as long as how you feel about yourself is at the effect of succeeding, or not.

If you only have two options, failure or success you are in a personal push-pull dilemma. Grinding is not necessary. Even if you succeed, while leaving who you are out of the equation, you may experience satisfaction, but fulfillment may evade you. Temporary fulfillment at best then off to chase another rabbit. You may experience burnout.

Men often share with me that they want to have in a relationship.

When I ask them why, they tell me things like this, "*I want sex, freedom, adventure, and someone to share my life with.*" Then the relationship becomes the vehicle to the goal, which is to experience *sexuality, freedom, adventure and connection or collaboration.* If you focus on these experiences and operate in the pursuit of your goal from these feelings, *you already are what you wish to become and accomplish.* That is owning it in pursuit of your goal, then it's no longer a someday thing.

Another perspective is this*: you are giving and participating in the energy you want to have.* If I am dating and I bring the energy of sexuality, adventure and connection to women, naturally I am going to create that. She has a choice, to participate in my energy or not. She can also choose to continue to date me as she enjoys the confidence in my energy and sharing it, but feels it's too soon to fully embrace it. Either way, I am remaining grounded in who I am.

Because I am coming from this place, or operating from within who I am. That means whether I have the partnership or not, find the right person or not, I still am who I am. That is enough. There is no failure or success here, but, the reality is in any two year period of focus you will end up with a partnership that reflects to you what you bring to it. The feminine will align to your energy if you are guided and present.

If you focus on what matters, rather than, the attainment of something like a relationship, there is less pressure and force. As you can imagine no woman or man wants to be a checkmark next to a goal, right? But the right person wants to experience a relationship that includes *freedom, sexuality, adventure, connection and collaboration, will exceed those checkmarks.*

Often my very successful clients, who have more time and financial freedom, want to pursue a spiritual life. They set goals to meditate, do yoga, and take spiritual type trips or retreats. Again, the goal is not meditation it's what they want to experience through meditation. Often men will share with me it's to experience more *peace, presence or calmness and sometimes even nirvana.* The goal then is to experience nirvana and the vehicle is meditation. Are you starting to get this? It brings to the forefront what you are really after and the reality of you having it now. That your goals are not subject to anything or dependent on anything or anyone.

My goal is to experience *presence and nirvana* and I do that through meditation. That is far more powerful than trying to accomplish nirvana. Or just another accomplishment amongst your list of many.

BE THAT WHICH DOES THAT. MOST MEN HAVE IT BACKWARDS. THEY DO THIS TO BECOME THIS AND THAT MODEL IS FLAWED AND LEAVES MEN DISSAPPOINTED.

Don't fall prey to the illusion that one day when you 'accomplish' something and therefore become someone. It's a lie. You have to show up and call forth what you are and know yourself in order to experience anything.

Let's review this in a different way before we begin to set new goals.

If $1,000,000 is a vehicle, then it's a vehicle for you to experience what feelings?

Now, put that into a statement starting with, **"I am (feeling), (feeling) and a (feeling) man.**

That may look like this, "I am a free, loving, and passionate man." Now attach the vehicle to that statement so it is more complete:

"I am free, loving, and a passionate man, achieving $1,000,000 or more starting right now."

Now you understand, BE THAT WHICH DOES THAT. Money does not define you, but it can help you. As a side note I always end my statements with some urgency or decisiveness so that way I am activated. My words are no longer just words, there is a charge to them.

There is a clear distinction between a man who says what he wants and one who speaks into what he says he wants. Speaking your word has a potency and energetic charge behind it, not just words. Rather than pick the right words, pick the ones that express what really resonates with you.

That's the difference between goals and vehicles; I start with the END feeling. This is the law of attraction. Start with the feelings; cultivate those feelings, which build momentum and drives actions that are congruent. Now there is no success or failure, but rather a journey of living on your terms, your way. There is freedom here.

Here is another example for men about wanting a relationship:

A partner or a woman, relationships or marriage is not a goal. It's a vehicle. It's odd to think of it this way. A relationship is a vehicle to experience what?

Love. Sex. Joy. Fun. Challenge. Whatever you are truly after is the goal, not the person.

Lets' consider this.

"If I want love, joy, fun and to take on challenges in a partnership, am I being that man right now?"

Now only a nimrod would say, "If I say this statement 10,000 times a day I should have this woman, right? NO! Be that which does that. You cannot have what you are not experiencing. I am suggesting you own this now. The love, joy and fun. That you are expressing it in your daily life. The partner that vibes with that will come chasing after you, but don't take my word for it. Experience it for yourself brother.

The goal is to experience sharing, giving, and exchanging feelings with someone you resonate with. You want to manifest a partnership, so you can experience the sharing and giving of the feelings you want. Now let's generate this into a BEINGNESS goal.

"I am a loving, joyful man who loves challenges and I am now manifesting a partner to share my life with." Versus, "I want to marry a sexy, honest, and fun woman." Do you see the difference between the two? One says, "I am what I want", while the other says, "I am not what I want," which is why men have to chase after it. Be the man who believes he is everything he truly wants.

The first is an epic man goal. The other is all the other men out in the world. You've been down that path. Not much can be achieved and fulfilled if you leave WHO you are out of the equation.

Let's go deeper into this and work through some examples of goals and vehicles. The list below represents traditional goals and the right are the feelings or experiences each of those goals creates when accomplished.

GOALS	FEELINGS
I want to make $1,000,000.	I want freedom, certainty, to feel valued.
I want a life partner.	I want sex, adventure, and connection.
I want a ripped body with 10% body fat.	I want to feel hot, sexy, and attractive.
I want to have 5 dream homes.	I want to feel important, secure, admired.
I want to have 3 kids.	I want to feel proud, have a legacy, and a family I love.

Now let's switch these up based upon what we learned in this chapter.

VEHICLES	FEELINGS
$1,000,000	I am a man of freedom, certainty who feels valued and loved.
Life partner	I am a sexual, adventurous, and connected man.

Ripped body 10% BF	I am a hot, sexy, attractive man on a mission.
5 dream homes	I am a valued, intelligent, secure, and admired man.
I want a family	I am present and ready to create a family.

BE THAT WHICH DOES THAT IN ORDER TO HAVE THAT.

Let's put this all together into a full statement. Taking the vehicle in line 1, the goals and combine them into one statement so your feelings, goals, and vehicles come together.

Vehicle: 1,000,000 and the goal is, to have freedom, certainty, to feel valued, and loved.

Statement:

I am a man of freedom, certainty who is valued and loved on a mission to $1,000,000.

Assignment:

1. Write down goals that you have.
2. Follow the format and change the goals into vehicles.
3. Write down what the vehicles give you and the feelings associated with them.
4. Then write them out into one statement.

VEHICLES: **GOALS:**

1.
2.
3.
4.
5.

STATEMENT:

I am a man of freedom and certainty. I am valued and loved. I am on a mission to $1,000,000.

The turning point in your comeback is bringing awareness to what matters. The 5 dream houses are not what really matters, it's what those houses represent to you. Those 5 dreams houses mean 5 mortgages, insurance policies, maintenance, and bills. Internally, where it matters, those houses mean freedom, adventure, value, importance, and recognition. You may start to realize there isn't much of a point to having 5 dream houses if you already feel free and valued. Thus, they will never define you.

And that is the point!

They do not define you the way you once thought success did. Having them is just added value, for most men, it is the value. This man may never feel the joy of being alive or being a man. What defines you usually breaks you, unless you're defined by what really matters. What really matters is that you fulfill your purpose.

CHAPTER 4 NOTES: THE HIDDEN GOAL AND VISION

» Lead from the beginning with what you want in the end.

» Operate from the place you want to end up, *If you want peace and power, start from this state of mind now.*

» *"I am free, loving, and a passionate man, achieving $1,000,000 or* *more starting right now."* This declaration is far more powerful than a man who is just after money.

» A goal is not just making money, it is usually the feelings that having money provides you. if you combine the two you can manifest more powerfully.

» Within each of your goals is a hidden desire to feel more valued, respected, recognized and usually ends with wanting to feel loved.

» The most powerful quote to remember from this chapter, **"Be that which does that. "**

END OF CHAPTER 4 NOTES.

I am with you brother. You got this. You can and will succeed at anything you chose to.

Let's move on to chapter 5.

Chapter 5

THE ULTIMATE MAN TRAP

#1 Do you overthink everything?

The ultimate sign you are not following your heart, gut, or feeling is if you are overthinking. Overthinking occurs when you are uncertain about something or fear you may not get it. As you dive deeper into your head, things become harder and less clear. When the mind is uncertain, it tries to win by thinking harder, thinking more, and hoping to find a way to solve problems, rather than creating a path to success.

The more you think, the less you feel. The more you think, the less inspired you are. Overthinking disconnects you from your body, your spirit and frankly it's exhausting.

A few years ago Hawken reached out to me on LinkedIn, he was a marketing consultant with ambitious goals. He took marketing programs, seminars, and workshops every weekend for years. He had more knowledge than he knew what to do with.

Hawken became excited about everything he learned and then added another piece to his business. Within 2 years he had 10 different titles for himself, 15 different products and ways to help people, and had no clients or money.

He spent more time thinking, learning, and hoping people would hire his company for marketing than he did understanding what he really wanted. Everything he was doing felt good and seemed right. That was until I questioned what he really wanted. He really didn't know why he was doing any of it.

Despite all the things he knew, he literally implemented NONE of them to make his business successful. Think about this, he knew how to generate leads for his clients, but used none of those strategies for himself. His was not in integrity of living what he set out to do.

MEN HIDE BEHIND THEIR THOUGHTS AND KNOWLEDGE WHEN THEY ARE UNCERTAIN.

Hawken and I talked through the clarity generator process, his goal was \$2,000,000 a year. Sadly, he has never made more than \$200,000; that is a huge jump and frankly not a realistic one.

What he really wanted underneath his ideas and knowledge was to be a man of influence and to be loved for what he does. Nearly everything he offers doesn't make him feel influential at all, and since it's not selling, he doesn't feel loved or respected.

He thinks too damn much and is constantly reaching for the next best thing, all the while NOT checking in to see if this is really for him. Once we took away the stuff and let go of over thinking things, it became clear that Hawken is the ultimate strategist. He loves to consult and turn around companies' strategy for success. A very important skill set. That is what makes him happy and feel respected. He realized he overthought things when he wasn't in alignment with his strengths and passion. This is true for most of us.

The ultimate mantrap is when we do one thing, but it's not backed up with your strength. Your strongest vibration as a man rests in your greatest strengths. When you are not in alignment with this, men mentally trap themselves into figuring it out mode and rarely see the light.

OVERTHINKING KILLS YOUR VIBE AND LEAVES LITTLE ACCESS TO INTUITION.

Life is NOT a thinking game, if that were true we would all be slim, rich and gorgeous. We would have it all because Lord knows we think about having it all more than we experience it.

Solution:

Full body decisions are the only way to get into alignment. When you decide from your vision and full emotional engagement, you shift your conscious and subconscious mind to alignment. Your mind begins to operate as a tool, rather than a devil's advocate. This is hard for men. The masculine makes decisions, the feminine prefers to collaborate, and neither wants to be wrong or fail.

The more frequent you are with your vibe and feel more powerful, the faster the decision-making process is. Think of the movie Rocky, each time he decided to fight his next opponent, despite feeling like a bum, he found a way to ignite his fire. He set himself on fire. He did that by accumulating feelings and a vibe that turned on the warrior inside himself. Then he saw this opponent in his mind, he lived and breathed through the training process. He pushed himself extra hard. He came alive and we came alive watching him. It didn't matter how many times he got hit, he got stronger. That does not happen living in your head!

#2 We Sell Out on Ourselves

The biggest way we sell out on ourselves is by being on a path that isn't right for us. Often disguised as convenient, easier, and less confrontational. We lower our value as to avoid feeling unworthy.

We also wait until we have to do something, while you are waiting, and you're selling yourself short from living on top of your game. It buries us even more into feeling stuck and that's why we do it. It's a mental game; waiting builds tensions, which causes us to act. No different than cramming before final exams. Once something is urgent you act like a hero; except you are not living like one. Sadly, it's the most painful approach to get us to act. Despite our true nature, "to not be told what to do," we want to do it because we have decided to. That's power. The more you sell out, you may find yourself in a world where people "tell you what to do" or worse, no one is around to support you at all anymore. Selling short is self-degrading.

NOT ACTING IN YOUR BEST INTEREST MEANS YOU NEED TO BE TOLD WHAT TO DO, WHICH MEN DISLIKE; AVOIDING ACTION MEANS YOU CANNOT BE TRUSTED TO CARE FOR YOURSELF. EITHER WAY IT DEPLETES YOUR MASCULINE POWER.

Rarely does a man come home to his wife when everything is working well, and says, "let's work on our relationships more, I want to get to know you better." (Laughing) No, he waits until he has to, until enough pressure has built, and problems arise. But the best time to make improvements is when things are working.

Convenience is another way we sell ourselves out, we take the easy path to getting something or fixing our problems and rob ourselves of the growth process. Brave man recognizes opportunities to direct success and also recognizes the road ahead. If you want to be unique or different on your comeback, don't settle for convenience, that is where far too many men live.

Solution:

Be 100% responsible for your space. This is your life; if something is off, take it on. If you're not getting what you want, address it. Own the space you are in every moment. That is when men are the happiest and most fulfilled.

That means right now, anything that is on your plate, stuff, stress or tension, begin to clear it out. I have found in men who have made comebacks that they have spent amble time clearing out the past that is still interfering with their present. This space creates freedom and room for NEW things to show up that are more in alignment with your future.

#3 We hide behind knowledge

A mentor of mine years ago told me a fabulous joke, "there are 5 assholes sitting in a tree and 1 decides to jump out, how many assholes are left?" 4, right?

WRONG! Assholes confuse making a decision with taking action. He decided to jump out, but he didn't. He is still sitting there. Often times making a decision confronts us and we pull back or hold back at the last second. Just because you know something or know what to do doesn't mean anything, especially if you are not pulling the trigger.

DECISIVENESS TRUMPS CONFIDENCE AND COMPETENCE.

We hide behind what we know, and then fail to act on it. We hide behind what we think, dream about ideas and don't speak directly about manifesting them. Searching, testing, and validating your ideas and theories from a place of indecision is nothing more than grasping for enough proof you won't fail. The knowledge we gather has become sedative. It comforts us into a safe zone of non-action, rather than living our lives.

We get off on knowing stuff more than experiencing the result of what we know. Our need to feel intelligent makes men feel better for not acting; *at least I know what to do, at least I have the knowledge.* Unfortunately, with this thinking, men end up know-it-alls with no results. These men are left with a head stone and shortly are forgotten except, maybe on holidays. I will choose the decisive man to win any contest over a know-it-all. Even if he doesn't outperform the know-it-all, he will win people over and act fearlessly in the pursuit of what he wants.

At some point, you know enough to get started and to decide.

A SELF TRANSFORMED MAN TAKES THE NEXT STEP EVEN IF HE IS NOT SURE HOW THE NEXT STEP WILL BE RESOURCEFUL FOR HIM.

Two years ago, I spoke with a consultant, he had 3 partners and they were working on their system to make their consulting business grow. When I challenged him about why he thinks the system is the reason his business is not growing, he became defensive. Why is the system not working I asked?

He continued to tell me it was not perfected and that he was still searching for the missing pieces to finalize things. Despite it's been the same story for two years, something felt off in my mind. I have heard this one many times.

Finally, we got to the truth as I listened intently, I said to him, "when you talk about your business I don't hear any fire?" He said, "well I am a little tired today."

Really? Does that have anything to do with your speaking the truth from your core? Does feeling tired mean you cannot be who you are? This guy had no balls or courage to say what was true.

Gregory is hiding behind his systems and knowledge because he lacks confidence. In his mind, the business is not working because of the system -- as if it has nothing to do with his leadership or energy. His system is about generating leads for his business, meanwhile he could easily pick up the phone, network, or email people to acquire new clients. Given its been two years, a driven entrepreneur is not going to wait to make money.

I took this a step deeper and shared with him that men try to build competence to compensate for the fact that they are not ready to pull the trigger. The system does not make the man, man is the creator and builder.

Waiting to see how that works out before he puts his fire power behind it is a sign he is not trusting himself. A part of him is holding out, waiting to see how the system turns out before he owns it. Your purpose and the system must fuse together.

I refused to work with Gregory; I cannot help someone if they are not open to the possibility that they are responsible for their life. His life is on stand-by until the system works for him, rather than him work the system.

A year later I saw him on my Facebook page touting about the launch of his business, again. Now it's been three years. I laughed. In three years, I have worked with over 100 people with my lead generation system. It took one month to put the system into action, it's simple, pick up the phone and share your passion and enroll people. Even if you are building a system of automation, you don't have to put your life on hold for it. Never put life on hold for something and not act on what you can do simultaneously.

WHILE BUILDING YOUR FERRARI, KEEP DRIVING
FORWARD LIKE YOU ARE ONE.

SOLUTION:

Get clear about when you know enough to start or change something, there is no such thing as being 100% ready. Making a decision and doing everything you can to make that decision right is what is needed. The best way to get clear is to have someone you respect challenge you in a conversation until you are 100% clear.

Here is how you can do that, have someone ask you what you want and why? If you answer them each time then you're fooling yourself. It's not about getting the answer right. It's about how well you show up in your response. Do you believe what you say? Can the other person feel your passion and strength for it? When your responses flow in a way that causes the other person to light up, then you know you are ready. Until then it's just head talk.

Chapter 5 Notes: The Ultimate Man Trap

» Overthinking things is an indicator that you are not trusting your decisions.

» Hiding behind your knowledge is not the answer, it creates a false sense of certainty. There is no better sense of certainty than success.

» Trusting yourself raises your vibration.

» Powerful men don't sell out on themselves, they don't mess around with things that are not their purpose.

» If you avoid doing things that are in your best interest, someone else will be forces to tell you what to do; a man does not like being told what to do.

» Decisiveness trumps confidence and competence every time.

» A man who makes a comeback, who is in the process of transformation takes the next step even if he does not know how it will be resourced.

» You can spend your entire life building your Ferrari, but if you don't have a strong enough purpose (or fuel for it) it will just sit there.

» Keep speaking what you want with a passion and a purpose that lights up other people when you speak; if you're words don't then you have a lack of clarity or expression of your power.

» Practice speaking what you want until you and others light up. Then you will know you own your word.

END OF CHAPTER 5 NOTES.

I am with you brother. You got this. You are more powerful than you think.

Let's move on to chapter 6.

Chapter 6

LIMITED IDENTITY CRISIS

It's natural to want what you've lost, it's also natural to want nothing to do with it ever again. Masculine energy swings the pendulum under stress. One minute they want back what they lost, or they say, "*the hell with it, I don't want anything to do with it again.*" Either way it is fear based.

It's also important to discover your story about what happened and why. The first identity men take on after a failure is the ***I was guy. He*** had it all, or close to it and now he doesn't. Whether its business, marriage, sex, a job or family, he had something he wanted and even worked hard for and now he doesn't. In some way shape or form, this guy often feels shut down, bummed out, or has given in all together. If he is hurt deeply enough he won't want anything to do with his failure or pain again.

We have all experienced some like this before, sometimes it happens at the "40 mid-life crisis" or when men get divorced, etc. We start to wonder what happened and find a new path that is more fulfilling, if we know how.

The other limited identity crisis is the, ***I want it back guy***; he is ready to fight at will to have it back. No matter what it is he won't settle and refuses to believe that he has failed. For better or worse, denial or acceptance he believes what he had is supposed to remain his. ***The I want***

it back guy is operating from a fear of loss; not realizing it's his identity he is trying to get back. He may not realize he has lost himself, rather than get clear on chasing after the stuff he sees he is losing. My view is simple, get you right first and the rest will follow.

IF YOU FEAR LOSING WHAT YOU GOT IT'S BECAUSE YOU HAVE ALREADY LOST YOURSELF IN THE PROCESS OF SUCCESS.

Believing you can get things back the way they were is a source of frustration. Living your life trying to go backwards is delusional as thinking that material success makes you a man. You cannot go back and get it. Our compartmentalized mind thinks, "you want it back" referring to the good things and good times, but that also includes the all pain that came with it. Why would you want that back?

Making a comeback is not about bringing the past back to the present or fixing the past to relive in some new way. Even if you try to get back what you lost, it won't be the same because you are not the same. Fighting for it is not the same as standing for it. Fighting for it is man's short-term way of fixing something so he can keep it. Standing for it means embracing pain and love, expressing vulnerability and forgiveness, it means healing and honoring the journey and ultimately stepping into more of your authentic self.

TO TAKE A STAND FOR YOURSELF MEANS FEELING EVERYTHING,STAYING WITH THE FEELINGS UNTIL YOU OWN IT. REAL MEN LIVE HERE, SMALL MEN FEAR THIS.

Let's look at where you are currently. How is your identity currently set? When a man fails, he usually falls into one of the two identity traps. ***I was guy or I want it back guy***, both of these identities are not useful to your comeback.

In my late twenties and earlier thirties, I was earning more than $1 million dollars per year, with a private plane, family, exclusive high-end home and many other benefits. I was also unhappy, the more I built my life; the more responsibilities came with it, causing feelings of overwhelming and burdens. Rather than living in joy I was in misery. A misery I created for myself, but did not want to admit. I built a world I wanted, that most men want, but I was not equipped to keep it all together.

A few years of this stress and I filed for divorce and walked away from it all, it was then I felt like the **"I was guy"** and yet, I tried my hardest to get it all back before discovering it wasn't what I really wanted. It was not who I was, but how the world thought I should be. A conditioned belief that what I had equaled what successful men do and have. It was not the case at all, even my closest friends often wondered and inquired about what I was up to and why. I didn't want to hear them attempting to remind me that it wasn't who I am or what I was about.

A couple of years later, while on a humanitarian trip in Africa, someone was asking about my journey and suddenly I felt like a **have been guy.** There were parts of my life that were amazing, shortly covered up with the many parts that brought out the worst in me. I built something amazing and continued to add more stuff to it. The easiest thing to do was follow what was true for me. Never would I have thought this early on in my life I would be feeling like I had accomplished so much and a 'have been' at the same time. Acting out of character or truth is more painful than any financial loss. Money can be remade; losing character takes its toll.

The **I was** guy unknowingly finds himself unmotivated, even things that may once have excited him causes an energy loss in other places. At the core of his life force he has been depleted or deflated. Often times trying to grasp new ideas is hard and he loses excitement for them. Naturally, wanting to seek comfort is more appealing and dreaming about what you want, brings solace, not motivation or commitment. I remember shortly after I walked away from it all, that I struggled to feel. I was numb. I forced myself to go to the gym and when I arrived I had no energy for it. I would sit in the lobby and order a pizza then go home; at least I showed up.

Nothing seemed to speak to me; very little resonated with me except doing nothing. It was a scary time to suddenly be stripped down to nothing. It's *no man's land*, the place we all fear experiencing. Yet, if you are patient and sit with this you can move through it quickly. You cannot push or force your way out of this space. I discovered it's a **reset** button for me. Sometimes we just need a break from it all to feel like nothing and **trust** we will pull through it.

While sitting in no man's land, I experienced intense boredom, weird carvings, I stopped eating meat and started watching TV. I attracted new friends that experienced the same things I had. Even while feeling like nothing, I was meeting people and having experiences like the world thought I was amazing. Yet, I still felt numb and I want you to know there is nothing wrong with this. It's just part of the journey, we all have to face. In order to break the mold and make an authentic comeback you have to face the stuff that no longer works. This too will pass.

Which one resonates with you? The **I was guy**? or **I want it back guy**?

Either way it is a mind game, only the mind experiences loss. What is more important is to read the rest of this chapter from the perspective of **your core, or the essence of who you are.** *Read this considering the question, "how was I showing up that created my own loss?"*

The *I was guy and the I want it back guy* are playing small. They cannot tell the difference between playing the game of life or business to win, or if they are playing the game to avoid losing. To avoid losing you are never fully in the game because you are more committed to the fear of losing than you are for the love of winning. As an example, if you watch a UFC fighter who fears striking another opponent because he knows if he does, his opponent may fire of a counter attack and win. The fighter that hesitates, holds back and does not fully engage. He isn't playing to win, although he wants to, he is playing to not get beat up. Rather than true champions, they take on the game fully and move forward without holding back. Everyone loves winning when they are winning; comeback men love it even when they are not winning.

Once you have experienced failure and disappointment, your mind will do everything to avoid it happening again. It's no different than putting your hand on a stove -- rarely do you do it again, but you can only do what you believe yourself to be, hence your identity.

If you don't shift your identity, you will only repeat the pattern. Most men blindly think that if their body is unhealthy then somehow their relationships, business or even sex life is good. "It's just my body that needs work."

Really? You don't use your body anywhere else in your life? Of course we do, yet we try to hide, ignore, and rationalize why it is okay to be out of integrity in other areas, while claiming we are men of integrity in others. And that no one is perfect. It's really not about perfection, but claiming reality instead of creating epic lies to battle.

You cannot put a nail in the tire and believe the leak is compartmentalized. You cannot trap or control an area that is not working and pretend it is not impacting the rest of your life. The nail will cause the entire tire to go flat – just like in your life and business. When your finance department reports there is no money left, don't pretend the rest of your company is *fine.*

Your identity is everything in your life and it's everywhere in your daily life. Who you are shows up everywhere. You may have different attitudes or emotions expressed in different areas, but your underlying identity is still the same. You have heard the phrase, "how you are anywhere is how you are everywhere?" Or "how you do anything is how you do everything." This rings true because they center around one's identity.

When you shift your identity, you shift all dimensions of your life-business. If you don't shift it, your mind will figure out ways to avoid the exact things from happening, while repeating the same pattern in different ways. Instead of putting your hand on a stove, you might trip over something. You may "burn" your relationships. You may get shut down in conversations. You might run red lights. The symptoms may change, but the reality is you are locked in an identity that is not your destiny.

Your failure is not who you are! Do you get that? It's not who you are. You have attached the results or lack thereof to your identity and now you are showing up like the identity you claimed. Stop claiming it right now, stop claiming and referring to yourself as the ***I* was guy**, **I want it back guy** or **I have failed guy**. Once you identify with it, it's time to shift. Just as you would not label a child for dropping a glass as clumsy. Nor label a child dumb because he struggles with reading; don't label yourself as the **I was guy** or **I want it back** guy.

The I Was Guy refers to himself through the eyes of the past. It's easy for this guy to feel down, numb, depressed, lonely and angry. When this guy sets out on a path to become someone and fails, whether it is financially, in his marriage, or with his kids, what he has really lost his is identity. A new one has not been claimed, so he feels a hole. Almost like a silent no one.

After my divorce, I was crushed; I didn't even realize how numb I was. I mistook how dead I was as calm and relieved. People noticed how calm I was, but the truth was I was in a bit of shock and dismay. I had no motivation. It felt like one moment I was the cross fit guy who trained 5 times per week, had an amazing diet, generating $35K per month working 3 days per week, to the guy who couldn't get out of bed.

Nothing inspired me, I was able to get mentally stimulated at times and feel excited in short bursts, but nothing really grabbed me anymore. The old Carl, the old identity of dad, family, and entrepreneur was gone. If it was ever me at all.

WHEN YOUR IDENTITY AND LIFE IS IN TRANSITION YOU MAY FEEL NOTHING. THIS IS A GOOD SIGN THAT YOU'RE IN BETWEEN THE OLD PARADIGM AND IDENTITY AND A NEW ONE. STAY IN THIS SPACE AND YOU WILL TRANSITION OUT OF IT.

Tate, a middle-aged man, attended my workshop in January of 2016. Tate was not in the best shape of his life. He seemed like someone who didn't believe he was attractive. Albeit a great communicator, huge connector, and lover. Tate roamed the room and sat next to every pretty girl hoping for their attention, mainly so he could feel good about himself.

Tate was recently divorced and in the process of losing the home he desperately wanted to keep. To make matters worse, Tate gained 20lbs and often battled loneliness. As he described, "I have this feeling of *why bother getting out of bed anymore.*"

In his mind he had once had everything he wanted. The wife he dreamt of, the house, his own wood shop and studio, solid consulting jobs and lots of friends, but he is passionless now. After working with Tate in coaching, it became clear that Marc was trying to get back all he had lost, to reclaim his identity that he was loved and has his life in order.

Tate built up a life he thought he wanted and should have had. That is what men do, get married, buy a home, find a good wife and live out life, but it did not fulfill Tate. It was exciting at times, but it lacked a higher purpose.

BUILDING UP A WORLD THAT YOU THINK YOU SHOULD HAVE, OFTEN LEADS TO DESPAIR AND DISAPPOINTMENT.

When you build up the energy to create a life, you lose all energy when it's gone. Tate was living this image he built up in his mind. It seems so real and worthy, yet the "honey do this, honey do that," way of life is noble, but not all fulfilling. Tate was not serving a purpose larger than himself.

Tate had to reach back and see who he was underneath it all. When we reconnected him to what he really stands for, what he is great at, and what really turns him on, Tate began to come alive again. It was a battle for him. While reflecting at what is underneath this, Tate still has to pay his bills, attend to his clients and occasionally run into his ex-wife and her new husband.

EMBRACING YOUR REALITY JUST MEANS FEELING IT A LITTLE DEEPER AND ASKING FOR THE TRUTH.

A year later, Tate has generated an additional $80,000 income, he lost 25lbs, is dating again, he healed his hurt and sadness. Tate became a badass and started asking for what he wanted, no matter what.

Tate began charging his clients more money, and was asked to sit on the board of Mars World, a two billion dollar hotel and Mars World theme park in China. He was the lead operator at mega cars shows across the U.S. and South Korea. You see Tate was living for others, for women, to please and have it all figured out, but not for his purpose. The nice guy does well for others and turns weak when taking on themselves and their mission.

When the 'I was guy' upgrades his purpose to the attitude of, "I care so damn much about who I am, I don't care," he is a free man.

It's time to upgrade and it all starts with a decision. Then you can build enough energy to generate momentum to move to the next level.

The 'I want it back guy,' is in for loads of pain. He doesn't realize he isn't playing to win or for freedom, he is playing to avoid admitting what happened. He lost and is hoping to piece it all back together. That way it looks good, feels better than what he is experiencing now. We have to approach it from a place of love, passion and purpose.

The 'I want it back' guy would be better served looking at his reality from a few thousand feet above the ground. What is he is trying to get back? What does he think he lost?

It's always a feeling that was lost. Men don't make the distinction between the two, they think those things and feelings are one in the same. Money equals power and without it I am powerless. It's an inaccurate perception, but it feels that way.

Everything has a lifespan and things do end. Allow that to be okay or face fighting for something that may no longer be for you. Your purpose doesn't end. You may have to repurpose things or re-elevate your purpose, but purpose never ends.

When man defines himself on the bedrock of what he has instead of who he is, reclaiming or attempting to get back what he perceives he lost, he is missing the lesson. The patterns that led to the loss in the first place are still at play. You can manipulate, fight or push your way back to it, and the patterns will resurrect themselves again. Too often men fight the good fight, but with the wrong approach and cannot figure out why it doesn't work.

YOU CANNOT GET BACK WHAT YOU HAD BEING THE SAME GUY THAT LOST IT, OR ELSE RISK LOSING IT AGAIN. THIS REQUIRES SHIFTING YOUR IDENTITY AND THAT TAKES TIME. SADLY, WHEN MONEY, A WIFE AND KIDS ARE INVOLVED YOU ARE PRESSED FOR TIME.

A client, Stan was in a situation where his business and marriage were falling apart. Everything he built was shaken when his wife grew tired of his lack of presence in their marriage. His business was stressing him out and he could not fix it while profits continued to sink.

He fought hard and did not have a successful outcome. His wife left him and his business was barely surviving, and then suddenly, he was ready for a change. When he called me, his conversation was not about change, but rather how do I make changes to fix my business and get my wife back. He thinks it's a task to do and nothing to do with "how he shows up."

If he looked at the patterns that caused his wife to feel left out, lonely, and his business to struggle, it all could have been cleared up and re-routed. But Stan wanted a temporary "pull it off" strategy, rather than look at how controlling and fearful he was of disappointing himself and his family.

If Stan can accept his reality, he can shift it. If he cannot, he will struggle more and push away the things that matter to him. And what really matters to him was not his family, although he claimed they were, or his business. When I asked him to consider what mattered to him, it was to always have money and to not disappoint anyone or he became unglued. Now we have the truth! He felt called out and realized he couldn't hide the truth anymore.

What you don't deal with, will deal you a hand bigger than you can handle. Stan was smack dab in it. Now the coaching can begin.

Stan had to get clear on what he thought he had and he revealed that he deeply cared for his family. He loves them and they also represented some status symbol of protecting and providing for them. That very symbol of what he learned a man should be was also his greatest fear. Unresolved fear within man never gets solved on its own.

Stan also admitted that when family things got difficult, he poured more energy into his business. Business makes him feel amazing, but once it started to head south, he was stuck, *does he stay and work through it, or does he go home and work through the issues? Either way, it was not going to be fun.*

Underneath it all, our values called family, health, finances, relationships, and our spirituality are a set of feelings we want to experience. When things change, we either experience growth or loss of feelings.

Stan wanted to get back his safety net in business, his sense of importance and his family was his status of feeling like a man. Although, socially noble and honorable, Stan was tired of keeping it all together. His identity was a mere label called Dad, husband, and CEO.

Stan made the shift. We spent an entire weekend together and he radically shifted how he saw himself. He identified key patterns about what being a man is and how difficult he made it. From the depths of his bones, he finally admitted what most men never do, he admitted he just wanted to be LOVED and never did anything to create it.

The **I want it back** guy is unloved; that is what gets to shift before he can succeed at getting his life-business back. When he began to approach everything from here, people, struggles and profit numbers would start to shift. Once Stan shifted his energy, everything else around him began to shift.

Men Who Rise:

During my comeback I had grown incredibly frustrated, the more I tried to get my life back, the worse it became. The more I tried to engage in new activities or passion, the less I felt. Regardless of which direction I took, I was duped. For once in my life I gave myself a few months break from business. No matter what the costs were I had to create space just to feel again. I called it a spiritual cleanse, to let go and give myself permission to feel like shit and experience the ultimate low, so I could rise again.

Doing this provided me a clean slate. Taking out the garbage in the form of a cleanse renewed my perspective, how I saw myself and ultimately gave me breathing room to create again. This feeling of emptiness has more peace to it than anything I have ever felt. By emptying things out I felt full and alive again, this is important for me. We all want the full package. In business, job, wife, and family. The entire kit and caboodle, but to have that we must be that.

By operating from fullness you will find your experience of greatness is much deeper and powerful. It makes no sense to man's logical brain to embrace the bad and believe that somehow your life will be richer. Yet, your brain or mind is not where embracing occurs. It's in your heart that it occurs. Feeling the stuff allows it to "leave." It depletes the negative charge so it does not run you. No man enjoys having anything run him, yet our stuffed stuff does run us.

A MAN WHO EMBRACES ALL OF LIFE IS A MIGHTY ONE.
A MAN WHO EMBRACES ONLY CONVENIENCE IS A MERE HALF MAN.

The man who rises must not allow suppressed drama to continue, waiting to deal with reality until you have to. Avoiding taking care of yourself until you get sick. Waiting for his wife to breakdown before he listens to her feelings. That includes not making time for what cannot be replaced, and money is always replaceable.

The man who rises must connect to a new part of him that is unknown or left behind. For me it was accepting the reality that my primary strength is courage and empathy. My courage was dead, and empathy suddenly became a DNA flaw that was not deserving of wealth, but rather more pain.

SOLUTION:

The risk of not checking in each day is that you work harder than you need to, and you work against yourself. Living by to do lists is not living, it's living for one day. Grinding it out means you're not connected to your truth or your purpose. Hustling hard is necessary at times, but you won't survive for long without a higher purpose feeding you limitless energy. You have to accept that you are enough right now to have what you want.

Commit the first 20 minutes of your morning to the creation of energy. Personally, I meditate on my vision until I experience a peaceful adrenaline rush. What happens for most men is a pattern of **excited-excited-exhausted/tired.** What you want is **excited-excited-relaxed** in your vision. This sets the tone for the entire day and allows me to operate from what is aligned within me, not live in reaction or the past.

The Rise Begins with a Capitol C: Courage

There is nothing bigger than you, it only seems that way when opportunity over shadows your inner strength; your courage. A client of mine Nathaniel had a slew of tough circumstances in his life. He was in the middle of a divorce, a new business and felt as though he couldn't move forward until his divorce was complete. There was just too much going on for him, although, rationally this makes sense to men, focus on 1 or 2 things at a time. It's how we limit our lives to feel we have control, and we move other important things to a later date. The divorce and new business was not bigger than him, but it does have a hold on him.

The willingness to activate courage summons an energy that says you are willing to do what is required of you, while feeling fear. It allows you to experience a freedom, while freeing yourself from a future date or limiting your life to 1 or 2 things. Courage is acting not to spite the fear, but embracing it and acting in congruence with what you want. It ultimately expands your capacity to handle anything.

COURAGE IS REQUIRED TO EMBRACE FEAR AND ACT ANYWAYS.

I experience fear often, but it's not an issue unless I allow it to hold me back. If you are not used to skydiving, fear is a natural response. If you jump, fear dissipates, and freedom takes over. All that is required of you is courage. Courage is not a mind game, it's an actual experience that is summoned for a situation demanding you to expand who you are. If you hold back moving into an uncomfortable situation, then you never develop or embody the courage for it. It seems like supply and demand at first. When you need more courage it's there, but only if you allow yourself to be in a situation that requires courage. You can spend your entire life trying to build up the courage, but it will never be enough until you act.

COURAGE IS THE PREDECESSOR TO BREAKING THROUGH.

Men have balls for a reason. Rarely do we use them to seek out raw, deep vulnerable and powerful states of consciousness, but mainly for short-term pleasure. It's not just a metaphor, but also the very essence of creativity and procreation. You may not feel you have enough power until you act powerfully and decisively. The vulnerability of starting over or cleaning up a mess is uncomfortable. No question about it, we don't like vulnerability. Courage is a gateway to act while feeling vulnerable.

Until you decide to slay the dragon and take on your vision, you may experience fear. So, what! Keep moving forward and summon what really matters to you. As you stay engaged in any moment you will activate more courage. You are an endless supply of courage and can summon more by staying engaged with the fear and vision.

THE SELF TRANSFORMING MAN TAKES THE NEXT STEP EVEN IF HE DOES NOT KNOW HOW HE WILL BE RESOURCED.

Years ago, I use to vomit 20 minutes before public speaking events. Before I put my tie on, I would head into the bathroom with a pillow and throw it down to kneel on, and hurl. Brush my teeth, tie my tie and walk into the room packed with hundreds of people, and deliver my talk. It was an odd ritual I didn't enjoy.

I stood on stage praying no one would see how flushed my face was, and I delivered my greatness. Five minutes later, I was as relaxed and unstoppable as I envisioned. Getting to that place was miserable, it was both a calling to speak publicly and a breakthrough. I continued to lead with courage no matter how the road blocks manifested. If you meet challenges with your greatest strength you breakthrough.

The longer my speeches went on, the more courageous and powerful I became. I couldn't get enough of it, so much so, that on days when I wasn't speaking, I felt down. I had to get back in the game and on stage. I was willing to endure the pain with courage to free myself from the fear. Courage and willingness go hand and hand. Seventeen years later I don't bother to prepare speeches. I trust what I say and what the audience needs to hear will be perfect.

THE COURAGE TO ACT & THE WILLINGNESS TO TRUST WILL CAUSE A BREAKTHROUGH.

By summoning courage, the willingness to trust is when breakthroughs occur. Before you decide to do something, courage or lack thereof must be activated. What stops men is thinking too far into the future, which they have no control over. In other words when you doubt what is going to happen and you cannot control the outcome, you stop moving forward with trust. Trusting the process is where most of us fail.

The Rise Continues with Trust

Children are very trusting. During our pre-toddler phase our intuition, ability to feel, and our instincts are at an all-time high. When I was 3 years old my dad was holding me in his arms. We were outside by the garage. We were watching his friend cut some wood for a bird house they were building. I remember a silent voice saying, "move." Every time I moved my legs it inconvenienced my Dad from having to put his cigarette down to re-adjust how he was holding me. My father kept pushing me back not realizing I was sensing something.

Then the loudest gut-wrenching scream came out, as his friend slipped and hit my ankle nearly severing it with an electric skill saw. That was the first time I allowed others to push my instincts away. That moment was the beginning of a battle of when to trust my instincts and when I was made wrong for having them. The truth is your intuition may not be convenient for others, your instincts may not be understood, and your life is about honoring them anyways.

In sports, I maintained my intuition at high levels, but it was more difficult with my family. They lacked self-trust and were controlling, so they never understood why I felt what I felt or did what I did. I had to explain myself constantly, but to no avail. They had no faith and always worried the worst would happen, even to the point of making the worst happen. Then they would say, "I told you this would happen." My family only wanted to be right and not honor the path of others. Sadly, they didn't realize my path is not about them. If you have people in your life that do not honor your path, or are uncomfortable with it, you must upgrade for people who do.

Life became a battle of trusting myself and standing in self-trust especially when others could not understand it. I made many mistakes and succeeded at failing many times. All the while, knowing in my gut what I was about to do was going against my own intuition. I did it anyways until I finally surrendered and let my heart lead. As it turns out, keeping my head out of it was easier and more freeing than I thought.

Still, today my family cannot figure out how I can walk away from the perfect life and started over doing what I love. It makes no sense to my family to follow your own instinct and intuition.

The most powerful CEO's I work with trust themselves beyond measure. At insanely high levels, they do things others think are crazy. Visionaries and intuitive people are often ridiculed for their unrealistic ideas or logic. We live in a world that only trusts what seems logical or reasonable, but not someone else's intuition.

There was a day when people laughed at the thought of a car instead of a horse for transportation. Or the idea that the internet would run our lives, let alone technology. Many of the most powerful CEO's or inventors were not believed when they started. When my male clients look for validation and get it, I often tell them those are red flags, not a green one's. If no one challenges your idea, you won't necessarily grow stronger. Starbucks got laughed at, Yahoo, Amazon, and Myspace. Which was sold for hundreds of millions of dollars by a farmer. People thought they were nuts, and that's a good thing!

RECEIVING NORMAL FEEDBACK ABOUT YOUR IDEA IS NOT A GOOD THING, UNLESS YOUR IDEA IS JUST ANOTHER NORMAL IDEA. WHEN YOU RECEIVE FEEDBACK THAT YOU'RE IDEA IS CRAZY--- YOU ARE PROBABLY ONTO SOMETHING GREAT!

The more mental or analytical and even confused you are, the less access you have to your own instincts. When your energy goes into your head, you lose your balls and the masculine energy that has allowed you to succeed is limited. You cannot experience life in your head. Nor does the mind inherently trust anything it cannot figure out, back up with knowledge or evidence. The mind's job is to protect you, not create happiness or success. The mind can only direct your vision once you fully engage in it, but make no mistake, the mind is not the primary source of your success.

For men, we are torn between two polarities. Men often have experiences like this, "I feel this but," "I know this but," or "I think this, but I am not sure how I feel about it," and we bounce back and forth, in and out of knowing and not knowing. Sometimes they even oppose each other, in other words, you are not listening well enough and you're uncertain.

This is where a powerful man sits and listens to his gut or heart and waits to honor his truth. A fantastic example of this is Gandhi. He fasted for weeks in order to shift an entire country into independence from the British. Upon coming out of his fast, he marched to the Indian sea, made salt and freed India from British control. He waited courageously for the truth; most men wouldn't dare sit for an hour to discover their truth. If you want an epic empire this is an example of acting epic.

I am not suggesting starving yourself for weeks. I am suggesting you reveal the truth that you're hiding. If you sit and listen to your truth it will set you on fire. When this occurs, every obstacle falls out of your way. It will feel like you are not doing anything, but you are!

Primarily, we learned to live in two heads. Our sexual head feels a lot when we are sexual, while our mental head talks a lot. When the sexual head feelings are strong enough we convince ourselves mentally to rationalize our actions. If the mental head figures out its strategy, we decide to act on it, no heart required!

Where is the integrity to our vision? The goal is to feel your entire body all the time. Feel your feet touch the ground when you walk, feel the depths of your balls, your heart beating, breathing and while watching the thoughts and feelings emerge that you want to experience. This is man's way of mastering embodiment, rather than myopic focus on one or two things; we have to take a 360-degree connection.

Bouncing back and forth is a sign of disconnection--a looping state of mistrust. Just as a child who has no direction and is left unattended makes a mess, man who is disconnected and left alone to "overthink" creates a mess for himself. Meanwhile, you think you are figuring it out. The part of you that is figuring stuff out is denying the part of you that already knows. Here is an example:

Bill Bartmann was a billionaire client and friend of mine, he passed away in the midst of writing this book. He was the most amazing man I knew. During our time together, he realized it was time to rebuild one of his companies. It had been over a decade since his billionaire business was forced to shut down. As you can imagine this epic failure resulted in thousands of people out of a job, serious financial loss and a great deal of stress. Why would anyone go back and do it again?

During the financial crisis starting in 2008, the amount of debt in the U.S. climbed to its highest levels ever. Bill had a strategy to collect that money.

One Sunday he and his wife were driving to their favorite pancake house and he leaned over and said, "It's time to rebuild CFS II. I want to ask you if you are good with that?"

His wife's response was epic, "I knew this day was coming years ago, what took you so long?"

MEN ARE WIRED FOR FEAR OF FAILURE. IN OUR DNA, STILL TODAY, IS THE BELIEF THAT WE ARE HERE TO PROVIDE AND PROTECT. IF WE FAIL, WE LOSE OUR FAMILY, LEGACY AND MONEY. SADLY, THAT IS A LONELY APPROACH TO LIFE NOR IS IT A TRUE ONE. WHAT WE FEAR THE MOST IS THAT WE WILL RUN OUT OF EXCUSES AS TO WHY WE DID FAIL.

Have you ever noticed that women tend to know things before men admit them? Women usually know the heart of the man they are with. They often drop hints at us, and avoid "telling us "what to do." Then if they really care, they will get louder or more obvious about it. Then they surrender and wait patiently for men to "get it." Your inner knowingness is a lot like a woman giving you a heads up in advance.

That same part of you that knows, is getting covered up with your need to ***figure it out.*** Let that go! You must trust yourself and demand to see the truth. When you get certain about something, when you get clear and empowered, you see what to do and how.

THERE IS A PART OF YOU THAT ALREADY KNOWS. WHILE YOU ARE BUSY TRYING TO FIGURE STUFF OUT, JUST ADMIT THAT A PART OF YOU KNOWS AND LISTEN TO IT!

I could give a man my exact strategy for building a one-million-dollar business and he will fail 90% of the time. The reason I succeed is because of how I show up, it's my personality, my strengths and my mindset that are not easily duplicated. You see, who you are matters more than what you do and how. If your heart and soul are not behind the steps, you're playing the robot game.

I spent the first part of my coaching career showing doctors exactly what to do, step by step, to grow their practice and communicate with their patients. Doctors are notorious for "not wanting to take risks." Rightly so, there are huge liabilities if they are wrong. So, they rely on science only. Because of this they are NOT offering who they are to the process to avoid failure. "It is not me it's science." Unfortunately, holding back from offering who you are to the success process, means you're not showing up. If you are not fully showing up and available for the process, you won't be fully available to experience fulfillment.

As if a part of you doesn't already know! Wake up my brother, you are a powerful source of intuition and instinctive sense. Stop trying to play chess with life and figure stuff out. When you know your vision and purpose, life is not about figuring stuff out, but rather manifesting and staying true to it. Your vision and purpose inherently KNOW what to do. Your mind will always run out of things to do, except that which it already knows. Same old same old.

IF YOU WANT TO AVOID FAILURE THEN LISTEN TO THE TRUTH IN YOU NOW. OTHERWISE I PROMISE YOU, TRUTH WILL ARISE LATER.

I know I can handle things in my life even when I don't know what they are. How? It's not a how, it's knowingness. This knowingness is called trust that I can handle me, my reactions, and access resources to find out what needs to be done in the event I don't know in that moment. Does that mean I always will? Does that mean I will always find a way? No, it means I am strong enough to embrace the risk and move forward in trust.

Just as a top CEO doesn't always know what will happen in business, they trust themselves to adapt, re-strategize, and work their game and often without time to think or get stuck.

TRUSTING YOURSELF MEANS DECISIONS CAN BE TAKEN FASTER AND WITH MORE CONFIDENCE.

Beware of making decisions when you are not grounded, a decision from this state creates sabotage. How you can you authentically decide out of mistrust to make a situation workable for you? You are smart enough to know that making a decision when you are upset is not the best time. Grounded decisions require you to breathe into your body, take as much time as required for you to sink into your gut and listen to what is true for you. The more you practice, the quicker your ability to handle decisions in urgent moments.

For me, trust means deciding from my vision and then acting to make that decision prove right and productive. It means trusting and not judging my intuition. Even if the mind screams otherwise, it is my duty to let the mind know what I have decided, and it is to align with my decision. Thinking and mulling things over is not a decision making process, that is a head game to avoid confronting the real issue or opportunity you need to decide on.

Early on in my career, while coaching for Tony Robbins, I ventured into stock market trading in-between client phone calls. I really didn't know what I was doing. I had taken some training and other coaches were educating me along the way. I started with $500 and watched the stock graphs and stayed true to my investing rules. Mainly, "don't lose money and cash out every 10% increase in value."

I invested in Ariba software and bought it at $22. Within a month the stock climbed to $42. My rules for selling were met and I sold them. I then reinvested at $41 and held on. All the indicators for holding on to this stock were in alignment with my rules. And my gut said to stay with this and invest more money. I went to Bank of America and got a loan for $2,500 and I invested all $2,500 into ARIBA. What? Why would you do that? This is what my mind said, but my gut was calm, clear, and knew exactly what it was doing despite my lack of experience.

Then I made a huge mistake, and it's not what you think. I knew based upon my strategy and this tug I was feeling, that something was going to pop. Something told me to ride this out.

The mistake was not setting a stop loss to protect my money if the stock had dropped. I was leaving for Cabo San Lucas on my honeymoon for two weeks, with very limited internet access and no computer. I acted irresponsibly and frankly, like a rookie.

When I returned ARIBA had a quarterly earnings report that came public. I had no idea quarterly earnings reports existed, but, ARIBA jumped to $129 per share, then I sold it at $144 before it returned to $122 and stayed at that price for many months.

I nearly quadrupled my investment because I had the courage to trust my gut and my strategy. Even while making a mistake, and yes it was a mistake despite making money.

Now here is the mantrap. What if I had lost all that money? Would that have been a wrong decision?

In one sense, yes, I made a negligent error in not setting my stop loss; but if I hadn't received the results that does not mean my gut was wrong. It's almost always human error that gets in the way and it almost did for me. Here is an insight for you, will power feels like excitement and a rush of energy, head power feels like dopamine or a mental high. Both are red flags; deeper insight is a green flag. My excitement was not a trigger for taking a loan out. The 'hit it big' attitude did not cause me to make this decision, it was pure insight and the strategy aligned with me.

Just because something did not work out, does not mean your gut was wrong. It just means you did not get the result and that is what happens in life. Sometimes your gut will inform you to do something and you may or may not know why. You might find out later why your gut wanted you to act. Sometimes the real magic happens later, but you would never know if you didn't trust your gut. I can count the times my gut led me to do something and years later I discovered why. The masculine part of you fears this.

You are here today because of the decisions you made. Men who read this book have emailed me stating, "I was just thinking I need to return to reading your book again after my divorce, and I looked up and the guy next to me was reading your book."

If you map out your life path and look at each decision you make, it alters your path and direction in life. Your life on paper would look like a holistic spider web. This is something I do with men that are wondering or lost in life. They can see which path they took and why and how it all leads back to their vision, or at least finding their vision. It's all connected to the very fabric of who you are. Feeling pain or power are not factors to whether you are on your path or off your path, you're always on the path. Nothing is coincidental, nothing is random, and nothing is useless. All of it or any of it can cause you to rise up.

The most successful men I know, live in their vision and act out of it. Your vision does not live in either head, it lives in your entire being.

The Rise Completes with Embodiment

The embodiment of your WHY is felt everywhere. Embodiment means you have saturated your body with your vision. You own it and every move you make is from a grounded, solid place of ownership of your vision.

Gerry is a client and lifelong friend, in his mind, he felt it was important to tell me that, "If I were standing in front of him I would agree he is not the best-looking guy. Women are not going to notice me or check me out." At the same time he is a highly sophisticated guy, a goof ball, and yet, very successful, but looks like he has not worked out in years.

He still had the courage to try and impress women while knowing in the back of his mind he has no chance. To overcome this, he would settle for a less attractive woman to avoid feeling like a complete reject. He was the guy that built a huge real estate empire and in just a year closed its doors and lost his wife on his birthday.

Gerry called me at midnight on his birthday in tears. Hearing a man cry from the depths of who he is, is a beautiful thing and a scary one. It's the ultimate alienation of our manhood and leaves us vulnerable. Yet, it's the most powerful place for a man to let go.

Gerry was shocked and yet, a part of him was not surprised. He built up a grandiose business vision and he was so close to it all clicking together and reaping massive rewards for his efforts and brilliance and suddenly it all shattered. He was committed to having it all and like most men, they have no way of keeping it all together, long term.

After working with Gerry all through the night he was able to admit his life was driven by the fear that no one wanted him. No matter what he did, he was afraid he wouldn't be wanted by others. That revelation is also a deeply embedded story, and that is all that it is. Our stories shape our world and they can all be re-written.

Most of the brilliant CEO's I have worked with all had some level of desperation, hurt, and disgust in their life. They are the most powerful forces in a man's life. We want to prove those feelings wrong and anyone who doubted or questioned our true nature. Material success is evidence we are worthy. If you're going to create a story that you are amazing because of your empire, then you also need to admit in your story that your empire owns you. That your empire defines your worth, or else risk feeling like a fraud. If your story is one sided, it's probably not authentic.

Growing up my father and I did not get along. I was the youngest and most exciting in the family, so he lived through me to find joy and meaning in his life. This created an unwanted pressure for me. Before sporting games, he would always say something that would piss me off. Those games were my best performed games. It became a running joke as I got older, before a championship game my teammates would ask, "did you fight with your dad today?" If so I was destined for an ESPN type day.

Gerry, like most men, has had experiences in his life that led him down the path he is on. Gerry built up a story and convinced himself that a beautiful wife, a successful real estate empire, and financial wealth would prove others wrong and that he was not the unwanted reject. That his parents could no longer reject him with this kind of evidence. If they did, then it would be noted that he isn't the one with issues, it was his parents.

This revelation changed everything. It shifted him from living a story he made up, to operating from passion, respect, contribution and the sheer fulfillment of making his clients dreams his number one priority.

Today Gerry walks into a room and lights it up, people notice him. Women now respond to his conversations because his focus isn't on achievement, although that is what is happening. He sold $23 million in real estate last year, while traveling every quarter to a 3rd world country for vacation. His shift was operating from an authentic vision and his deep desire to contribute. When he operates from commitment there is openness, love and he is never disappointed, nor fears failure because it is about empowering others.

Gerry rose up! 8 years later he is still growing and now married. He adopts abandon dogs, often injured, and cares for them. He recently returned from a two-week trip to Spain, while his office continued to grow without him. He owns it now.

WITH EMBODIMENT THERE ARE NO BARRIERS, YOU ARE UNSTOPPABLE.

Our next step is to become more embodied, but first I want to share with you a story. It is about a prisoner of war who was held captive for 7 years and tortured. He found a way in the most extreme conditions to find both freedom and embodiment when the other men captured chose to slowly die.

Colonel J was captured in the Vietnam war. He was an African American soldier. During his capture he was placed in a small homemade cell barely big enough to sit Indian style in. He was not given the luxury of a simple pillow or blanket to stay warm. He was fed minimally at times and starved on many occasions. I think we can both agree that water didn't flow from a clean sink into his cell. Imagine that, 7 years of contaminated water. After 7 years the Vietnamese prison camp decided to let him go. Here's why.

Each day as part of his captivity Colonel J was beaten and whipped. Soldiers tied him up to a post and whipped him daily to force him to talk. Yet, he refused to. At one point, it occurred to him that there was no way out, but through each day after being beaten he was tossed back into his cell. With flesh wounds and blood dripping down his back and severe pain, he refused to go numb or give in. He began a push up and sit up routine. Multiple times per day he did hundreds of push-ups and sit ups. He created an affirmation that said, "whip it on!" Since no medical care was provided he decided to embrace this pain and take it on, rather than fight against it.

Whip it on! With each passing day of yelled, while he was tied up and getting whipped. His fresh flesh wounds from the previous day ripped open even farther and deeper, he would yell, "whip it on!" With each whip. Alchemizing each painful whip into pleasure and motivation.

Then stripped down off the whipping post and sent back to his cell he would commence even more vigorous push-ups and sit ups chanting, "whip it on." Meanwhile, the prison guards thought he was crazy or at least going crazy. Why would anyone want to take it on? That answer is simple, with embodiment you can alchemize pain and generate power. While most, even on a less stressful and emotional scale, go numb and suppress their lives, he chose to expand.

PAIN CAN RAISE YOU UP OR SINK YOU.

With each whip he gained more passion, power, and determination. At one point, he shared experiencing more peace, like there was nothing they could do to beat him or cause him to surrender. He continued to rise up and get stronger each and every day. Meanwhile, his comrade Gunther whined, complained, and resisted the pain. He fought against it instead of rising up. He encouraged Gunther to say, "whip it on" and to join him in push-ups and sit ups, but he was going crazy, numb, and in pain. He refused to find ways to get clear on the goal of surviving and getting home. Or to do anything that would facilitate a direction other than looking forward to more beatings.

Gunther died a short while after, while Colonel J was getting ripped and powerful. He was so connected to his body and solid, they discontinued beating him because it wasn't working. To add humiliation to his torture, prison soldiers began urinating on him in his cell. As you can imagine, acidic urine on flesh wounds, burn. While they urinated on him, he continued to chant, "whip it on." Shortly after they fed him less, while his body continued to grow in ways most men who go to the gym hoped for.

After a while they left him alone to just sit in jail. No one could figure out what to do to break him. Seven years later they opened his bamboo cell and set him free. He made his way home and now speaks about his experience.

He never lost his swag or his ability to feel or his ability to act. He chose to stay in his body and own his experience no matter how great the pain was. You see, it's easy to feel like you are in your body when things are working. Staying within your body is where the magic happens.

Let's look at some steps to embodiment.

3 Steps to Embodiment

Embodiment is powerful, it means you are SAFE, CONFIDENT and feel freedom in your body. Embodiment happens when your vision is so strong that you can feel it when you walk, breathe, and move. The impact of this is that "who you are" speaks louder than anything you could say.

Here are the 3 steps to embodiment.

1. Engage your swag

Every man has his own unique swag, this swag begins with the strongest inner stance about your vision. When you visualize your vision, it alters the way you stand, breathe and move your body. When you pull in the emotions created from visualizing your vision, a natural movement begins to occur in your body called swag. As you walk in that vision you express a swag. Therefore, living in your head does not help you win, nor can you manifest from your head. Your swag and life force must come through your body.

YOUR BODY IS THE MANIFESTATION OF YOUR MIND — HOW YOU MOVE YOUR BODY IS DETERMINED BY THE TYPES OF EMOTIONS YOU EXPERIENCE AND INTENSITY OF THEM.

Here is a simple analogy, think of the greatest moment of your life or that you just received a client check for $10,000,000. You are ecstatic and every single cell in your body is alive and vibrating. You walk into a restaurant; do you think people will pick up on your energy?

YES! Of course they will. Conversely, on tough days your swag is stiff, and rigid with no movement or freedom coming from you. I find it hysterical when men tell me they want freedom yet, their posture is stiff, rigid and has no "freedom" like movements exuding from their body. Their mind says one thing, but their body says the opposite; it's called incongruent.

We are a three part being, mind, body and spirit. Only ignorance thinks they can experience liberation with a stiff body and no spiritual path. You may know or feel in one part of you, and feel you should have results. But, you want all three parts of you to experience that knowingness. Then results occur effortlessly.

Now reverse the above scenario. Are you willing to experience having $10,000,000 right now? In your body and let it manifest in reality? Most men say yes, but rarely do they sit quietly for 15 minutes per day intensely focused on it. Yet, they keep chasing the white rabbit.

Your swag is the expression of the vision you stand for. It's the most stunning characteristic of man. Your ability to be in charge, in control, and express your vision through your body. It speaks volumes about you to women, your market, your tribe, the people around you and it's your brand speaking on your behalf.

All that is required of you is to fully feel your vision and allow it to move your body. Athletes do this well. Have you seen football and basketball players when they are in the zone? They move in amazing dynamic ways, versus a guy who is in a slump, who moves like he is stuck. Even football players being accused of "showboating" are expressing the commitment to winning through their body. Their intense emotions and charge come through their body in full expression. Only a weak man stands still and rigid during times of successful and epic accomplishments, afraid to let his emotions exude from his body. Yes, we all celebrate in our own way, but holding back the amazing feelings from moving your body is not how you embody or express your truth.

Your swag is both a way to live and a way to shift yourself in each and every moment you feel disconnected or not in the zone. And yes, you can still have swag when things are not working, or you feel stressed. It's takes practice. But to say you want a million-dollar empire while your body is stiff, and rigid is incongruent. It won't happen hiding your emotions from your body, they must be expressed.

2. Breathe life into every cell

What is the very first thing a man does right before he loses control of his emotions? Or has an orgasm? Or begins to over think?

He STOPS breathing and this act alone changes his swag and his vibe. Cutting off your life force is the ultimate no-no. Think of life as dynamic as the actions of a boxer. A boxer can move in any direction with quickness, power, style and instinct and has a deadly swag. They never stop breathing the entire time; or fueling their swag.

Years ago I was hiking in the mountains and I was struck in the leg by a vicious rattle snack. This guy meant business. He was big, and he gave me no warning sign, at least that I heard.

The moment it struck me, massive pain took over. My heart began pounding, and my leg felt like it was on fire. To make it worse, the snake couldn't retract his fangs and he was stuck in my leg. I grab the snake around his head and tried to maneuver his fangs out. Finally, I got the fangs out and tossed him into the bushes.

I had no idea if I would make it back to my truck. I was already miles into my hike, and this had to be the worst day to forget my cell phone. Not to mention its 90 degrees out.

I was dizzy, and light headed. I started to walk as fast as I could, but I tired quickly and the faster I went the faster the venom travelled through my blood. I began deep breathing. I breathed all the way into my fang wounds. Then I would walk for a few minutes. I stopped again to breath for a few minutes. After about thirty minutes of this, something profound happened.

The pain started to dissipate. I could feel my leg throbbing, but the pain didn't impact me. My heart began to relax and slow down and a rush of energy helped me continue down the path back to my truck.

My dizziness went away. Given that I have a low tolerance for pain, a bee sting would knock me down for a day, I was stunned by this. I finally reached my truck and drove to the emergency room on my own. When I arrived, and told them what happened, the front desk lady asked, "are you sure, you seem quite calm?"

The action of breathing, not only keeps you calm, it keeps you present. It provides you access to all parts of you and your potential. It is your best agent for healing.

This is the experience you can have when you are embodied. It's one of the most unstoppable experiences because you realize you are in control of the only thing you can control, your energy.

3. Visualize your purpose

Now that we covered the swag expression and breathing, bringing in your purpose adds spark to the fires of your identity. Let your purpose take on a life of its own. Let it have its way with you as opposed to allowing your masculine wiring fight for control. By doing, so you enter the flow or the zone that men crave to live in. For example, when you were a child watching a movie, you were so into it, that nothing else existed. The movie was in control of your brain and occupied you. Let your vision do this for you. The difference is the vision is more empowering than a movie and, yet our mind is a movie. You just want to install the vision that supports you.

When you add physical movement to breathing and the visualization of your purpose, you have fully engaged your primary senses, sight, sound, and feeling. Think of this as pulling your purpose into the rest of your body.

At first, I used to visualize everything on my visualization board by sitting in a meditation pose and starring right at the center of the board. After 10 minutes, I would close my eyes and watch the images appear in my mind.

While staring at the center of this board for 10 minutes, my brain was literally reading and scanning the entire board and committing it to short term memory. Short term memory lasts for 3-5 seconds. Doing this for 10 minutes continues to build the memory. This way when my eyes do close I can consciously capture all the images from the board and focus on them.

As I focus on them I am generating a strong mental focus for another 10 minutes. Can you imagine the state of mind I am in when my morning ritual is done?

I am alive, fully engaged, and in my body.

Your Embodiment Assignment

This exercise does not require much effort at all, and yet the results are profound. Make a large black dot in the center of a white piece of paper. For men, they find their ability to let things go, their thoughts, feelings and stress are best done in this exercise. When you are done, you can add in a vision board or quotes or pictures to fill you up with inspirational food.

Here is how it works:

Place that white piece of paper 3-5 feet away from you at eye level. Stare right into the black dot for several minutes and toss every thought, feeling or internal dialogue into the black hole. Until you have some clarity and inner silence. You can spend as much time as needed on this. Think of it this way, your daily thoughts are in the tens of thousands. It may take more than 30 minutes the first few times you do this.

Once you have emptied yourself out, you can now place the picture on top of the black dot. Start your 10-minute stare down of that picture on the visualization board. Once you are complete, close your eyes and focus intensely on all the images that have now been imprinted in your mind. There is no time limit on this one; there is no reason to have one. Once you are committed to the vision and can feel it fully in your body you are complete. You can continue to go deeper into those images and feelings. It will only sharpen and enhance your experience.

I used the word complete, did you notice that? There are days when I meditate and 20 minutes into it I have a vibe of completion and I stop. There are some days that last longer. It is not important to stop for time or when you feel done, but rather complete. Completing the exercise means you have gotten what you needed and have a full circle experience and some level of "it's finished" and I can move on. The opposite of this is like leaving a tough conversation before it's complete and now it's up in their air as to when you will come back to complete it. That feeling is never fun.

The **I was guy** will find great value in this because he is numb. It will ignite him and clear out feelings of disappointment, pain, or regret. The **I want it back guy,** will find authentic inspiration to reclaim his personal power and begin manifesting again.

I recommend doing this daily. You have every reason to commit to this until it becomes a habit. Think of it as your personal "non" think tank, where you are aligning your world, so the outer worlds follow you, forms to you and makes way for your purpose, rather than the opposite, which you have already lived through. This process is invaluable. You may discover that some days you do it and it works well, compared to the days you don't do it. You may also discover many issues you can clear up by sitting than by acting. That is the power of it.

Chapter 6 Notes: Limited Identity Crisis

» During a set back or failure, its your identity that feels attacked. And that identity can no longer work for you, you have to upgrade how you see yourself in order to make a comeback.

» Take a stand for yourself, that means feel everything no matter what until you own your feelings. When this happens you will feel unstoppable.

» There are two types of identities, *The I Was Guy and the I Want it Back Guy.* It is up to you to determine which one you are.

» Your identity means everything, it determines how you feeling, how you behave and ultimately determines who well you success or not.

» During a time of transition, you may feel nothing or unmotivated. That just means you body and mind are learning how to find healthy and more empowering ways to live. Stay with it, you will pull through.

» Embracing your reality means that you accept the truth about your reality. Then and only then can things change.

» Courage is required to embrace fear and act accordingly anyways.
» Courage is the predecessor to having a breakthrough.
» The courage to act and the willingness to trust will cause a breakthrough.
» Trusting yourself eliminates doubt, hesitation and withholding yourself.
» The best way to avoid failure is the listen to the truth.
» When you embody something you become unstoppable.
» Embodiment is about regaining your male swag, breathing life into every cell in your body, and then visualizing your purpose until it takes you over.

END OF CHAPTER 6 NOTES.

I am with you brother. You got this. You are more powerful than you think.

Let's move on to chapter 7.

Chapter 7

FEEL YOUR WAY THROUGH

If you think in terms of everything having a pulse, your main role as a man on a mission is to do everything with a pulse. That means feel your way through it, into it, and keep your pulse close to you. One of the biggest challenges men have is understanding the difference between their biological sensations, thoughts, feelings and hormones, and their heart calling. For most men, it's like swinging the pendulum, one moment you are excited about something, then suddenly you feel otherwise. Understanding these differences means avoiding another breakdown in the future, instead of running into one and learning the hard way.

A friend and client Aaron was suddenly struck with the worst thing that could happen to him. Aaron was indicted by the U.S. Government for bank fraud. But before you judge made mental assumption, I will tell you as will Aaron, it was all perfect. It was meant to happen and his two-year prison sentence was life changing.

Now the back story, Aaron was always a high achiever. A powerful young lad who started his entrepreneurship path at age 17. He was great with the ladies, so much so, most men would be jealous if not standing in line asking, "how does he do it?" Aaron is fit, great with money and people. So why or how did this happen?

Aaron was addicted to achievement, he had to drive to the finish line and in some cases not enjoy the process until he got what he wanted. Like many men, he used control, not trust, used drive, not divine fire, and used his head, often leaving his heart and truth at the door. Although he thought he was doing the right things, and it felt right, those are the biological reactions, not necessarily the heart callings.

One would argue that although winning drove Aaron, he was more driven by not losing. He didn't want to end up alone, hence the heart is our great protector from this feeling. A sign we're disconnected from our heart if we fear loneliness. Aaron's greatest fear was losing everything he built.

WILL POWER CONFUSES MEN INTO FEELING LIKE THEIR HEART IS CALLING THEM.

One day, while in a taxi cab waiting for the light to turn green, the FBI opened his door and asked, "are you Aaron?" He said, yes and they arrested him. He was among several who were indicted.

The bank was offering lines of credit to businesses and created errors in the process. Aaron was an expert in this field so the FBI believed he should have known better. He had done months of due diligence on this company and began referring clients to them. His assets were frozen as part of the indictment, which forced him to have public representation.

Now the real story begins, was this a lesson or opportunity? Aaron was now faced with his greatest fear, one that, all men face them at some point. They all come in different forms like, prison, divorce, drugs, depression, and obesity and nonetheless, we don't get out of this life without facing them. The question now for Aaron was, "how to be free in a process that takes your freedom?" If he didn't get the lesson or opportunity, prison would be a waste and a hell.

Aaron's experience in prison was similar to that of life for men, feeling trapped in a marriage, relationships, business or having to conform and not win. Prison was defensiveness and survival with ultimate intensity. You have three choices, join sides in a gang or face yourself or both.

Every day Aaron prayed, meditated and listened to his heart. After experiencing sadness, anger, hurt, and regret, he found a way to find peace in a non-peaceful environment. He realized that love is all that matters. Soon this would prove to be very true, as he was tested by a psychopath.

At one point an inmate darted into his room and began choking him out because he did not believe he was a good guy. Aaron yelled back, "I am with all people and I will not conform." That way of thinking does not work in prison. Rightly so, neither was telling a psychopath while being choked, "I LOVE YOU." Aaron chose love while getting choked. He rose up. He may have been beaten, but he was not conquered.

It makes no sense, does it? To tell someone who is minutes away from killing you that "I love you." Most men would rather be beaten than to surrender and love the insanity of another. There's freedom in what Aaron did in prison.

NO MATTER WHAT HAPPENS, LOVE IT.

Aaron's response and how he chose to see the world at that point was with an "I love you." He said that to everyone silently and out loud, especially when it came to violence or racism or judgment or having to take a win-lose side. He began liberating himself each and every moment, in a captive environment. Aaron realized the man-made stuff about success, winning, money, status and material gain was just a cover up. That he lost everyone because he refused to let love in. He saw this as a personal journey to his own freedom. The key takeaway from this story is to have this truth realized before we get sick, before we get divorced, hooked on drugs or in some cases head to prison or down a path that causes us to wake up. You are here to love brother. Behind every action love is what we are after, we just call it ridiculous names to cover up that truth.

MAN CAN EXPERIENCE LIBERATION REGARDLESS OF HIS CIRCUMSTANCES. OTHERS GET DEFINED BY THEM.

Surrender is not giving up, it's simply saying, "I am who I am and I am free." You cannot control most of which you have tried to control. Aaron took the most conscious approach to living and came out better than ever. His time in prison was what he needed, and it was only his choice to land where he landed. If you don't let go of your fear and trust your own heart, then you may face an opportunity or lesson to have to surrender and let go. To let God or let heart live through you, rather than pioneer yourself through every wall, barrier and to every goal, thinking you will be a better man because of it.

Whatever happens "love it." Are kids going to push your buttons? Will a marriage cause you pain occasionally? Will work? Money? Yes, it all can and probably already has. You conceptually know to love, but it's not your default response to love either. You do want to embrace or go with the flow, but you don't. It's easy to say I will love you or life no matter what. That you will do whatever it takes, then there is reality. You don't.

You cannot fight your way to epic living or through epic challenges. If you pour your greatness, your love, and passion into this moment, into everything that is right in front of you, you are masterful. There will be very little that can take your freedom. You have a choice in any circumstance or situation, that choice is usually an indicator of your character. Choose well, choose to love the hell out of it all.

Let's break this down:

Aaron did one remarkable thing after another, mainly he *felt* his way through everything. In a hyper Alpha Man environment, he became more feminine and balanced. Which is counter and darn right illogical. He shifted his alpha side to his heart side and no one in prison could force, coerce or beat him down, even when they tried. No one of the many hardcore criminals could force Aaron to succumb to anything. Even while facing violence, he stood his ground in love and repeated the "I love you" process. No one else messed with him after that.

Now imagine you are on purpose and stuff like this showed up? Many would give in, give up or move on and not stand their ground. Men wonder why they don't ultimately get what they want? How can you wonder why? None of us knows what is going to happen on our path and I am here to tell you it doesn't matter. You get to take it on and trust the process. The path will never intentionally hurt, humiliate, or force you down. Although, it may appear like it is, the path itself is always neutral, giving you free will to choose how you want to experience it and take it on. That freedom is the liberation I am speaking of.

Aaron had 2-3 hours per day to sit and listen to his heart. Just as Aaron had to "fight and find" his liberation and so will you. Feeling your way through everything is a practice of becoming a fully embodied man. It's not something you schedule next Wednesday to practice. That is saying "next week I will get to know myself, but for now I am ok." It's a lie to avoid being 100% responsible for who you are. To think next week you will connect with your spirit, but right now you have more important things keeping you from it. Really?

Aaron discovered through this process that because he refused to listen to his truth, he had to crash and burn. His biggest fear in life was losing everything and exactly that happened. He was driven for freedom, but was without it, and he found it in a way he never planned.

I would not recommend his approach, but every man has felt imprisoned at some point.

FACING YOUR EPIC IS RARELY AN IF, IT'S A WHEN;
MAKE IT YOUR CHOICE TO FACE IT.

Man cannot achieve more than what he knows of himself. If he tries to create a world beyond his capacity of knowing himself, he risks collapse and failure. If you create more than your capacity to hold together, you have created a burden, not a haven. It is not wise to put a janitor in the CEO position, or the catcher in center field or ask a 9-year-old boy to act 14. If you place a janitor in the position of CEO, or ask a 9 year to act like an adult, you're placing a weight on them that cannot be lifted. It's setting up a failure, not an opportunity for grow.

Stretch yourself enough to step forward, and not collapse yourself before you start.

King of Your Reality

Feeling through your circumstances, means becoming the KING of your reality. Yes, this is your life whether you like it or not, want it or not, or even agree with it or not. It's all yours brother! Facing your reality means experiencing it, just as you want to fully experience a woman or an orgasm, to have an "orgasmic life," man must fully experience all his emotions. Remember, you cannot shut off from one aspect or experience of life then claim you are an open person. Being open to one thing while closed off to another is not open; that's conditional and compartmentalized living. It's a lie. If a nail goes in your tire, it's in your entire tire.

When I first introduce this to alpha men or businessmen, they don't quite understand it. Mainly because they keep trying to understand it instead of trying to experience it. The last thing a man does when he is experiencing an orgasm is analyze it; even the most analytical men don't. Powerful, integrated men feel all their experiences deeply. When the feeling is deep, go deeper. It's total self-control and embodiment, it's how we expand our experiences. In other words, when you're really happy, embrace it. When you're feeling really down feel all of it, so you can let it go. This way nothing owns you, you want to own it.

It also takes practice and at first it won't make sense if you've been living in your head for so long. The most powerful men can bring emotions up to the surface and let them go. I learned this in acting class. Some of the most powerful actors can fully experience an emotion during a movie set and express those emotions, on demand. They do it so well the audience can feel them, whether it's happiness, sadness, tears or love. An actor's training is among the most powerful training I know of.

Let's look at ways in which we avoid feeling our way through it. This way you can identify what you may be doing.

"Honey, I'm fine." Yet the truth is you're not. It's man's way of escaping reality and frankly lying.

"*I will be okay.*" Yet in that moment you are not okay with something. You're avoiding reality.

"*I just need to rest.*" You mean rest in peace? Rest in love? Rest in silence? Or do you think sleeping it off is going to turn you into a powerhouse man?

"Things are going good right now." Is that the goal? Things' going great is one thing; you being awesome about the process or journey is another reality.

"I will figure it out." Except life is not a chess piece to figure out. It's operating a mind game instead of a heart game. Nor can you figure out anything with the same mind that created it.

"*I will think about it.*" Another way of saying this is, "I haven't figured out what chess piece to move." Pushing things away forms a delay and keeps you from living decisively.

These justification, albeit sound true, are covers ups to avoid emotions. This is not how great men approach their life, business or family. It robs us of our own freedom and the ability to shift gears and make simple changes. There is no access to NEW results in denial.

Facing reality is much easier after you practice a few times. Until then, these examples are what we do to avoid taking on reality because it's more convenient and comfortable. Choosing the safe way out cheats us of our potential. It also means women, kids, and business partners cannot fully trust us. Who can relax and trust someone who does not reveal or feel their own emotions? Let alone know what to do with them. When men are upset, the people they love to feel it. When they hear you say, "I am fine" they know you are lying. It raises a concern flag with others. The more you do it, their concern slowly turns into mistrusting you.

Why? Because you have yet to learn to trust yourself.

Let's talk about anger.

The first emotion to cover up is the denial of your reality. Anger is what men do to protect themselves and cover up pain, and they don't know what to do about it. We fear that if we feel anger or talk about it, we are going lose control or something bad will happen. I can promise you that if you suppress it, the same will happen.

EMBRACE YOUR EMOTIONS. THE DEEPER YOU GO THE MORE POWERUFL YOU BECOME.

The Alpha Path to Feeling Through It

At first the Alpha Man will feel like he is going through withdrawals sitting with his feelings. His mind will be running 100 miles per second, while sitting still and feeling nothing. His mind will create distractions and reasons why he has to do something. Then, if he has the courage to sit with himself, he will feel nothing then dismiss the value of this. Once he starts to feel, he will find something to laugh about. Finally, he will reach a place of calmness and insight. Therefore, I recommend salt floating to all my alpha men. Salt tank floating is known as sensory deprivation and it is very empowering, destressing and brings a serious amount of clarity.

I can promise you, if you sit still and feel, a significant part of everything you do will all come together with the insights you generate through this. Life becomes easier for you.

When I refer to feeling through it, I am suggesting that underneath the emotions you predominately feel, there are more subtle and gentle feelings that are not being felt. As you learn to connect with the dominate emotions and let them go, the subtle feelings rise to the surface. This subtle rising has more wisdom and insight than finding the best kept business secret. In fact, it is your best kept secret and the patterns of grinding, fighting and pushing your way through stuff start to fade.

McDaniel was a former CEO of a large company; I will honor his name and company by not using them here per his request. He was in the midst of a class action lawsuit, a real estate investment company worth over $20 million that was falling apart. McDaniel is the Alpha Man who loves people, moves fast, and wheels and deals. He is the guy that drops $2K on drinks for people he doesn't know, and he can easily afford it.

During this time of chaos, every strategic move he made created more roadblocks. There was no way to save the real estate deal and his staff was feeling the heat. Within months he became ill and started drinking and putting on weight. When he called me, he demanded answers and solutions. He even stated, "I will pay top dollar to the person who can solve this, I need answers."

The other coaches and consultant on the line scrambled to come up with ideas. I laughed out loud on the conference line. The last thing he wanted to admit or hear is that he was the problem and was making it worse by operating out of fear. The only thing he cared about was his own tale and losing money. He was playing the game of NOT losing, rather than asking himself, "how did this get created?" "What can I shift in me to shift all the chaos?"

Suddenly he was faced with becoming the "**I was guy** and the **I want it all back** guy" at the same time. I had not seen it this intense before.

I spoke out on the call and said, "I can give you a solution while the rest of your team here finds a strategic move to solve this. However, first let's admit you've had a breakdown, then let's look at how this happened. If you are not open to that, I am wasting my time here. You can shift all of this, but not with this level of stress."

I hung up and he wasn't interested in what I had to say. An hour later he called me and asked, "what did you mean when you said if 'I shift' this can all go away? How?"

I laughed again because he was so hooked on fixing it and making it right not realizing that if he doesn't operate from being right, being great, being at peace and finding ways to repair damage and mistakes he has to succumb to moving chess pieces. It's the infamous theme men give women when she wants to leave, "Honey, I will change and make this right." But you're still the same guy in the end, who can only re-create a better version of the same problem.

I told McDaniel this, "If you entertain me for a few minutes and get clear I can help you shift this, otherwise your consultants will find a way to strategize your way out of this mess." He reluctantly agreed.

I had him close his eyes and just breathe. It took almost an hour before he could relax, then I asked him, what is the one thing all these upset people want?

His list began:

1. Revenge
2. Money
3. All these people are greedy useless bastards.
4. To drain me
5. My lifestyle
6. They want me to pay for their mistakes.
7. What does everyone want from wealthy people, their assets because they don't appreciate what it takes to do what I do.

What is interesting here is that I can draw a parallel between what he said, how he lives, how is wife feels, and how these people want to be treated.

I said, "okay, now tell me, has your wife ever complained of not being appreciated?"

His answer,

"I buy her everything, all I do is for her and the kids and she just enjoys it." He shortly followed that story up with a "no, she often tells me she doesn't feel appreciated."

"Great, thank you." I then asked him, "what do the people in these laws suits feel?" And what do your employees often complain about?"

That really opened Pandora's box and for the next 30 minutes, I heard an amazing amount of anger come from him to finally arrive at the following statements:

1. My employees think all I care about is money.
2. My team doesn't feel respected; in fact, they think it's all about me.
3. Everyone says I am consuming and overwhelming.
4. These people are suing because they think I was out to screw them.

I said, "okay, that explains it then."

How you show up is pretty much like the feedback your family, employees and customers are treating you. Like a greedy bastard and here you are complaining that others are the greedy bastards. It's hard to want to sue a genuine person for being a greedy bastard.

If you are willing to work through this I can promise you, the energy and circumstances will shift. Everyone in your world just wants to be a part of your world, to feel valued and respected. From your wife to your employees and customers and you are a "fix it - alpha ass."

"What is missing in all of this McDaniel?" What is the one thing that is missing in all of this?" I asked.

McDaniel went on to tell me that growing up he was the odd one in the family. And not much has changed; he is the odd one in his own business and his own family. No one believed he could do anything and that he was worth nothing. His brothers and sisters did what Mom and Dad wanted them to, while he pursued his own path.

All he ever wanted was to get revenge and prove his worth to them and win respect. Pretty much the same problems those around him complain about. Interesting.

That is when I jumped in and said, "you mean you wanted revenge?" You wanted them to not just appreciate who you are, but you wanted them to pay for how they made you feel?"

Thinking.... Thinking....

"Yes, I guess so," he replied.

Hence your first response when I asked you, what are people feeling that are suing you, and you replied with "revenge." Only to find out it's you who wants revenge.

"Wow, you're good," he said!

"I know McDaniel, I know." (Laughing)

A huge weight was lifted in this moment. He took ownership of how he felt and discovered why he was having a gut-wrenching experience. Now we can rekindle all of this by re-connecting him to his primary purpose. His why.

In short, he said the primary reason outside of gaining respect and wealth to show his family up, he wanted nothing more than to build a company with values he didn't have as a kid. Those values included collaboration, respect, kindness and everyone having a chance to grow within his company.

I challenged him to hold an emergency companywide meeting at a hotel nearby and to openly discuss what was happening. In that meeting, I suggested he show up raw and open about his life story and how his worst fears are happening all through is company and his personal life.

He shared his vision and gained the support of his hundreds of employees, then addressed the lawsuits and customers. He crafted a win-win deal with all of them. They resigned their lawsuits and forged a better partnership and paid restitution where it was deserved.

The lawyers on the other side said, "I've never seen anything like this, if all CEO's were like this we would have less cases."

McDaniel said, "don't worry, most CEO's don't face their reality or their emotions, you'll be in business a long time." (everyone laughed).

WHEN AN ALPHA MAN FACES HIS EPIC, HE SOLVES PROBLEMS WITHOUT HAVING TO MOVE MORE CHESS PIECES.

The Lionheart Path to Feeling Through It

Lionheart men love to sit with their feelings, in fact, they sit with their feelings so darn much they fall short in productivity. They are so heart centered, a disguise as "comfortable," they won't act or follow through, at least with a level of gusto that sets masculinity on fire. Why would they, in their experience they are happy and everything is good. Despite the fact they are not fully embracing and living their purpose.

One Lionheart client of mine, Lane, has been doing spiritual work for a decade. He is married and has written a book on relationships. He is so calm and at peace with everything, even when he has no money. He spent two years on a simple lead generation website, branding and colors of his logo, before he could get a single client. Lane does every single small thing to make himself feel "more connected," rather than living in action.

A Lionheart faces his reality through his emotions and is terrified that if he takes the leap, he will lose love and connection. So much so, he no longer feels safe during the time of action or change. It shows up everywhere in his life as well as his business. In life, his wife may be forced to be more decisive, masculine, and even the money maker. In business, he won't ask for the sale, he will give more than he gets. He ultimately comprises his raw masculine power for the "nice guy."

For the Lionheart, "courage" is the answer (not to sound like the Wizard of Oz here). The courage and the willingness to ask for what he wants, speak what is true without edifying himself, and to stand in his power, risking that someone may not like what he stands for.

The Lionheart differs from the Alpha Man. In essence, the Alpha Man sees himself in the world creating, building and taking it on externally. The Lionheart thinks he does the same, but he does it internally. The Lionheart needs to connect his internal world to manifesting it externally that way he moves into action.

That means learning to maintain love, joy, and passion, while taking on challenges that he may or may not be good at. For example, Stu was a client of mine from New York. He was a healer and the ultimate nice guy. He always believed "good things were coming" and if he just focused on his meditation and prayer work, then his business would grow. Except that never happened.

Stu did not like the thought of having to sell his services. He felt that the business side of things killed his passion. Stu needed to be able to see that he can use his heart and soul in the process of selling and not lose anything.

I set Stu up with a new enrollment process that was about supporting people to say yes to his advice. Rather than pay per visit to see Stu, you could pre-pay $1,000 and have 10 visits, which would be cheaper than a per visit rate.

The following month Stu collected $12,000. This was double his monthly income at that time. The best part is the courage it took for him to do this, to dance outside his "viewpoint," that he would lose love and connection was an illusion. His patients gave him great feedback; they loved the pre-paid package idea and were thankful for the discount. In fact, many patients expressed, having to pay-per-visit and charge their credit card numerous times per month, was frustrating for them. They preferred this method.

Lionhearts must act on their desires and flex their masculine power. Knowing there is risk, that you could be turned down, upset someone, or be called a sales person. However, the Lionheart grows more powerfully through action than he ever will hiding behind his heart. In other words, Lionhearts have to learn to explode their power; bring the very essence of who they are by infusing their energy in uncomfortable activities. Plain and simple, don't hold back anymore.

Alan is a dear friend and colleague; he is one of the best and most powerful Lionhearts I have seen. He truly has it all, except his business isn't a reflection of his genius. Alan has had some success selling a $15K program, but he never knows when that is going to happen next, and meanwhile, is hot wife wants to quit her job and have babies.

Alan has all his websites, funnels, brochures and scripts down pat. He has more tools and toys for business success than I do. Yet, he tests marketing way too much, dabbles in phone calls and emails and has not fully unleashed himself in his business. The underlying fear is that he could fail or let his wife down. So, staying comfortable and making 5 sales a year is plenty income for him and he doesn't have to fear losing himself or getting stuck in his business.

He is so happy, and satisfied that mentally he has a fire, but not one that burns six or seven figures. The challenge with Lionhearts is they know so much, feel so much that it's easy to hide behind it, and not live in the fullest expression of it. That means, heart-centered and consistent action towards the fulfillment of his desires.

LIONHEARTS ARE BETTER OFF JUST SAYING, "I AM THE BEST AT WHAT I DO, MY FEE IS $15,000, TAKE IT OR LEAVE IT."

Lionhearts need to know they are not alone and have accountability partners that are more alpha or integrated. They have to trust their greatness and start to lean into the alpha side. Lionhearts or alpha men are half men, but they neglect one part of them hoping to have a fuller successful experience of life. Just as an Alpha man must lean into his heart; a Lionheart must lean into his alpha side and start penetrating the world with his purpose.

It's the only way to become the complete man. Having access to all of you without holding back is what makes us happy, fierce and accomplished. That means engaging fully in everything you do, not casually or like a nice guy, but actually moving with purpose and authority within your space.

Later we will discuss the rebranding process. This process is about operating in your space with more integration and less one sidedness. You want to bring together the alpha in you and the Lionheart, that's a powerhouse.

Surrender Brother!

As the Alpha man McDaniel had to surrender his story and be vulnerable and open up. The Lionheart needs to surrender and trust his abilities to live in action and follow through. Both men have the same challenge just different approaches. The Alpha man wants to conqueror so he can live in peace and vacation and the Lionheart wants to conqueror his inner world, then wait around acting like life is a vacation. All so they can feel safe, certain and know they are loved and worthy as men. They operate opposite of each other for the same reasons.

The best way to let go is to face your reality. A comeback requires you to just do what is required of you. If courage is required of you on this comeback, then you act out of courage. If it's openness, then you act out of openness. If it is inspiration, then you act out of inspiration to create the results you want.

Let's be clear here. If you summon the courage to act and you don't get the result, a "Gunther" will say, "it didn't work," but an epic man will become more courageous, not less. Just because you do not get the results right away, does not mean it didn't work or it isn't right, it simply means you get to become more courageous. You do not sell yourself out or sell yourself short after a few occasions when something did not work. Especially when this may be a new way of operating.

For McDaniel his requirement was to open up and level up with his team. For Stu, he had to level up and face rejection and ask for money. **Be that which does that,** is the path of surrender and how Alpha and Lionhearts can and must take on their comeback. **Be what is required of you and do that.** Cut the rest of the nonsense out.

For men who want to repair their marriage and think talking to their wives a couple of times to reset their past fights will fix things. That she is supposed to say, "okay everything is good," is nuts! When men are faced with a spouse who wants to leave, trying to be more present to keep her is NOT **being that which does that.** Being that which does that, is a shift in your operating system. Not just a one-time shot to save my marriage or business.

Chapter 7 Notes: Feel Your Way Through

» Will power can confuse men into thinking they want something because they feel it so deeply, so much so you think you can feel it in your heart. That may not be a heart centered.

» No matter what happens, just LOVE IT!

» You can experience liberation due to your circumstances or get defined by them, its your choice.

» Facing your epic reality is not an IF, it's a when. Its better you get on top of it now before it comes after you.

» The king of reality does not offer lip service to his wife, kids or partners. Saying you're "fine, its okay, I will figure it out," is not necessarily the truth.

» Alpha man thinks he can move chess pieces to solve problems. Most of the time he needs to step back and have a reality check within himself.

» Lionheart grow more powerfully through action than hiding behind their heart.

» Just surrender to the process.

END OF CHAPTER 7 NOTES.

I am with you brother. You got this. You are more powerful than you think.

Let's move on to chapter 8.

Chapter 8

COMEBACKS, TRIUMPHS, AND MEN WHO LOVE.

To honor your comeback it helps men to connect with other men who have. To be inspired by others who have altered the course of mankind, not because they succeeded, but because they have failed. Men who have failed miserably have also comeback with an epic fire.

What is most important about comebacks, is not necessarily who failed and made a comeback, but rather why did they. Everything in life occurs for a reason. This is an overused statement and the least understood one. Mainly because most people don't see the reason why, they just act like there is one. The common denominator for many is their purpose; it's always been purpose.

I remember decades ago watching Mike Tyson box, talk about a purpose, Tyson had a unique purpose, mainly to prove to others that no one can hold you down. Tyson did not grow up in the best environment. His boxing was driven by his why and it showed. He was dangerous and didn't hold back in the ring, in fact, many of his opponents were knocked down within 2 rounds. They didn't nearly have a fight or purpose in them, or at least at the level that could stand toe to toe with Tyson.

THE PERSON WITH THE STRONGEST ENERGY ALWAYS WINS.

One day, boxer Buster Douglas found himself in the ring with Tyson. Douglas went down early in the fight and somehow managed to get back up and continue the fight. Many couldn't believe he got back up. Anyone who dared to get back up against Tyson was knocked down again. How did he do it?

The answer to that is simple. He sat up, put one foot on the ground and pushed himself up. How do you get up every day? The same as the rest of us, right? That answer to how, is always a simple one. The real question is, "why did he get back up?" Douglas was safer on the ground. If you don't know the why, you will always want to know how, despite its simplicity. The how isn't relevant if you're not committed to rising up again.

What Douglas did was represent all of mankind in that fight. A part of each of us was inside Douglas that night. The courage to act, the willingness to rise again and step back into a reality that is defeating you. But that is what comeback men do, step back in the game.

Tyson was in disbelief when Douglas got up, he went back on the attack and began punching him in an attempt to take him down one final time. Tyson didn't succeed. The bell rang and both fighters went back to their corners.

Over the next few rounds, Douglas summons the courage and the passion to fight back, grinding down Tyson who nearly won the fight. Somehow Douglas generated more power after getting knocked down and depleted. Something was accessed in that moment. Was it a wakeup call? Did he have the fear knocked out of him? Did he have sudden clarity he was fighting for something more than himself?

Something shifted. A few rounds later Douglas knocked out Mike Tyson and won the fight.

What you may not have known was a few days before the fight, Douglas' mother passed away. The worst thing that could happen before his big fight. Douglas had a reason to be in that ring, whether it was to take his pain out on his opponent, to honor his mother, or to fight Tyson for the things his mother sacrifices. Only Douglas knows the answer, but he had a purpose that got him up and caused him to summon every bit of energy, passion, and determination to fight on.

Little did Tyson know he wasn't just fighting Douglas. He was fighting against his mother's death, his history, his pain, and a hole in his heart. Douglas' purpose was far more empowering than Tyson's. Douglas recruited more power by honoring his purpose for being in that ring. In order for Tyson to win he would have to knock out Douglas, his mother's death, his history, his pain and his will to honor his mother's death by having a victory. This was far too much to knock down, even for Tyson.

Little did the viewers know they weren't just watching a boxing match.

I have seen this in sports, business, marriage and life far too many times to believe, people just do things to do them. For example, the most unlikely man to win the 800 meters in the Olympics, Dave Wottle of the U.S. Wottle was the only guy wearing a hat while running and he lagged 25 feet behind the other racers. He was so far behind he wasn't in camera view, but he came back to beat them all in the last 200 meters. That's epic! It is interesting to watch how people prejudged him before the race as "unlikely to win" and judged him to "not win" during the race, and then fanatically cheer for him when he won.

AT FIRST THEY IGNORE YOU, THEN THEY LAUGH AT YOU, THEY THEN FIGHT YOU. THEN YOU WIN!

~ GHANDI

You can see this with gymnasts and divers, with serious injuries, pulling off perfect maneuvers in the Olympics. People are inspired by watching this, not even realizing that it fuels their courage to live on purpose. Usain Bolt is the newest star in the track and field arena, another epic man on purpose. He clearly loves running, so much so, he turns his head and smiles at his opponent as he breezes by them. He runs in freedom, for freedom, not just to become someone.

A fierce lover of mankind, W. Mitchel was in an accident and suffered third degree burns over 90% of his body. Yet, while he was healing in the hospital he flirted daily with his pretty nurse. By the time he left the hospital that nurse was with him and they later married. Sadly, a few years later he was in an airplane accident and became a quadriplegic. You would think that this was the final straw for him. That living an EPIC life or making a comeback was out of the question.

If so, you would be dead wrong, he later decided to run for Governor of Colorado and won. And still had his pretty nurse, now his wife by his side. Who has time for an ego?

Now, tell me, why are you struggling with your comeback? It's a choice. There are no requirements or prerequisites for success. Be on purpose, be engaged, and do what is required.

Robert Downing Jr., **a serial mistake man,** had a five-year setback as he struggled with a drug addiction. He made his comeback, and is now one of the richest and most respected actors in the industry. People remember Ironman, not his addiction, right? He is one of the most intelligent men I have heard speak. His setback was the best thing that happened to him.

Steven Whitzeniger is a public speaker who has no arms and no legs and uses prosthetics. Having been on drugs most of his life, he stumbled into the woods during a snowstorm. He passed out and hit the ground, nearly freezing to death. By the time he was found his arms and legs were frozen, then later removed. It takes him an hour every morning to get ready. Imagine having to put your legs and arms on without legs and arms to do it. He is epic. The first sentence out of his mouth when I met him was, "this is the best thing that ever happened to me."

Josh Hamilton, the former centerfielder of the Texas Rangers baseball team, now with the California Angles, sustained several injuries and became hooked on medication. He made a comeback after his friends developed a plan to help him. This, coupled with his attitude, allowed him to make a full comeback. Josh is one of the highest paid athletes in baseball and fun to watch.

Ulysses S. Grant, quit the army and decided to go into business. His venture failed spectacularly, forcing him to re-enter the army. After rejoining and lifting himself up, he led his troops to victory. Later he up leveled and became President of the United States. Not once, but twice. It's interesting how we remember him as president and not a comeback failure to the highest office. Well, some of us do remember him for his journey.

Nic Vujicic, a man born without legs and arms, is now a world-renowned speaker. He drives a car, has a wife and children now. He loves his life and has from day one. He is also an avid swimmer and surfer, in his mind, he never had a setback nor was his life a failure. Nic believes life is about how strong you finish.

Kurt Warner is an NFL quarterback who did not get drafted into the NFL. He was bagging groceries at $5.50 an hour, but continued to improve his skills and keep his mind on the prize. He got another chance to play NFL football and struck gold.

Michael Jordan, well known for his intensity, offense, defense, jumping, and leadership, did I leave anything out? He was cut from basketball in high school. He flat out did not make the team. Who knows if he would be the Air Jordan he is today had he not been cut. My guess is he would not have been but the best thing he did was use the pain of that experience to his advantage.

Albert Einstein failed Algebra. Go figure! He was also considered autistic and didn't talk much as a toddler, in fact he mumbled and was told he would not amount to anything. Would he have become the Einstein we know today had that not happened? You see, failure can activate potential. And with your mindset and commitment can cause a whole new level of manifestation. Imagine how he felt after he cracked nearly over code to life including, $E=MC^2$.

Daryl Davis, a black man who befriended 200 members of the Klu Klux Klan (KKK) and ended violence. Today he is known for his work with "black hate groups." White angry men invite him to meetings, talks and consider him family. He converted them into nonviolent towards blacks. He simply showed up at the door of hundreds of KKK members and asked to talk. That's epic!

Jim Ziolkowski, former head of finance at General Electric left his high paying and established position to start a nonprofit. BuildOn, has built hundreds of schools in third world countries. People thought he was nuts or just living in la la land. Now, he is one of the largest and most respected in the industry. I have toured Africa with his company for nonprofit work.

The list goes on and on. Men who hold up hospitals at gun point when their son is denied a new kidney because they cannot afford the co-pay. Later, insurance companies reevaluate their policies. Men who lose arms and legs that climb Mount Kilimanjaro. Or cut off their arm to save their own life while stuck on a mountain. Or black and white coaches, coaching a team of the other race, become championship teams that change the way we operate globally.

The only difference between these men and you is not how they are made. It's not genetic. Their family, money or upbringing, but rather whom they decide to become and their ability to let go of the failure that exists in the form of pain locked inside them.

So ultimately was it a SETBACK?

Whatever the hell you make it. Everything in life is an interpretation and you own that interpretation. The meaning you give to it, is what it is, the meaning you give to anything determines your experience. If you interpret your failure as a man who is now a loser or worthless, that is done unto you and those around you who love you. You have a choice to also view it as a "thank you, I am grateful that worked out the way it did, because it was not for me anyways."

Do not attach your identity to your failure or your success; it's the cause for your pain. When you win, you think you're amazing, when you lose, you feel like you are a failure. That is a roller coaster for suffering. Who you are is not dependent on anything and who you are does not rest solely on one deal happening.

Setbacks for some are nothing more than a zap to your excitement. It can feel like a loss. In one sense it is, you lost energy, excitement or feel a bit let down. But, that is energy, not necessarily the deal or opportunity. On the other end of the spectrum, it can mean a step forward, gratitude, or a "thank God" that didn't work out. It's a choice and you get to own that choice.

A Setback in Disguise

In 2004 a company from Texas called me to consult for them. Their clients were not succeeding, and they asked me to coach them to drive more sales.

Rather than pay me a monthly fee, I requested a percentage of profits and sales and they agreed. Instead of a $10,000 per month contract I was getting $5,000 per new client. On average, they closed 12 new clients per month with a low of 9 and a high of 19.

In other words, I was knocking out $50,000 months and my best at the age of 25 was $90,000 in one month. But, things turned sour, unbeknownst to me; their real intention was to use me to save their clients from filing legal action. They had a contract with their clients that offered guarantees. If the client did not receive so many new clients of their own, due to the Texas company marketing system, they would not have to pay their bill for that month. Well, each client paid $25,000 in advance and often on a loan. Sadly, as time went on I was having to coach the clients using my strategies, but meanwhile they were stuck with a loan payment every month for a system that was not working. I spent more time keeping them from pursuing legal action than coaching.

I stuck it out for a year, only to get destroyed emotionally. Until one day, a client, Dr. Marv from Aspen Colorado, called me on a Sunday while I was driving home from the airport. He had shared with me that there were 200 clients on a conference call asking for my help. He told me they were filing a class action case against the Texas company and wanted my support. I was their only hope.

Unfortunately, my hands were tied. I was on non-disclosure contract with the company and they drained their financial resources every month, and then closed their corporation, leaving no money for claims and escaped responsibility.

When the company crashed, it was worth $16 million, and I was 5% owner. The company was in dire straits. People were filing sexual harassment claims, having affairs with each other and the owners were getting high at lunch. They fired me stating, "I was not a positive person." Yet, all I did was put out fires with a smile.

At first, I was shocked and then hurt. However, I realized, "it was a blessing." A month later, a major medical magazine printed a full-page article about the company that read, "never do business with XYZ." The article had pictures of the owners and executive team. I was the consultant, and V.P. of coaching and marketing, but, they left my name and picture off the article. They called to let me know that it was intentional that they left me out.

Is this failure a blessing? I took it as a blessing, not because of the article, but rather this deal was not for me. Frankly, the reason it became that dramatic and interfered with my life is because of my own greed. I had a chance to leave quietly and on good terms after a few months and a couple hundred thousand dollars in my account. I chose not to, I wanted more. That was my only failure or regret, but I can live with that.

REMEMBER, NOT EVERY DEAL HAS TO BE A HOMERUN.
BE AWARE OF MILKING AN OPPORTUNITY AT THE
EXPENSE OF MILKING YOURSELF.

Is it a coincidence that a year after, the authors of the movie and best-selling book, "The Secret" hired me as their consultant? Nearly doubling what I was earning with the Texas company. There are no setbacks my friend.

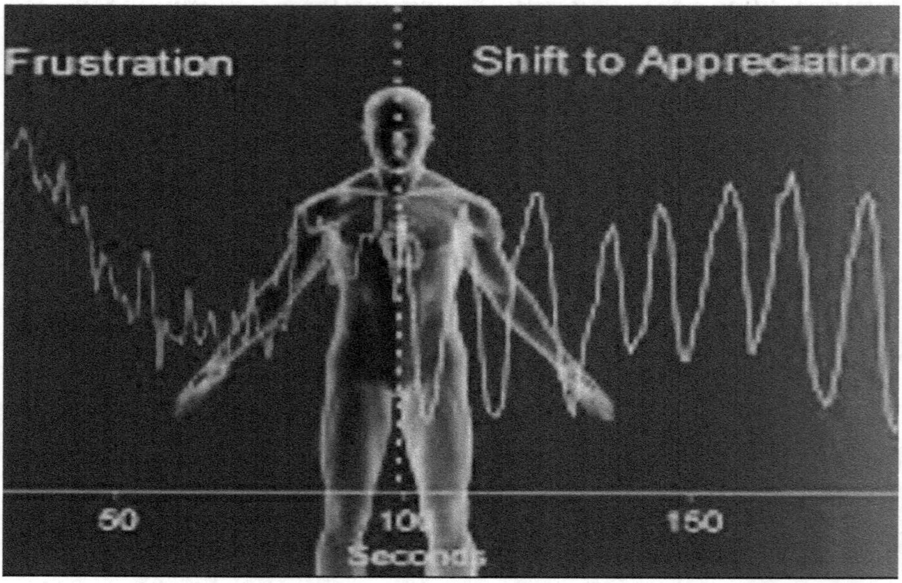

The only things you really have to come back from are the energy loss you experience. Money is energy. When men don't have any money, it's hard to feel motivated and passionate. When we lose money, it's a hard hit to take. Just as when we make a ton of money and feel elated. It really is nothing more than dopamine levels rising and falling. Testosterone spikes and dips, like all bodily chemicals, they are addicting.

Recovering and re-igniting your energy levels is the key factor in your comeback. The only way to get that back is NOT through excitement, but through letting stuff go and connecting to more empowering reasons to climb again.

The most powerful way to shift yourself from a setback or failure is seen here in this picture. Your heart shifts things more powerfully than anything else. When negative energy is felt in the heart, it registers with a vibe that "spikes." When you can "feel your way through it" and infuse a powerful emotion, you can shift your core vibration into a state of "flow." Hence the green line.

As men, we are happiest when we are creating, building, and making things. In order to access the flow, the ultimate state of creation, which only exists in the heart, we have to become aware of it. Heart energy can detect disharmony and harmony. It is up to you to detect with rhythm the heart is detecting and refocus your energy.

Buster Douglas shifted himself from knocked down and frustrated to calm, focused, and inspired to win. Dave Wottle was never frustrated, he continued to infuse determination and greatness into his running and came back to win. He became so confident, he intentionally started all his races in last place, while the rest tired out, he would gain speed.

When you avoid embracing emotions you're dampening your vibe. You cannot shift anything or find you way back to the flow. If you are experiencing stress, simply re focus your energy and mind on your vision. As you focus on your vision and connect with it, your heart will begin to gravitate towards that vision and shift the energy back to harmony. As seen in the chart, frustration came in, but what came out was harmony. When a man can harmonize negative energy into positive, from frustration to appreciation, he is unstoppable. Nothing will remain negative in his life for long, and he will engage in the flow for longer periods of time.

Action Item

No matter how high my emotions are, or low, I experience them fully by brining calmness to them. I ground myself in those emotions. How I do that is by centering my energy into the ground. I want you to consider practicing this exercise daily, mostly when you have high empowering emotions and high disempowering emotions.

1. Stand in dirt without shoes. YES, literally stand in dirt without your shoes.

2. Place your hands on the part of your body where you experience the emotions.
3. Breathe into your hands and expand that part of your body into your hands.
4. Now send the energy down to your feet, place your energy and focus on your feet as they touch the ground.
5. Keep going until the energy dissolves.

Once you practice this a few times, you can then do this in any situation. Without having to stand in dirt, the energy will dissipate and ground itself. You will become more solid in your energy. Most of all, your emotions won't drive you or cause you to make decisions because of them. You will simply be free of the emotions.

This matters because men cannot live in their thoughts or their emotions, but rather from their purpose. To be guided by purpose, rather than ruled by thoughts and emotions. Grounding yourself keeps you together, thus your life and business and nothing can break down until your energy breaks down.

Chapter 8 Notes: Comebacks, Triumphs, and Men Who Love.

» The person with the strongest energy always wins.

» Ghandi said it best, "At first they ignore you, then they laugh at you, then they fight you, then you win."

» Everyone fails. Even the best now, started out in the worst way.

» A set back is what ever you make it out to be.

» Setbacks might feel like a loss at first, until you are grateful it actually happened.

» Not every deal is life changing or a homerun.

- When you shift from frustration or fear to appreciation, you see clearly again. Practicing these simple shifts changes your vibration and flow.
- Men are happiest when they are creating and building, not watching others do it.

END OF CHAPTER 8 NOTES.

I am with you brother. You got this. Anyone can make a comeback.

Let's move on to chapter 9.

Chapter 9

STOP BEATING YOURSELF UP – REFRAME THE FAILURE

Men were raised different than women. Family was tough on men, we got punished for our behavior and rewarded for it. Rarely were we acknowledged emotionally. Having been raised on "what will you do," instead of "who will you become," performance became our path to respect, love, appreciation and feeling valued.

When things didn't work out, the paradigm already established early on was to beat yourself up. When things do not go right we punish ourselves as a way to improve ourselves. But it doesn't. The relationships you have with yourself also manifests in your relationships with others. It's impossible to beat yourself up then claim "authentically," you don't take it out on others or judge them. It may manifest differently than how you treat yourself, but, none of the less it's present in your relationships.

We do this only because it's the paradigm of men and raising boys and we have yet to learn how to shift or reframe things. Masculinity gets fixated on its point of view, then men lose their ability to shift or reframe their experience. Until we learn reframing, beating yourself up seems like the only thing that can be done, and yet, no matter how hard you try *not* to do that. Just as you shift your relationship to yourself, in how you relate to you, can you successfully reframe anything in a way that empowers you.

Reframing

Fact: You're supposed to fail. No one is 100% successful all the time. Even those who are "successful" are still failures in many other ways, and those who are failures are some of the most amazing men spiritually, as lovers and fathers. So, what is success and failure?

The difficulty with failure is not that it occurs, its being able to accept it and reframe it so you can improve your perspective. It's the willingness to let go of trying to fix what was done, and to shift your relationship to it.

IF YOU'RE WILLING TO ACCEPT FAILURE AS MUCH AS SUCCESS, YOU WILL FIND A SOLID BALANCE ON YOUR JOURNEY.

As much as success is taught, how to fail forward, how to fail like a pro, should also be taught. Failure is a guarantee, success is not.

Failure reframing is as powerful as it gets. When you reframe your experience, it opens new doors and allows you to release the heaviness of failure. There are 3 ways to look at re-framing so you can make new distinctions about it. A distinction is a new insight leading you closer to breaking the pattern of failure or setback, so you can trust your future comeback plan.

Three Insights

If you strip away surface conversations and look at, ***"how were you showing up,"*** there is always something to learn. Even if we don't want to admit it, it's there and it's time to overcome it.

"What was your goal?" You learned earlier in this book, the difference between goals and vehicles. Underneath it all, men say what they want X, but there is usually something behind that. Wanting to make a million dollars, instead of leading with your desire to feel valued and important, creates a conflict. This sets up your value based upon a money amount. Your leading with surface stuff and not necessarily your truth. Money does not create a sustainable valuable man, but a man with substance will have all things.

***"What actually happened*?"** If you filed bankruptcy and got a divorce, on the surface one might say that is the problem, rather than all the choices that led to it. There is a difference between what actually happened and how you currently see it. Most of all, if you can reveal the "why" behind why you made those choices that led to a bankruptcy and divorce is where the paradigm can shift.

For example, you know this to be true; 10 people watch a car crash and they all have 10 different stories to tell. If a car runs a red light and hits a person walking through a crosswalk, that is what happened. When you mix the story in about what actually happened you have to sift through the story to get to the truth. The same story about the car accident might also sound like this; "this car came screaming through the stop sign, he was blazing at high speeds and didn't see the person crossing the street and hit her, she was just walking across the street and now her life is over."

It's the story that causes the suffering. For all we know the lady woke up this morning thinking something was going to go wrong today. Perhaps she thought she saw a walk sign and walked across a red light. The person who hit her was not a man and was driving the speed limit. People don't know what they don't know, especially when emotions take over and cover up what actually happened.

Once you get clearer on what actually happened, you can pinpoint the actual breakdown and quickly feel in control of your life by reframing it. In each of these insights I can assure you there is a breakdown in how you showed up.

The Greed Factor

There is a great TV Show called The American Greed. Although I am not an advocate of TV, this show is a great example of how great ideas and businesses in the hands of ignorant men can create massive problems.

Jeremy, a client of mine in 2006 was a real estate investor, among other things. I advised him to read a book by Harry Dent called, "The Next Great Big Bubble Boom. Which basically said, between 2006 to 2020 or so, we will endure the greatest economic down fall ever. Harry mentioned in his book that apartments, trailer parks, retirement homes, gold, and among other things, will be the best investments to purchase. He also mentioned that dream homes would be less expensive and a good time to buy.

Harry was right, but did the masses listen? For the most part, no. My client had 7 rental properties, all with 5-year arm loans, which were coming due. Who would have thought Country Wide loans would file bankruptcy and sell their loans to Bank of America? Or the system would have gone bankrupt all together? His mortgage payments went up higher than his rent. His cash flow went from $1,800 a month to negative $1,200 per month. He had to lower rents and his opportunity to sell for profit tanked. His $500,000 in equity became miniscule.

Before he bought these properties, I coached him on his financial rules and selling strategy. His goal was to create cash flow, but also have an equity hold, then sell when each property yielded a 30% ROI. Well, before the economy tanked, we were sitting on a 45% increase in equity and he didn't sell.

He broke his own rules and stayed in wanting more without acknowledging reality; he already has more! If he honored his rules he would have cashed out 15% ahead of his goal.

He really didn't pay attention to the five year loan or the status of Countywide who funded his loan. He didn't pay attention to the market or the book he read. Mainly, when men think everything is good and money is flowing, they take their eyes of the goal, and the risk goes up. Who wants to think about money flow stopping? Yet, history has taught us otherwise, I mentioned to him that he may not want to live as though this is going to last forever. His response struck me, "I've got that covered, my guys are ready to sell whenever I call them." Like most men who think they have it together, but they don't and usually pay a price for it.

Jeremy decided to stop paying the mortgage, it was the only way to get the banks on the phone with him to modify the loan. He, in fact, was making too much money to qualify anyway and was willing to take the hit to his credit report.

He racked up cash flow for the year, then tried to short sell his properties. Some short sold and some were foreclosed.

He lost $500,000, but at least kept $20,000 in unpaid mortgage payments.

His mini-empire was gone. So where did he fail? Where is the problem? How did he show up?

Let's discover what happened instead of denying it. Let's dive in and see his pattern, because it's not a real estate pattern. The pattern is in his mind and not exclusive to real estate.

Jeremy and I walked through nearly this exact same strategy in this book. Here is what he realized.

During the process of his real estate there was a part of him screaming to sell and move on. He didn't listen to it because he saw the numbers and they were going up, if he could hold on for a few more months he could sell and reap 65% ROI on his equity, giving him more money.

He admitted that he was trying to maximize his return, and didn't honor his own rules. It's called greed. He was focused on getting more and missing what he had.

If we break this down here is the truth:

1. He failed because he didn't listen to his own gut.
2. He failed because he chose greed instead of integrity.
3. He failed because he didn't honor his own rules.

4. He failed because he didn't trust his own rules.
5. He lied to himself that he had it all together and one phone call took him out of the market.

MEN WHO DO NOT LIVE IN REALITY, GET CALLED OUT, FORCING THEM TO FACE WHAT THEY HAVE BEEN AVOIDING.

Jeremy was not present to reality, he had reached his goals. Reality slapped him in the face and suddenly this dynamo entrepreneur is shaking his head.

What happened was not the economy's fault. He could have reached his goal, sold his properties, protected his assets, and honored his pre-determined rules. But he failed. He failed by not having integrity and honoring his word. He also admitted that if he could just hang on, he could have made his wife even happier by coming home with a check for $750,000 as a surprise. Despite the fact she was against investing in the first place.

That wasn't the only place Jeremy used to do this. Remember earlier when I said, you have to learn how you are showing up and discover what actually happened? Well, the underlying goal was the need to make his wife wrong for not agreeing to invest. He risked his money to prove himself right and her wrong. In fact, he became a doctor because people said he wouldn't stick with it. His family told him real estate was risky and to not do it. No one actually believed he would succeed as an entrepreneur.

That was his driving force; his purpose was to say, "*I will show you.*" Instead, he ate his own words. But, when men embark on things for the wrong reasons, it often fails or leaves us unfulfilled. Even if Jeremy did the right thing, he never would have uncovered this. He would have upped his game, made more investments, and at some point, suffered until he faced his reality -- that purpose is not vengeance, it's about living who you are. When you operate without integrity it always crashes at some point.

Once you realize the failure is not something in the form of materials, but rather in the form of *how you were showing up,* you can then change your life and situation. You cannot reframe the economy, but you can reframe how you showed up and how you relate to it. Just as Jeremy lost money, others related to the economy as an opportunity. Many made millions, while others lost. How they framed the situation is what allowed them to win, while millions lost.

Failure Reframe

Only you can know what really happened or is happening. Only you can decipher what the failure was and come to accept it, the sooner you can reframe it. Once you reframe it, then you can be free from it. How you currently see or experience what happened is not serving you, the reframe can shift that to a higher perspective so you can make your comeback.

If someone presented the same money-making opportunity to you in 10 different ways, you might have 10 different experiences, right?

But all you need is one experience to accept that opportunity, right?

Reframing your life is the same thing as mastering your experience. Thus far, with the feelings of disappointment, failure, regret or loss, you created a frame of disempowering frame of mind. It leaves you unmotivated about your comeback What we are discussing next is how to set yourself up so your frame is unleashing your greatness.

If we bring back the failures and realizations from the above, we can work through them step by step.

1. I failed because I didn't listen to my own gut.
2. I failed because I chose greed and to squeeze out more money.
3. I failed because I didn't honor my own rules.
4. I also failed and experienced disappointment and regret by trying to prove to others they were wrong for not believing in me.

How would you reframe each of the above statements?

There is always another way to see things. Always! The best way to reframe is to get curious about all the ways that you can now see this experience.

For example, **"I know that anytime I listen to my gut I am guided to make intelligent decisions that support the best version of myself."** That statement is a perfect reframe to statement #1.

Statement #1:

I failed because I didn't listen to my own gut, *"I know anytime I listen to my gut I am guided to make intelligent decisions that serve my highest good."*

Statement #2:

I failed because I chose to soak more money out when I had what I wanted, *"I am certain that when I follow my word and operate from abundance, not lack, I win."*

Statement #3:

I failed because I didn't honor my own rules, *"when I commit to honoring my own rules, I protect my assets and secure my legacy as a man."*

Statement #4:

I also experienced disappointment and regret by trying to prove to others they were wrong for not believing in me, *"I am a man of greatness with nothing to prove to anyone. I trust that my will, will be done with respect and authenticity; I decide who I am and seek no approval from anyone."*

The ultimate reframe can reignite your embers, heal your pain, and put life into a simple perspective that causes you to come alive in new ways.

In 2015, I embarked on a humanitarian trip to build a school and new bathroom. The journey to Africa from California was exhausting. Seeing radical different cultures in 36 hours, different types of weather, and food then taking a bus through jungles, land, poverty and arriving at a small village in Lilongwe, Africa. The village included only 350 people who were dancing, singing and cheering as we arrived. I was in tears.

The outpouring of love from these amazing men, women, and children who appeared to have nothing was deeply touching. They had such honor and joy and were willing to share it. My experience in America is that we culturally hold back, hide, and are not openly willing to share this level of passion and joy for random strangers. Let alone the people we claim to love.

Many of us didn't wait for the bus to come to a complete stop. We escaped out the window into the arms of loving people and danced for the next hour in a celebration. That night went on for a while as we met the government of this city, and started our official humanitarian sign in and broke ground.

I was gifted a father and mother for the week and I stayed in their home. They even gave me an African name, Muay, called the "Lucky One." And that is exactly how I felt. When I realized I was the lucky one, my frame of mind shifted from making these people feel good about who they were and uplifting their situation, to feeling lucky that they are really here to teach me joy, love and unity.

The family I was with shared with me that the biggest challenge they have here in addition to the bad water was Monsoons. Each year during Monsoon season, many people in the village would lose their homes; literally watched them wash away.

Most homes were made from burnt mud. I asked, "what do you do when monsoon's happen?" His answer was brilliant and simple, "We rebuild. We start over." He said that without any ego about it. They just rebuild. In the US, we would end up in depression, shame, or anger. The stuff we lose is linked to pride and identity, when it's not. It's not that they don't know any better, or that our country is better. They just don't get hung up on reality, keep their joy and move on.

Anything we lose was once a choice and we make that choice pretending to not know it's temporary. That we are mortal in one sense. Your house, your money, your wife, even your kids are all temporary. When your journey ends you have either served them well, not enough or not at all. For the people in Africa it's just a journey and they stay true to that journey no matter what.

Brother, you can keep pretending you have time, but you don't. Time is the only thing we lose every day and cannot get back. You can keep telling yourself you need to get your ducks in a row, that you need something other than what you have, that you need to fix your system or that you're getting there and doing it. Or you can accept the reality that your time here is limited. Your journey is the only thing that matters. Your journey is unique to you, your voice, and your body and if you realize you have been sent here to live your purpose. Facing it, is all that is required.

You will succeed. It may not be like the illusive vision you created and how it should be. Success is rarely how you envision it. We have to be challenged to grow, it is what allows us to reach back and demand more of our greatness. When everything in life is OK, we don't expand in greatness, we actually stop it from emerging within us.

PRACTICE:

Create a series of statements that reflect your failure. Using the previous examples as your guide, reframe them to shift your experience from disempowered to empowered.

1. Name a time when you failed.
2. Describe what happened.
3. State what actually happened.
4. Now reframe the situation so you take 100% responsibility for it and feel empowered.

Chapter 9 Notes: Stop Beating Yourself Up – Reframe the Failure

» When a man is fixated on his point of view, he loses his ability to make changes.

» If you accept failure as much as success, nothing will stop you.

» Beating yourself up is part shame and part shut down. There is no need to inflict more pain as a way of teaching yourself a lesson.

» If you take an honest look at, *how you were showing up? what was the goal? and what happened?*

» Its always wise to call yourself out before the universe does it.

» Men often fail due to simple human errors, things that we overlook.

» Greed is a powerful force that causes men to overlook red flags.

» Failure reframing can radically change things for you, and how you relate to your past.

» Define your failure, then make new statements to shift your perspective.

END OF CHAPTER 9 NOTES.

I am with you brother. You got this. Be your greatest fan, and others will follow.

Let's move on to chapter 10.

CHAPTER 10

THE ULTIMATE WHY ~ YOUR SEARCH FOR EPIC

IT TAKES COURAGE TO START WITH YOUR WHY. Men who honor their why are rare. Anyone can chase money, but rarely are they able to sustain it. In fact, your why and your wealth must go together to sustain your future. If these two deviate from each other, creating wealth becomes a stressful burden. Men lose sight of what really matters and thus lose sight of the real value of wealth and accomplishment.

There are two noticeable times we become excited and highly motivated for achieving our goals. The beginning of the journey and when we face losing it. Here is an example:

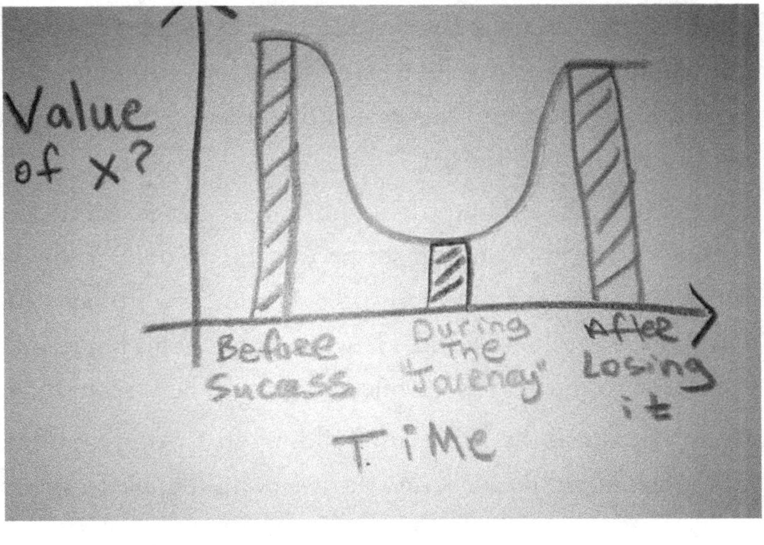

What occurs during the journey is what actually matters. While we are seeking achievement it's easy to lose ourselves in it. Disconnecting from our real purpose in the middle of our journey makes our lives harder. The tasks overwhelm us, while the drive to the finish line provides an adrenaline rush to push harder, instead of surrendering and trusting the process. A person can only operate from power if they stay connected to their why.

The willingness to surrender and trust the process is the elevated approach during your comeback. By the way this is also true with women, money, relationships, family, projects and business. At first a relationship is a thrill, sometime after making a commitment we lose value for it. Things get hard and issues arise, but if a man love's a woman and she start the process of leaving, the value of her goes up again. Does this make sense?

Aaron is a millionaire real estate investor and in 2015, he had a multi-million-dollar project he was waiting to get paid for. While it was in construction and waiting to be sold to the highest bidder, he was a wreck on the inside. His only focus was on this deal, while it was a wait and see game; he shut out everything else in his life. He would not date, take care of his health, or think about his future. This was a pattern for Aaron.

When Aaron got on the phone with me he apologized for being late. He began telling me his story about how times are hard right now. He is investing $50K per month in this deal and marketing to see his return is high and it's eating up his time.

Let's translate that, although it sounds amazing and good, Aaron is a victim to his own deal. You can see he is in the middle of the picture. Neither excited or inspired nor trusting the process. In fact, this deal owns him. It is controlling his life. He went on to say his house is a mess; he had not been to the gym in a while and frankly, he isn't sleeping.

Aaron is what I call the half man; building up a world he thinks will make him someone, while alienating the rest of his life. He lacks capacity.

He cannot hold his entire life together, experience it or have balance by putting it on hold. Hoping that if this works, then he will have time for a family, wife, and his health. While listening to Aaron I could feel his heaviness, there was no passion, joy or inspiration about his project. This is the point in the journey when men stop feeling and the journey becomes a grind. Are you getting this? He is in the middle of the process, where men are most vulnerable and begin losing themselves in the process. It impacts every aspect of their lives. The masculine energy puts so much emphasis in one basket he loses balance on the rest. The impact this has on children, spouses and your health may not be worth the pot of gold at the end. Money won't buy these things back.

The same reason we love women and are frustrated by them is because they have multiple experiences throughout their journey. Men have the experience of chasing and starting, and things ending or succeeding. We don't get better in the middle as masculinity is all about getting it done. However, if you connect with your feminine energy, you can sustain your drive, adapt and trust the process easily. This is what the feminine does. They surrender to the process and enjoy it.

Forgetting what matters by replacing it with your dreams is a fatal mistake men make. Men are notorious for placing their values on the back burner for the accomplishment of their dreams. For example, men express this to women, "honey, when this business hits it big, I will have plenty of time to travel and do anything you want." "Honey, I am trying to do everything I can so we can live well, I just cannot always come to our sons baseball games." It's an epic lie. Why would you ever create so much pressure on yourself? This is the ultimate set up for failure. Even if it works, you cannot get your time back and you cannot make up for the missed experiences.

Your future is not about putting areas of your life on hold, while another area works out. Without balance, men breakdown. When they do break, usually everything else follows.

This is a clear example of how men don't believe they can have it all, while pursuing a dream. There is no if-then life, or one-day life. You can have it all by making decisions along the way to be at home, to attend baseball games, to workout, to spend time with family or take care of yourself, while in hot pursuit of your dream.

In order for a comeback to be realized, you must start with why. The middle of the process or journey, is where the challenge is and where you are tested. Your why is the glue that holds it all together, and keeps you grounded.

Here is another example of what happens to large companies, entrepreneurs, and even their families. This example is universal across any culture, it's an inherent flaw in all humans. To have it all instead of choosing one or the other. To balance life and our values. To enjoy our path.

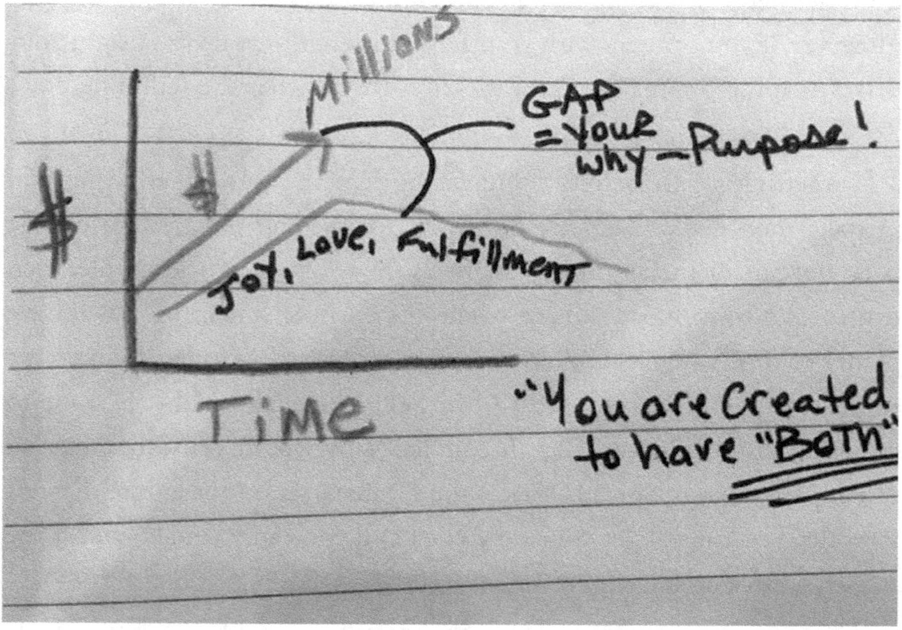

As we embark on a business or entrepreneurial path, we usually start with some level of excitement, passion and motivation. The longer we strive for business success the more bumps, frustrations, and let down's we experience, the more we deviate from true and purposeful living. The truth is we are created to have both, to have it all.

As entrepreneurs start to make more money and grow their business, the passion, joy and fulfillment often fades away. They get hooked on keeping the success alive, instead of the why.

Alpha men often get stuck with this one and cannot figure out how everything, meaning financially, can be going so well, yet their health is fading, and their wife is unhappy.

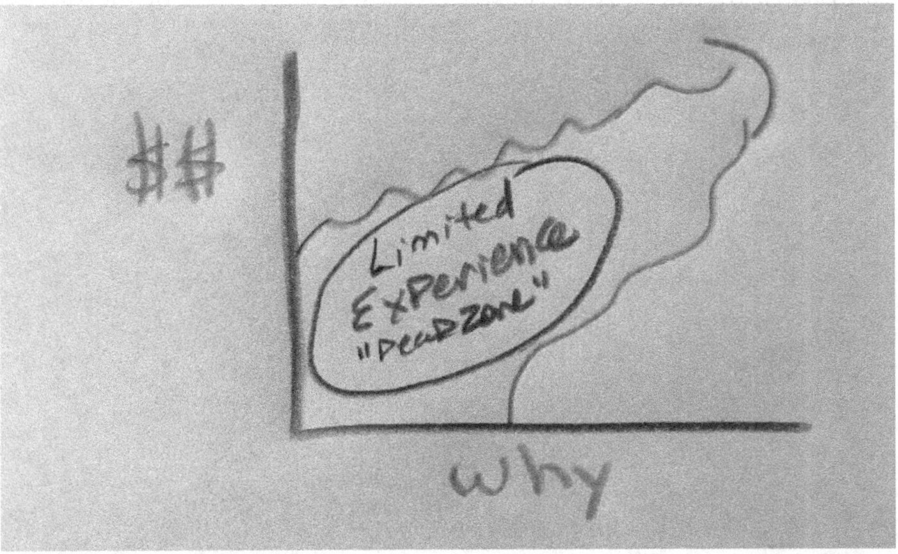

The gap between financial prosperity and fulfillment is what happens when you forget your why. Your purpose for why you started your business is a big dose of who you are. What you are standing for gets overshadowed by success or challenging times. If you lose your why, you lose yourself in the process.

Let's flip this chart from every day people, to Alpha Men and Lionheart. For men who are more heart centered. Here is an example of what happens with these men:

Alpha Man:

The Alpha Man takes his journey on with a significant focus on achievement and money, while leaving his purpose behind. If the financial rewards are achieved, Alpha man feels like he has lived out his purpose and the two meet, eventually.

Meanwhile, when he arrives at this destination he enters a safe zone and suddenly changes. He has now achieved a comfort zone disguised as happiness, freedom, and loving life. Now he is ready and able to take on family, kids, traveling, and so on. Yet, he still remains half empty. Noticeably, the "dead zone" is basically a non-experience of the success process.

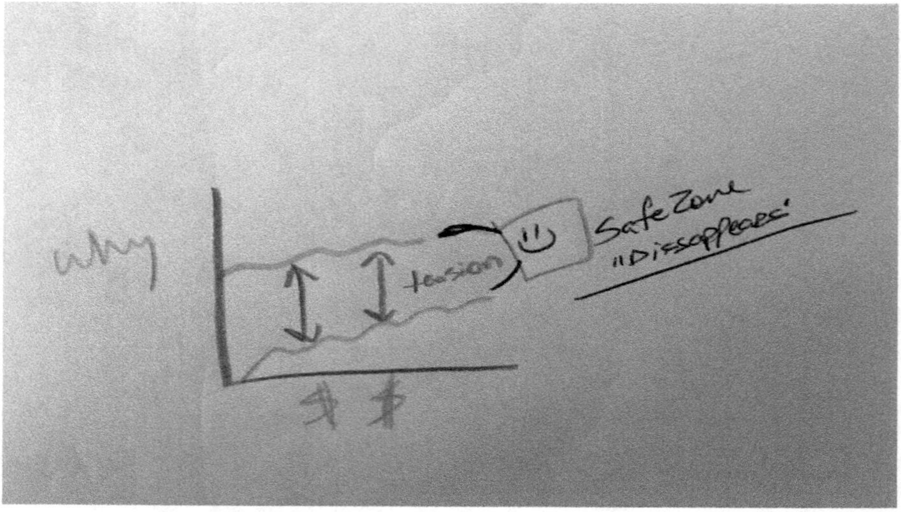

Lionheart:

Lionheart men start businesses out of love, passion, and to make a difference, then make money. They maintain their passion for it longer than most, but they risk severe burnout and neglect. They won't feel respected or worthy for a sustainable amount of time because financial prosperity hits and misses and then fades away.

You will know if you are a lion heart as people will tell you how amazing you are, and that your product or service is great. Except you won't have many results to show for it.

The difference between Lionheart and Alpha Man, is Lionheart doesn't have a dead zone during the process, he has a conflicted zone. He battles his emotions, focusing on purpose and having to deal with the reality of business. Not everything he does feels good and business requires you to do many things you don't like or are not good at. It's a flame that radiates high then low, back and forth, and forwards and backwards. He fears losing himself in the process and always chooses purpose and helping others at the expense of money, while the Alpha is the opposite.

If the Lionheart succeeds and his why and profits unite, he also reaches a comfort zone and then kicks back, enjoys his winnings and loses the fire a bit. It isn't until he fears losing what he has does he re-ignite his motivational engine.

With success, we all risk losing out on fulfillment and convince ourselves it's okay because we have succeeded. The goal is to maintain both at the same time by staying connected to your why. Your why lives in all aspects of your life, men don't make this connection. Rather, we justify how succeeding in one area will make everything else better.

Think of your purpose as oxygen, it breathes life into everything you value, that matters to you. Yet, men are myopic and experience their values as separate boxes they try to hold up. Purpose is what allows us to freely experience ALL our values, hence the phrase, "have it all." Your purpose should be fueled in each area of your life, not have those areas feel like a burden.

In other words, I can experience as much joy with kids, as I do in business or writing this book as I do taking a shower or picking up the dog stuff. My purpose is connected to all my experiences and through those experiences I become more empowered. It is not the task that matters, it's what I bring to the task that matters.

LIFE IS A PARTICIPATION GAME. IF YOU PARTICIPATE IN ALL THAT YOU DO WITH YOUR PURPOSE YOU ARE FUELED BY IT, NOT BURDONED BY THE TASK.

It's time to flip your operating system inside out.

Why ~ Inside Out

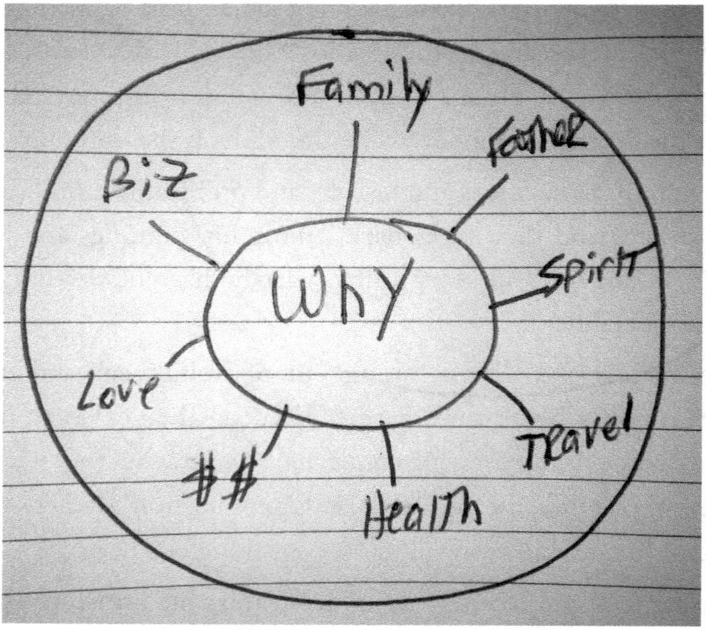

What is the value of knowing how to do something if you're not 100% engaged? For the past 17 years of coaching, I can tell you that when clients want to know how, they really want certainty. Which means they are operating from a lack of certainty. Shortly after wanting to know how, they want to know "if it will work?" I usually tell them the truth, "probably not until you determine why it matters for you." You are the reason things work and the reason they do not.

An indecisive man always wants to know how and makes his decision from the how-to, instead of the why to. He lives outside in.

How-to's are the last piece of the puzzle. Most of the time the how-to's are easily discovered when you are fully clear about why you are going to do what you want to do. 80% of your operating system is spent on the why and what, and the last 20% on implementation and execution.

I will break down the chart for your complete understanding.

If your wife wants you to listen more, how do you do that?

Most men would answer something like this:

1. Don't talk while she is talking.
2. Hear what she has to say.
3. I try, but when I do she gets more upset.
4. Understand what she is saying.
5. Make more time for her.

All of these are noble responses, yet they have nothing to do with listening. She is not asking "how" or telling you to listen. You could do any of the above statements and it won't work, leaving you wondering WTF!

If your why was to care, if your why was to love, if your why was to show kindness, if your why was to have compassion, you would know exactly what she is asking for. She wants to feel "heard." She wants to know that you "care." That is not a how-to, it's a feeling, a way of being, not doing. For you to be able to relate to her experience and feelings, it means she exists to you. Then she can return to balance on her own.

The feelings you may have that are difficult to describe, exist in your why, not in the how. You will come to know this as true when she asks you, "why are you with me? Why are you attracted to me?" She isn't necessarily looking for the "best answer," she longs for your feelings behind it, again, these only exist when you are connected to your why. Your why is your depth, the rest is surface level energy that wears off.

Do you get this?

Think of your how-to's as a vehicle for delivering purpose and not a place to live. If I want my wife to feel loved, I may extend my hand to hold hers, or kiss her. That is not love, it's a way to transmit my love to her and it's not the only thing to do that. A kiss with no why behind it is plain old surface energy with no depth. Nor will it consume her. She can feel the depth of you in that kiss. The way you walk, the way you move and the way you speak are all expressions of how you relate to your life and business. You cannot do what you are not. To do so is called fraud. You can only give what you are experiencing, and you can only connect with what you are connected to.

YOUR PURPOSE WILL ALWAYS REVEAL THE HOW TOO. MEN ARE NOT ROBOTS, BRING THE PASSION TO THE ACTION.

Most businesses, entrepreneurs, and men have this backwards. They start with a dream, then jump to the "what am I going to do and how." They search for the best how, instead of the most powerful why. It's the difference between struggles, hustle and making shit happen (the how to living) and living your why and all the how-to's are readily available.

Think of why as your reason for living, it's the warehouse of all your energy, passion, fuel, balls and fulfillment.

The what is what you are going to do to live your why.

The how-to's are the strategies to act on, to deliver your why or carry out the how to in order to live your why.

ONCE YOUR WHY IS CLEAR, THE HOW TO'S ARE SIMPLY A CHOICE.

Your Why

My why in the beginning of my life and business was simple: ***"Because everyone said I was not enough, strong enough, handsome enough and I couldn't do it."***

That is a strong why and it shifted over the years to, **"I stand as a catalyst for men to embody authentic masculine and realize who they are is a king."**

Now, having read that, is it obvious what I would do with that purpose? Like write this book? There are many things I could DO with that purpose, like building a school for men is in alignment with it, doing seminars for men is in alignment with it, building an orphanage is in alignment with it. Building a youth sports academy for boys, building homes and schools in 3rd world countries and the list goes on. What I will do is a matter of aligning possibilities that cause my why to ignite with more fire than anything else.

What to do comes next? I choose to write books, conduct seminars, coach, retreats, and humanitarian work because I cannot live without it. It sets me on fire, and frankly I hate writing. I am not good at it, but that does not stop me. I prefer speaking to writing.

How to do it is next. Well, since I don't like writing, how would I write a book? The question is why, then what, then how. Simple! My skill set is talking; therefore, I talk into a microphone, transcribe it, re-work it, and then send it to an editor.

Book done!

However, without my why, the book is as hollow as the action steps. There is no powerful reason to manifest a book, unless it's for ego sake and I can tell everyone that I have one.

Your Why

What is your why? Why do you do what you do? When you scratch the surface level stuff you will get to the truth. This is the most powerful place to start. When I ask most men this they often will say things like:

1. Because my family deserves more.
2. To provide a life for my kids.
3. To be happy.
4. To be free or financially prosperous.
5. Because I am married and have responsibilities.
6. Because my product can help people.
7. Because I am good at what I do, and I want to succeed with it.
8. Because I want to make $1 million dollars.

Look at each of the answers and tell me what you see? What do you experience when you read them?

They are noble. Nice. The right things to say, but lacks depth and most important, there is no why. Because "your family deserves more" is not a purpose. Your family will get what you create, plain and simple.

To provide is more of a 'what' you're going to do or 'want to do', not a why. But, if your child was sick and needed a new kidney, you have an instant why, but that why is temporary and a part of your journey; it's not the fullness of why you are here.

Here are some examples of powerful whys:

"Because no one had ever done it."

"Because I was told my gift was touching others."

"Animals need a voice."

"Life is empowered by music."

"Because art keeps me from hurting myself."

"Because I see the world as beautiful and I want others to see that for themselves."

"Because we all have potential."

"Because I didn't think anyone could love me."

"Seeing people come alive is the greatness gift."

"Because people deserve to see in 3 dimensions."

"Because I didn't realize the power of respect."

As you read those can you think of an image of each person?

Can you begin to connect with who the person is? Or what has happened in their lives?

They are very revealing and deep. A true why starts with opening things up, even for others.

All of these are examples of the WHY behind the how's. This is what makes men amazing. The how-to's make you like every other man out there. Frankly, the world doesn't need more of these guys!

There is only one way to discover or find your why. I suggest you repeatedly ask yourself and speak your answers from your core.

Your mind is an answering machine, your heart already knows the answer. When you get your mind out of the way, the answer can be revealed. Unbeknownst to most, the brain does not control everything. The heart is developed and beats before the brain does in a fetus. The heart sends more signals and information to the brain than vice versus. The heart is the part of you that feels the "unknown." There is a deeper knowingness that lives in your heart, and you have felt it many times already, so pay attention to it.

There is a question and answer exercise that can be done out loud. It is much easier in my retreats for men to do this, simply because there are no distractions and you have a guide. But, you can still achieve the results by following through here.

What are you the best at?

What are you deeply passionate about?

Now why?

Is there something you are the best at? When I refer to, "the best at" I am not referring to comparing yourself to others, I am referring to of all the things you know, learned and may be doing, what are you the best in "your" world at? (by the way, you may not be doing it at all)

____

____

____

____

What are you incredibly passionate about? As you make this list, do it unabashedly. Pay no mind to your current situation, if you can or cannot make money at it, if perhaps you failed using your passion before, it does not matter. List things out to get clear on what you are most passionate about. (there is no judgment here)

____

____

____

____

As you begin to notice your responses on both lists, you will get clearer about what you are passionate about and what you are best at. Something is driving this, there is something that occurred early in life that struck you profoundly.

Why do these things matter? What are all the reasons behind the overall theme of what you wrote?

____

____

____

____

A True Story About Purpose

I grew up in a family that was not very healthy, I felt responsible for taking care of them. Growing up my focus was always on being responsible for them. When I was little I collected first aid kits, and before I could even read I bought CPR books and even medical books from a place called Save-on.

Each time I tried to help my family I was always told, “you don’t know what you’re doing?” This fueled a fire and anger in me. Rather than give up, I found more ways to help my family. By the age of 6 I was calling family meetings, pretending to be a therapist after watching an episode of Emergency 51.

I was the expert! The more I tried the more they shamed me for it. I was convinced I would be a doctor and I also became a great athlete. The doctor side of me made me feel significant, the baseball side of me helped me vent my anger. Soon, my purpose in life was, “because you told me I couldn’t.”

That lasted for 25 years, then I was burned out. What I discovered was another purpose. A higher purpose. Realizing that becoming a doctor was just a payback for having my intelligences undermined; my mind had me convinced that was my path. Then I found myself in a Tony Robbins seminar, coaching became the best vehicle for living my purpose. A healthier and powerful way to help people that write prescriptions.

Once you answer the questions above, here is what you do.

What to do next:

1. Sit quietly.
2. Ask yourself out loud, "why do I do what I do?" and "what is my purpose?"
3. Repeat it every minute.
4. Wait patiently. This is the hard part.

The first few minutes, your mind will answer, disregard it no matter how important it makes itself out to be. It's not. Your purpose does not live in your mind. The feelings or vibe will reveal itself. Yes, I know it may sound spiritual or woo-woo, but it works. Many CEO's I have taught this to laughed at first, then they laughed at how difficult they made the process for themselves.

There is one common connection between all of them. I have discovered you will know when you see it because it may feel like you cannot live without it. If you were the only person living on an island and all you experience was your why, then you have arrived.

Chapter 10 Notes: The Ultimate Why ~ Your Search for Epic

» It takes courage to start with why. Men who do are a rarity.

» As men succeed financially, they often deviate farther from their purpose. This creates a sense of dissatisfaction.

» Alpha man deviates the farthest away from his why when he succeeds. He often enters a zone of comfort when he does achieve his goals. If he stays there he loses his power.

» Lionheart starts with his why, and if profits are not achieved, he loses his drive to continue the business.

» When your why and your profits have a large gap, the safe zone or success zone disappears and men question, doubt or become un-motivated by their business or goal.

- Success without fulfillment is not a success. Except for some.
- Your purpose will always reveal the how to.
- Once your why is clarified, your profits will soar. Get this right, and everything else comes together.
- What are you best at? What are you most passionate about? Now why? Use this process to help determine your why.
- Your why cannot be manufactured. It can only be revealed when you are quiet.

END OF CHAPTER 10 NOTES.

I am with you brother. You got this. Your purpose is the answer.

Let's move on to chapter 11.

Chapter 11

REDEFINE YOUR IDENTITY ~ REPRESENT YOUR BRAND

There are some unique steps to the branding process I am going to show you. The comeback version of branding means you have to brand a new version of you. During this chapter, we are going to look at elements that make up a personal brand, mainly what you stand for as a business man and entrepreneur. This helps shape your comeback and give it a framework for you to rise up again. Except this time you can do it with a renewed sense of passion and authenticity.

Always be in character! In acting class they teach actors to always be in character. It's a great principle to live by. Men often rise up to the occasion and put on a smile to get things done, then we change. This level of branding requires you to always be in character. To be in your genius mode.

Your comeback requires you to always be in your character, your most authentic identity. During my earlier years the only thing I cared about was anything to do with being a doctor. From the moment I could walk I collected first aid kits. You know my story. As I grew up people called me "Doc," it became an identity. As did the name "Ironman" for my pitching ability. I owned it so well even my opponents called me a machine. Ironman later became the name of a pitching machine. I should have made money from this. I showed no emotion as a pitcher and threw hard for a skinny kid.

These identities reflect what I was passionate about, had skills in, and a deep love for. When I stopped playing baseball and my doctor dream was forgone to pursue coaching, I had to shed these to take on a more authentic identity that would support my next level.

This new identity became the silent giant. I am highly introverted and intuitive, yet bold and passionate. The silent giant is who I am, it resonates with me. You can see it everywhere in my life and it serves me. People can feel my presence in the room and when I speak about it, people light up. Although, some may not enjoy or feel safe with my boldness and bluntness, that is just my character.

When we fail, we often forget who we are, and can feel disconnected from ourselves. Things seem off or we feel like we are wondering. When this occurs, we must return to our roots, our core essence and masculine nature.

Although we often get seduced by doing and having, we often do it at the expense of who we are. It's like venturing off to work and leaving your soul at home for the day. This is the part of you that must be called forward. There is an unlived piece of you that is yearning to come out, to be accessed and unleashed. Whatever that is, you can feel it. You don't need to analyze it or figure it out, you just need to trust. Your character is not a light switch that turns on and off. It is in every aspect of your life. The brand identity is about owning your true nature.

A client of mine Jens (*pronounced yens*) is a successful trainer. I've been working with him since 2013. He comes up with great ideas, hesitates and then shifts gears onto something else. Part of his mindset about creating success is about putting the best system together, making his ideas turn to profit, all the while negating to ask himself, "is this really my path?"

His training business finally reached six figures and by the end of 2016 he had reached $20,000 monthly revenue. Now he is contemplating a blog about sex, sweets, and recreational use of marijuana. He is in the love with this idea, but he is stuck on how to make money with it, position it and so on.

The real issue isn't his idea or implementation. If someone is really called to do something, the implementation process cannot be stopped. It's not the idea that succeeds, it's the inspiration behind the idea that causes success. Remember, it's the man behind it that creates it, not the system.

When Jens and I were talking, I asked him about his identity. Why are you taking this on? Why you? And why is this relevant? Outside of wanting his own yacht and one big idea to make him rich, he really didn't know. An idea without the backing of a powerful vision, usually never launches or brings profit

When I asked him to describe part of his character he related it to Cheech and Chong and body by suave. He wants people to have the best free flowing life, to be able to put life equal to or ahead of work. And what is required for him to be in that character was courage and boldness, to live it and call it forth without concern of judgment or criticism for his next venture.

He had to reveal his true nature in order for this idea to manifest. He could not hide behind the idea any longer if it were to manifest.

Jens has to be willing to access this greatness and call it forward, until his space is consumed with the energy of his identity. He has to be willing to recruit more power, strength, and courage and continue stepping into his character, until he surrenders to it. Surrendering to it means nothing more than letting greatness have its way with you; and don't get in the way. Keep yourself in check. Much like an orgasm can be all consuming, your true identity should permeate from the depths of your bones and be apparent to those around you.

Always Be Willing

The willingness to stay true to your identity and express it is essential to your comeback. Speaking your truth regardless of how others may respond or react. Just as we crave watching a sporting event and seeing any man on any field, step up and take over the game, we crave our own willingness to rise up for ourselves. When pro athletes are interviewed about their championship win they often say how grateful they are for God, trust, team, character, heart, hard work, and how they are committed to being number one no matter what. "Just be who we are and do what we do," is a repeated theme I hear when athletes in any sport are interviewed by the media. Never do they say, "do what we do and be who we are."

Your willingness is a clear and obvious demonstration of the quality of your character. When I work with clients who are moving through difficult times, they often feel like the only thing that is working for them is their willingness. And that may be true at times for you. Be willing to go to the mat for yourself. Be willing to get vulnerable to the point where you feel uncoordinated and awkward. Be willing not to know something or to feel foolish because that is part of learning. However, if you lose willingness, your character fades. There isn't anything about you that wants normal, or you wouldn't have chosen this book.

If you think of your life as a conversation and your willingness to have the conversation is your participation. Your vision requires you to participate fully. Participation means to be in the conversation with whoever, whatever, and wherever is needed to manifest what you want. Most are unwilling to take it this far and when they do, they are not fully participating.

Every result or lack thereof, is directly related to your participation in having what you want. A sales rep who isn't willing to make uncomfortable phone calls, while also stating he wants to make six figures, isn't participating at the level required. Although he isn't making near that, he can only run into a wall repeatedly and wonder why.

SUCCESS IS A MATTER OF HOW MANY UNCOMFORTABLE CONVERSATIONS YOU ARE WILLING TO HAVE.

There is usually an unwillingness that needs to be spoken. Men usually claim how willing they are for something, yet when it comes time to put it on the line, the unwillingness shows up in the form of a concern or fear. *"I don't want to fail, so as long as I participate to the point that concern doesn't show up, then I am ok."* In other words, we hold back, but playing the game to not lose is not going to create a win for you.

Men know the difference between winning and beating your opponent. You might win the game, but if you didn't beat your opponent then your fulfillment may not be as amazing as you want. Some men may pretend they are victorious and are okay with that, and some may silently feel they really didn't win. You have a choice, to be thrilled with your participation or hold back.

What Are Your Strengths

I have discovered that entrepreneurs who have built empires around their strengths have overcome incredible obstacles, while maintaining financial growth and profits. When I first began coaching, most of my clients were doctors. They knew what their strengths and gifts were. Some were great with their technique; so well they would forget to communicate with their patients. They loved working on patients so much that the thought of having to run a business was painful and often failed at it.

As their business grew, their office became more chaotic and the doctor would have to spend more time fixing business issues and less time with patients. In other words, they were outside their skills sets.

Dr. Loren attended my 3-day workshop back in 2004 and was a successful and skilled doctor – he was also burnt out. Literally fried to his wits end having to deal with every aspect of the practice such as staff, paperwork, and treating the patients. He had to wear all the hats. He couldn't even connect or talk about his strengths, it was as if he didn't know.

You can only split hairs so many times before you run out of hair. For Dr. Loren, had been burned many times with staff, experienced a divorce, and was trying out different business models to automate his business and became overwhelmed. He was ready to retire from the business he loved.

Sometimes we get overwhelmed by the next thing to do, and the next and how the next is going to work before we get one single step completed. Dr. Loren was not an implementer or executor of business. His best skill was diagnosing problems and assigning a solution/treatment. That is what his business looked like, a list of problems, and in most cases a remedy with no one to delegate to.

His greatest strength was now part of the issue. The more patients he saw and helped, the bigger his business grew the more pain it caused him. We had to find a trusted staff member with business acumen to take over for him and to free himself as a slave to his own business.

Eventually we found the right person, her name was Madison. Her greatest strength was following clear orders and executing them. She was a go-getter who could not get on her go-getting attitude, unless she had a leader who could delegate to her. Perfect!

We changed Dr. Loren's office hours to 3 days per week, giving him 4 days off. During the first 6 months, he was able to rest and rejuvenate on his days off. The final six months of our work together he was to travel. Freedom was his top value, and when he could not honor that it was a prison for him. Two years later, he now has another doctor treating his patients 3 weeks per month, while he travels. We set his office up to also do phone consultation and help diagnose patients with chronic illnesses and provide treatment plans. He charges $250 for the hour, plus the costs of products and makes an extra $2,500 per month while traveling.

WHEN SKILLS ALIGN WITH PASSIONS EVERYTHING GROWS.

When you align your business around your greatest strength then everything becomes manageable.

When you align your team around your weakness then you put your team into their greatest strength.

When you discontinue trading your strengths for the grind, you free yourself and revive your energy.

Let's go deeper on this one.

Expression of Power

Your strengths are part of your brand and how you lead your comeback. Each strength you have is expressed; it's called expression of your power. Usually men express those strengths in some areas well, not so well in other areas and not at all in some. If you are a strong strategist at work and with money, but you're getting blamed for not taking care of your health or solving family issues, it can be confusing for a man. How can I be called upon at the office to solve problems, yet I cannot solve my own? Sometimes we apply our strengths in areas of passion, and in other areas we disconnect from our strengths. Often not realizing those strengths still apply to all areas of our lives.

ALL YOUR STRENGTHS ARE APPLICABLE TO EACH AREA OF YOUR LIFE.

The goal here is to discover how your strengths are impacting your values, if at all. It's easy to feel powerful in one or two areas, and then feel powerless in others. To become more dynamic you have to connect your strengths to your values to have an impact.

The illustration shows the strength; in this case it's *strategy*. Someone who's strength is strategizing. How that strength is expressed is by asking questions, planning, giving advice, diagnosing issues, even solving problems and making connections to why things are not working. Now, how does this apply to a variety of values? How does it show up and create impact?

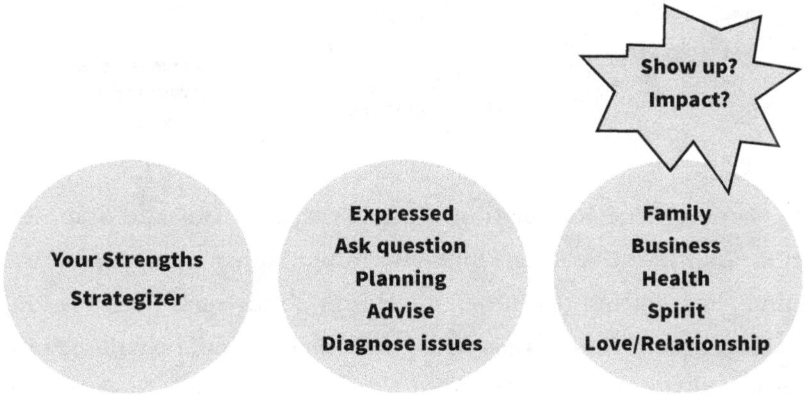

A person who loves to strategize may be good at work and with money, but how do you strategize with family? Health? Spirit? It is actually very simple. For family dynamics to work it is important that everyone has a strategy, something as simple as, "when someone is unhappy, we talk things out with each other." For spirit the family might use prayer or attend church. For health the family might have a few strategies to improve health, like family walks, hikes or meditation. We tend to think of these as action steps, but a strategy is designed to produce a result or experience that has impact.

Assignment:

Complete this chart for yourself all the way through to discovering how your expression of power is showing up in your values and the impact it's having.

Bart is a friend of mine; he is amazing at offering people strategies to grow their businesses. Yet, his relationships and health are a constant struggle for him. How can his strengths be applied to his values? If Bart carries his strategy ability to his health it might look like the example below:

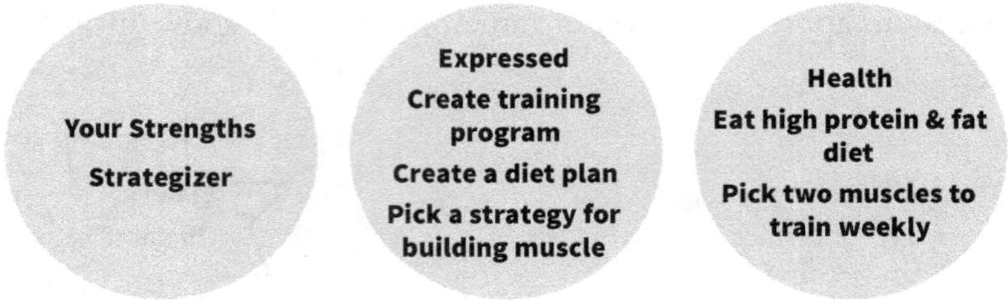

The same is true for relationships, perhaps he can add some of his strategic abilities to dating. Like listening, asking fun questions and spending time getting to know new things about each date. As long as Bart is clear about the ways his strengths are expressed, he will see how he can impact all areas of his life. What is important here is to see how men do well in living some of our values and linger in other areas. It is not a time issue, it's simply a matter of calling forward our identity, character, and strengths.

What Is Your One Thing?

Many of my rock star clients believe they are good at several things. This seemed to be true for me too, until I had a wakeup call and realized it was my need to be in control that led me to feel I was good at several things. In fact, I was passionate, curious and loved to learn. I confused that with being good at several things.

For two straight years, I was so busy that even my assistant struggled to create my schedule and see that I followed it. My schedule looked like this:

6:30 am – Wake up and Hour of Power.

7:30 am – Get kids up and spend time with them.

8:30 am – Off to school, first meeting via phone.

9:15 am – In office meeting.

9:45 am – Coaching clients.

11:30 am – Finance and Marketing meeting.

12:15 pm – Lunch

12:45 pm – Leave for airport – conference call on the road.

1:30 pm – Wheels up for San Diego.

3:30 pm – 2-hour seminar – Business Growth.

5:45 pm – Dinner meeting and closing the room.

6:34pm – Head to airport.

9:30 pm – Home with kids.

10:30 – Emails and Social media.

Midnight – Lights out.

Next day- Repeat

That didn't include interruptions, other meetings or people needing my time. After a while I thought there had to be a better way. When I looked closely, I discovered, in a way, I was no different than Dr. Loren. While his greatest skill was diagnosing, mine was communicating. Yet, my entire day was spent communicating and there was still not enough time in my day.

I decided to raise up the two people closest to me. Their job was to communicate, qualify and set me up to make decisions with others so I did not have to talk with them. This was to allow me to talk through my team. I also routed my coaching clients to spend a day in person with me, rather than 3 hours per day each week. That gave me back 12 hours per month of my time just in coaching calls. Meetings, conference calls, and social media took up another five hours per week, and 20 hours per month. I boiled it down to 1.5 hours per week and got back 14 hours per month. Then I made a huge decision to travel less, have someone else speak on my behalf, which was 50% of the time. Giving me back 3 days per month or 36 days per year. I just extended my vacation time to over one month!

After I made this shift my ears were going through withdrawals. They didn't know what to do without ear phones in them!

It finally occurred to me that I could knock out my entire day with one skill. That skill is leveraging my communication; I corralled my meetings into one. It cut my days nearly in half, freed up my time, and allowed me to spend more time doing what I am best at, while raising up others. I spoke to more people in one meeting to maximize my time. I set up new rules for meetings and phone calls and text messages, so people knew what and when to communicate to me. Best of all, I shut off my phone and computer when I was at home and in the car.

The stress involved was not because I was taking on too much, although that is an accurate statement, I was not inserting my greatest strengths throughout my day. Once I got into alignment my time and energy were replenished.

If you include your day around what strengthens you, you will be a sustainable man with an empire. I have now condensed my days from 6:30 a.m. to 12 p.m. in production, creativity, and clients. 1-2 is health and sex, 3pm to 8pm is family, friends, hobbies and living my values. Lights out around 10 p.m. Does this happen every day? No. Some days when I have retreats, books or projects, I might use up some of my 3pm to 8pm time for it. However, this is the new norm for me.

This is how men create a comeback and continue to live out their lives, and experience their values. Making decisions around time and having a structure you are disciplined to follow, makes the difference.

Who Are You at Your Best

Another key ingredient is knowing who you are at your best and for me, my best is courage, boldness, fire, passion and willingness to stand and deliver.

That is who I am at my best. Now imagine, your strengths, willingness, and identity all working together with who you are at your best.

You have had moments in your life where you were at your best. Begin to review those moments and see who you are that causes those moments to happen. I bet it is your energy that allows you to create these moments. They are not moments that happen to you. You and you alone choose your experience in life.

So, who are you at your best? As you make a list based upon what you see when you imagine it, you will start to see a pattern or a primary way of being that is congruent with your identity.

Larry was a successful man, but he ran into a few problems. Larry became diabetic, his business was slowing down, and his love life pummeled when his wife left him. This all occurred in a few months. When Larry reached out to me, he was confused and uncertain. For a highly intellectual guy, who likes to figure things out for himself, you can imagine how hard this was for him.

After one half day of working with Larry in North Carolina, he finally recalled and revealed a time in his life when he was at his best. Despite not feeling this way for a while. This is why coaching is so valuable; we don't let clients off the hook when it matters.

Larry said the following,

"I am creative, alive, joyous, happy, wealthy, rich, I am rich, I am filthy rich and happy."

Then Larry ran out of answers and didn't know what else to say. An hour past and he was disconnected again and short on answers. I reminded Larry that in the beginning it was easy to say all the right answers, but it's not what we know, it's what we own that matters. There is no answer to this, it's just the way you are. There is no right or wrong, there is only what you naturally are.

As we processed through this, he was able to access more. Access is key here. Whenever a man runs into a wall, or is short on answers, he can start to access something greater. His own being. Access to your being, bypasses the mind, which seems to know everything. This is where things are no longer a puzzle—but revelations start occurring. A revealing of yourself.

Later, Larry blurted out the following; as you read see if you can identify where he accessed his own being.

"I am a loving, creative and happy man, I am happy, I am rich and love being rich, money is always coming in, money loves me and I love money. I love women, women love me. I am a happy rich, fun man. With every cell in my body I live, and nothing can take my happiness, I love mankind and I trust with all of me that I will live a long time, and nothing can take my happiness, nothing can take my happiness. I am a loving joyous happy man, who attracts wealth, true wealth, everywhere I go. I am amazing! Life is amazing, I want more of this."

Did you see the access point? Just after he stated, "every cell in my body" he was accessing his own being and left his mind, or as I say, he is not living in either head, but his heart flew wide open. He was shouting out verbal rhetoric and crap like most men do. He fully engage in it and left his mind, his need to be right and give the right answers, to opening up a deeper part of him.

In a workshop with 30 men, this process is amazing to experience and with hundreds it's even more amazing. Everyone gets it and soon men start to experience life for the first time without thinking or avoiding feelings, but totally connected. It becomes obvious that their internal reality is created by them and they always have access to a deeper conversation.

Now it's your turn, who are you at your best? Make a list by writing down everything that comes up for you. Try to let go of your mind answering. After several minutes you may notice that you run out of answers, just keep writing. You may notice a shift from head to feeling or vice versus, but at some point you will access something greater.

Once your list is complete, start to look for one thing that really represents who you are at your best. Then integrate this into your life on a daily basis.

Represent Your Brand ~ The Final Piece

You have been representing your brand most of your life, whether you know it or not, your every action or non-action you take, sends a message to those around you~ your brand. Everything you say and do or not say, can be experienced in the form of vibe. When you have an impact on someone, either positive or negative, you have branded that person to remember you based upon how you showed up. Your brand is not some switch you can turn on and off, your power is not a switch either. You are always representing yourself, or who you are not. Either way, your brand is at play.

Now that we have covered a few key pieces to your identity and what you stand for, we can now put them all together. Let's review this chart and begin to start filling in the pieces to it.

Strenghts	Passions	One Thing
Character	BRAND IT!	

In each section I want you to write in the final piece that you discovered by completing the previous assignments. I will break them down for you here.

Identity- What is the single most important thing that has been a constant in your life? For me it was the silent giant.

Strength- What is the single most powerful strength you have? For me it was courage.

One Thing- What is one thing you can do to be productive? For me it was communication. This is where you spend most of your time living. This often goes hand in hand with your strength. For me it was the,

"Courage to Communicate" hence the Silent Giant Identity. Do you see how my identity fits with my strength and one thing? I could not be where I am today without the courage, or willingness to communicate my identity.

Best At: This is your being question. On your greatest day who are you being? This becomes your operating system, how you roll, how you show up and what you experience.

Let's take Bart as an example:

You will find when you complete this chart that you have a brand new image, title and so on. Your comeback requires you to "come alive" and take on what really matters to you. This is your next level; *what you stand for becomes what your brand.*

Strengths	Passions	One Thing	Character	BRAND IT!
Diagnosis	Decoding words	Language Master	Goofball/Intellect	Word Detective

So, what do you represent? What do you stand for? When you review this information in the chart, it can become apparent that you stand for something and can now represent this in all that you do. This will set you on a mission.

Here is an example of a client of mine whose name is Sunwolf, Sun has had an interesting life. He grew up a small kid in Brooklyn and later became an engineer who was told he could climb the corporate latter, fill up his 401K plan, and retire. Well, that vision got shattered along with millions of others, and he had to become a broke entrepreneur.

During our coaching session, I asked Sun to share with me a nostalgic moment in his life. I asked him one single question, **"why do you do what you do?"**

Your brand is driven by the answer to this question. You learned this in earlier in this book.

Sun told me that from a young age he was always going against the grain, if kids were doing one thing then he created something else against the flow. He challenged authority. He did not like growing establishments that took advantage and forced their way into people's lives. He also is very anti-government and believes they should just do the right thing for the people and not have their hands in our pockets. Sun has more energy than a 20-year-old and he is 65.

It became clear that Sun was an iconoclast and that's what he stands for.

His strength is connection.

His one thing is sharing wisdom.

And his identity is the Iconoclast.

He is at his best when he is teaching others. The Whimsical teacher.

His brand became Whimsical Teacher.

Sun also does a lot of things, from speaking, vegetarianism, and successful in Purium network marketing. He can juice anything that your body needs to heal. The man is a walking magic bullet blender and people love him.

The iconoclast fits well and his sub brand is "Juice It." Because he loves to maximize everything. Food, juice, time, this moment, his connection to people and sharing information that transforms people's lives.

That sets the tone for his website and marketing. Just by understanding who he is, you can start to create images of what a website or brand image would look like. That sets up his business and how he operates in pursuit of his comeback. Clearly, he won't be posting to support politicians. Except, it would be congruent for him to post things like, "*If Congress juiced more, they would actually understand healthcare."* His iconoclast identity can speak volumes for him.

Epic men make comebacks because they make a shift on how they operate as men. Even if you think you have done this before or tried it, you must shift perspective and create something even better.

Chapter 11 Notes: Redefine YOUR Identity ~ Represent Your Brand

» Representing your brand means you should *always be in character.*

» Always be willing to express and own your identity. Who cares what anyone else thinks.

» Success is a matter of how many uncomfortable conversations you are willing to have.

» When strengths align with passions you have a winning formula.

» The expression of your power is where manifestation begins. Don't hold back.

» All your strengths are applicable to each area of your life. Your strengths are NOT just good for one thing.

» What is your one thing? If you could invest your life into living for this one thing, what would that one thing be?

» Knowing who you are at your best, can reveal to you a winning state of mind.

» There are 5 parts to creating your brand. When all 5 come together you have invented a new approach to your comeback. One that sets you on fire.

» Rebranding yourself means that you won't repeat the past failures, because you are no longer that guy in a pattern of failure.

END OF CHAPTER 11 NOTES.

I am with you brother. You got this. Represent yourself like a KING!

Let's move on to chapter 12.

Chapter 12

GENERATE CONCISE GOALS

Early on in this book I shared with you the difference between goals and vehicles. We often lose ourselves in the goal and miss the fact that goals are really vehicles to experience something. If you have a goal of earning $1,000,000 by a set date, that would be a goal. It's also a vehicle because why you want that money is the ultimate goal. For men that amount of money is *freedom, power, and a life without worry.* What that money means to you is the real goal.

I want you to keep this in mind so you know the obtainment of the goal without the understanding of why and what it will provide, may leave you unfulfilled. If freedom is what one million dollars will give to you, can you experience freedom right now without it? As much as you believe money creates freedom, it's not the only way to experience freedom. You want to show up accordingly, having both the freedom to pursue a lofty goal and experience more freedom when you achieve it. But don't be mistaken, you can be a free man with or without the exact money.

Let's reverse this process so you are operating from what you want so you can create it.

Lets' break down the old model of goal setting.

Goal: I want to make one million dollars.

Why: Peace of mind, freedom, to quit my job.

When your why is strong enough, it can lead you to the creation of money. Unfortunately, creation requires you to experience the feelings of your why now, so strongly that it creates momentum towards your goal. This way you are operating from your why, rather than scarcity.

For example, if I want to meet a beautiful woman to marry, that would be my goal. And my why is to have love, sex and happiness. Then I ask you, how can you create that if you are not feeling love, sexy or happy now?

You can't. What you are trying to do with your goal is to obtain something, so you have *feelings.* That is operating from scarcity. Then you wrongly assume that you have what you want and that you own it, after the fact. Owning your life, means you own who you are and your why, right now. It means you create the experience, so you can **continue** to experience love, sex, and happiness and most of all have someone to **share it** with.

You cannot attract what you are not experiencing. You already are, in feeling, what you think, you will become. I am suggesting the idea that if you believe life is lived from the inside out; you operate from the inside and stop lying to yourself that having a million dollars is really the only factor that can provide you freedom. You have free will to choose and experience freedom right now. You're just stuck on an illusion that you cannot have it without the goal.

Let's break this down further in the context of fulfillment.

Goal: I am a free and peaceful man creating one million dollars.

Why: Because "I chose to."

Vehicles are anything you think will support you in experiencing your why. My car is a vehicle to get from point a to point be. What men unknowingly do is make the vehicle a status symbol and attach it to their sense of worth. You're worthy with it, and unworthy without it.

If you want a million-dollar business so you can retire, then your vehicle for retirement is one million dollars. The goal is to retire, worry free and happy and your why is because you promised yourself you would.

Because you "chose to." In other words, my will, will be done. You don't need a reason, just a clear why and the ownership that you chose it because you said so and your word is gold.

Do you know what the definition of abracadabra is? ***"I will create as I speak."***

Let's add in all three components to goal setting.

Goal: I am free and a peaceful man creating one million dollars.

My Vehicle: To promote my business to seven figures.

My Why: Because I said so.

Enough said! You are clear and connected to your why. In tune with your soul purpose. There is nothing to justify or explain. Notice there is no drama, long winded explanations or stories behind it. You have created a direction, a vibe and have crystal clarity about your comeback.

Let's assume for a moment, that you remove the vehicle from the above process, what would happen? **There would be no path to create it.** Can I count the times men have told me they want to generate $15K per month, and they had no why . Or they don't have a vehicle that can support the goal. If you remove the vehicle from this process, then you're just living a pipedream.

YOUR VEHICLE HAS TO BE CLEAR FOR YOUR DREAM TO BE REALIZED.

Do we not live in a world where people feel they have to justify their choices? That people have this need to explain themselves for doing what they do? This starts in childhood with parents who really do not understand why their kids behave the way they do. Parents either punish kids for their behavior or tell them they are wrong and then kids justify their actions out of defense.

Rather than understand or talk, they ask, "why did you do that?" But nothing really comes of it. Most parents don't get "Children want to be loved." And most children are not going to say that, if they have the capacity to understand their own motivation. If people lived curiously about knowing why others do what they do, we would have a more compassionate and in-tune world. If you know why you are doing what you are doing, you will have an in-tune world in you, and that's all that is required.

We all have a purpose and we all do what we do to serve our own needs. We do not need others to understand our purpose. For men, we do what we do to feel valued, respected, appreciated, and worthy. For women, it is often to feel safe, loved, connected, and wanted. It's the source of all human behavior. Spiritually, something is calling you. Although, many men say, "they don't know what that is," on the inside we all know what it is. You know what it is. You are just afraid to fail again.

There is no need to explain yourself. If you feel you must explain yourself, don't! You are not here to validate the feelings of others. Explaining things does not create results.

Can you imagine if your child came home with straight A's? And when you asked them how he or she did it, they said, "because I chose to?" That wouldn't make sense, who talks like this? Yet, that is exactly how it happens. You have to choose it. Just like a woman wants to be wanted and chosen. Just like wealth and money, you have to choose it to have it. Just like love, appreciation, and respect -- you have to choose to have it for you FIRST!

WANTING IT ISN'T ENOUGH, YOU HAVE TO CHOOSE TO EXPERIENCE IT AND BE WILLING TO CREATE IT.

If a child hits another kid and you ask why and they say, "because I chose to." That would be ridiculous. Yet, it's the actual truth. What parents fail to understand is that they want an explanation or story. Somehow this makes it better to understand and nothing changes as a result of it. If a child tells you they hit someone because they hurt their feelings, then a parent would punish them anyways. Rather than build emotional resilience or strength.

For example, "well, he made fun of me, and hit me, so I hit him back," is not an answer that suffices. The explanation is followed up with, "You're a bad person and you shouldn't have." Yet, there is not a mention of what choice he could have made to change the direction of his life in that moment. Just as you have results in your life, you chose to be where you are, now you get to freely choose to have it the way you want. No one runs out of choices. You may feel limited, but choices are available.

My point is, we all want explanations from ourselves and from others. We give explanations and demand others explain themselves as a dramatic way taking responsibility, "I made a choice, and this choice did not serve me." Once you own that, you can choose again, but the moment you head down a list of explanations, blame, shame and fault, you never get to responsibility. Then we try our best to keep that from happening again, which is choosing to avoid, not choosing to have.

VICTIMS ALWAYS HAVE EXPLANATIONS, EPIC MEN SPEAK THE BONE CHILLING TRUTH.

We rarely operate in ownership and a knowingness of clarity as to why we do what we do. And when we do it, it's a choice you have made.

The Strategy

The how-to comes alive when you do and when you choose to have what you want, the way you want it. Now that you have reached this far and have learned enrollment, context, contents, goals, and vehicles, your *strategy* is most important. Hopefully you remember reading about your *why* and next comes the *what* and the *how to.* Now we are heading into the *what*, what is your strategy? What is the strategy you will choose to take on your goals?

Early on in my business, my main strategy was to talk with potential clients on the phone. My strategy in life was to practice daily meditation, yoga, training by body, and having coaching sessions so to start my day in my genius mode.

Your strategy is the way you will now operate to achieve your goal. It is your undying commitment to never give up and manifest what you want. Keep this strategy close to you and know it's what you invest most of your time on. This is execution time.

Goal: I am free and a peaceful man creating one million dollars.

My Vehicle: To promote my business to seven figures.

My Why: Because I know I can, and I will.

The Strategy:

Let's continue to work through this process.

When I made my first million I focused on a few core strategies. It was my playbook.

» Phone calls

» Joint Ventures

» Speaking Engagements

» Referral Programs

There are so many strategies to choose from and I chose the ones I am best at or would be best at. This way there wasn't a big learning curve to make my comeback. I already had the competence, confidence and decision-making abilities to leverage these three strategies.

The list of strategies could go on, right? They are endless; ponder all the possible strategies that are available. Then choose the ones that are in alignment with you. Alignment is based on what you are competent, confident and decisive about. It is also important to pick the strategies you can move on right now, not ones you have to jump through hoops to get to.

As you begin to isolate the strategies that call you forward and you are both competent and confident with, the next step is to prioritize them in a sequence. It is important that you are focused on doing what is best right now.

When clients tell me they are, "working on the best website ever," I laugh. I laugh because I know a website without traffic is nothing but an online business card. If no one sees it, you have invested money with no return or a plan for that return. A website without a clear purpose, message, and way of getting people to either buy your product, call you or start a relationship, is an investment without return. I do things backwards from the norm. I build a traffic and profit plan first, then the website. I ensure I am clear as to why traffic will go to my site and why they will buy. Until that is rock solid, my sequence is off.

A strategy for a comeback must be one you can act on and see results. Putting up a website is one thing, having it make money is another set of strategies entirely. We want a direct approach to wealth. If your comeback requires you to make a website for an online business, go lean. Eliminate all bells and whistles until you are in the money.

The Sequence

Goal: I am free and a peaceful man creating one million dollars.

My Vehicle: To promote my business to seven figures.

My Why: Because I know I can, and I will.

The Strategy:

» Phone calls

» Joint Ventures

» Referral Programs

» Speaking Engagements

» Website

The Sequence:

As I charted my path to my first million, my goals were clear, my vehicle, my why, and now my strategies were in alignment. Now I had to sequence my strategies so I could act, this was most productive thing I have done. This way I was investing my energy into the right things, the most aligned activities.

My strategy for phone calls was my most powerful tool. I was great over the phone. I began making hundreds of calls each week.

My strategy for joint venture required me to make phone calls to already successful businesses. I asked them to promote me to their contacts, doing an interview of me or sending an email about me. While I was working on my phone calls and generating new clients, I also had to make phone calls and send emails for joint ventures. This worked hand in hand. Joint ventures would make much more money for me. My phone strategy was first because creating and launching any joint ventures takes more time. I needed to generate money, while the joint ventures came through.

My strategy for referral programs came next, simply because with each new joint venture or client, I have businesses to use referral programs with. Without some level of new prospects or clients, I do not have a referral program.

My strategy for speaking engagements takes less time, but the wait can be lengthy. Since someone else makes the decision to have me as a speaker, I was at their beck and call. This was a very profitable strategy, but a competitive one. There are many speakers to choose from. Without knowing who I was, seeing me speak, and without a website, this would be challenging, unless I was referred by someone.

My website strategy came last, simply because while I was doing the above and generating revenue, I could fund a website for people to research me. You might think this should be first, but I wanted a direct approach to money, while staying lean and investing little of my own money. When any of the above strategies creates money, my website is paid for without coming out of pocket.

The sequences of my strategies are equally important as the strategies themselves. If I switch these up then I am not producing the results I want, in fact I would be scattered.

Now comes the easy part. What actions will I take in alignment with it all? During your comeback, I recommend spending more time in these processes than in action. This way when you do act, you are acting from knowingness and not trying to figure it out. That is what I do, at least until it is clear what actions I am taking.

The actions are obvious. To implement all my strategies there are specified actions that can be measured. My first strategy is phone calls. I know at least 100 calls and at least 10 conversations will result in 1 new client per week. 400 per month or 4 clients at a sales price of $999 per month income, gives me nearly $4,000 per month revenue or $60,000 per year revenue.

My action step for this strategy is as follows:

1. 90 minutes of phone calls each day.

My second strategy is joint ventures. To implement this strategy, I need at least 5 businesses to call and their email addresses to email.

2. Locate 5 business phone numbers and emails.
3. Prepare email requesting a joint venture phone call.
4. Send email.
5. Call five businesses following up with email.
6. Repeat process weekly with new 5 businesses.

My third strategy is referral programs. For each new client, I simply make requests to refer them. I also add referral programs to my consulting contract with each new client. This states up front that once they get results with my consulting, they will refer three people they know who will benefit from my consulting.

7. Add referral program to contracts.

8. Call all past clients and new ones and ask for referrals.

My speaking engagement strategy is next. Here I ask all clients and joint venture partners for engagements.

9. Ask all clients and joint venture partners for speaking engagements.

The final piece of my strategy is a website. Once I generate 3 clients, I pay someone to put up a website with the sole purpose of prospects, doing their due diligence on me and my consulting services.

10. Build out framework 1 page at a time for website.
11. Find a freelancer online.
12. Budget for $350
13. Hire a freelancer.

My action assignments are clear and simple to execute. I add these to my daily calendar in short time blocks. No one task takes more than 30-60 minutes per day to execute.

Let's put it all together now.

1. Your Goal is ____________________________.
2. Your Vehicle is ____________________________.
3. You Why is ____________________________.
4. Your Strategy is ____________________________.
5. Your Sequence of Action are:

____

____

____

____

Chapter 12 Notes: Generate Concise Goals

» Generating clear concise goals means that you know what you want, and why.

» The definition of "abracadabra," ***I will create as I speak."***

» There is no need to explain yourself. No one needs to understand your why more than you.
» Wanting is not enough, you have to be willing to create it.
» Victims always have excuses; epic men speak the bone chilling truth.
» Your strategy comes after you generate concise goals and a clear why.
» Sequencing is power. Do the right thing at the right time. This helps to avoid overwhelm and keep you in genius mode.
» Once you sequence, your action steps become obvious and simple.

END OF CHAPTER 12 NOTES.

I am with you brother. You got this. What you speak will become reality.

Let's move on to chapter 13.

Complete this action assignment.

Chapter 13

HOW PRO'S MAKE EPIC DECISIONS:

Decision-making can be a battle; while decision-making occurs unconsciously, true decision-making is a muscle that is flexed by being rooted in your why. Why you do what you do is the source of the muscle behind your decision making. **Act accordingly.** Always inquire, is a decision in alignment with my why? You will be amazed at how much freedom you have.

When men are excited about something they instantly try to justify it in order to look "good" so we know what we are doing. "I know I don't have the money, and I am saving it to invest, but she is gorgeous, and I want to spend more time with her." That is a good example most men can relate to. Although it's fun to make spontaneous decisions for pure pleasure, it comes at the expense of not honoring your purpose. In the process of your comeback if it doesn't align with your purpose, be aware how you can manipulate your perspective to 'make' something fit into the purpose box.

Indecisiveness is a disease rooted in the illusion of failure. Indecisiveness is the opposite of playing to win, its playing to not lose. That is a safer path in disguise. I say in disguise because "not" deciding causes opportunity loss, time loss and often drama. All of which are usually costlier than deciding to act. The illusion of failure is that men project the fear of dealing with a loss or bad decision, yet not deciding does not change anything. Nor does it increase momentum towards your vision.

No one knows the future and fear and faith are projections of the same energy. When men are uncertain about something they can feel fear, project it in the future and stop themselves. Faith is the same projection with courage and trust that things will manifest.

Not deciding is a decision, it means you have chosen not to flex your muscles and trust your vision. There is no such thing as "what if this fails?" The question is what are you willing to do to follow through and ensure your decision yields results?

DECISION MAKING IS ABOUT DECIDING YOU WILL FOLLOW THROUGH TO ENSURE YOUR DECISION IS RIGHT ON!

The masculine is the decision-making element of who you are. The feminine element in you, avoids decisions and ponders all the options, choices, and often gets overwhelmed with it. There is a way to powerfully integrate it all. Is this decision divinely right for you? Is the decision I'm making in the best interest of what I stand for as a man? That is a powerful structure in which to make decisions from. I have often found that men know what needs to occur and they are not making the decision. It is easy to pretend you "don't know," but often times you do know. Often, the decision is sitting right in front of you.

Here is an example of what a decision maker at high levels goes through from moment to moment.

Tony Larussa is a legendary baseball coach and is an analytical man, and yet a grounded guy. He was being interviewed about his decisions during a game. I recall him stating that, "He has a plan before the game, that plan may change during the game and he has to feel the situation out. The game plan doesn't always work, and he has to be able to adjust at any time." Remember, a plan only works until someone disrupts it." Then it's a gut level improv game that requires you to stay in the moment.

As a coach, Tony has to analyze the game two or three plays ahead in order to decide what to do in each moment. There are moments when he can only decide to work with what is right in front him.

Here is what goes through a coach mind during the middle of a baseball game:

"Man, on first base, he loves to steal, watch his hands for the giveaway that he is stealing."

"The batter hits the ball in the gaps, he loves fastballs, if we throw a curve ball it will give the runner at first more time to steal, and move the outfield to cover the gaps."

"If we can get a ground ball double play, we can get out of this inning without runs scored, if he steals that changes the game, a base hit will score a run and we lose the game. Keep the runner close. Any curveball counts he may steal."

That is a lot of stuff! Every 8 seconds this is running through his mind. He has to analyze the situation and decide. Now, here comes the fun part, if his gut says the guy at first base is stealing, after he makes his strategic decision and prepares his team, he has a tug of war battle going on. Does he stay with the strategy and baseball percentages? Or does he trust his gut? Even if it's counter to his strategy?

This is where men get tripped up. Are you one to sacrifice a proven strategy for your gut? Do you lead with your gut? Or do you lead with strategies and facts? Either way you chose, there is an issue, simply because it's not a complete decision-making process. It's half man decision making when only a part of you decides and not all of you. You must own it and the way to own it is that all of you is in alignment. Go with what truly resonates with you the most!

I watched Tony during an interview; I have paraphrased his response here to sum up this point.

"I take in the information about each player and the situation, then I check my gut, what I sense to happen, I compress the information as quickly as I can, and I make my decision. It still might be wrong or right, but I have to trust everything I do."

If you don't trust your decision-making abilities, the natural response is to take in as much information as you can to make the best decision. Perhaps you won't check your gut at all. This process makes decision-making more difficult. Sitting in a sea of information only to find out that your decision-making pattern is still going to choose what it always has. Until you get clear about why you are making any decision, it won't matter how much information or how strongly you feel about something, your process will lead you to do the same thing anyway. How many times has a woman in your life known what you were going to decide before you did? Women see it before men do. Your decision-making muscles rarely change unless you change where you are operating from. In this case your purpose.

MEN OFTEN MAKE DECISIONS BECAUSE OF SOMEONE OR SOMETHING, RATHER THAN BECAUSE ITS WHO YOU ARE AND ITS YOUR PURPOSE.

Men make decisions based on their wife, kids, job, time or others. Rather than, this is my purpose, and this is my vision, so therefore, I am acting accordingly. It sounds noble and nice to do it for your family, and that may be a motivating force, but if you leave your purpose out of the decision-making process, you're depleting your masculinity.

Whichever part of you is authentically screaming, calling, pulling, or nagging, is what you go with it. Understand what is just in your head, the strategy, and feel your way through it, instinctively and decide. This is how a comeback man works with himself the best. The more consistent you are working with yourself, the more consistent your results will become.

What is a decision?

First, let's look at what decisions are not. Decisions are an act, not an emotion. Decisions are not facts; they are an act after you choose what will be for you, based on your purpose and direction.

A decision is nothing more than giving your word. The act of decision-making is drawing the line and taking a stand for implementation. Your goal is to manifest your purpose through this decision, until it takes the form you envision.

Once you flex your decision-making muscles, commitment comes into play. Commitment is also not a feeling, it's an action that will only move towards you having what you want, no matter what. Most of us feel like commitment is a prison, when really, it's locking you onto your vision.

Once that decision is made you continue to ensure that decision comes through. Men often get caught up in the result; trying to control it, rather than take the actions that ensure your decision is correct. No one really knows if the decision you make will work. You may have strong feelings about it, or you may be uncomfortable with it. No one can control the future, but what you can do is decide and continue to show up and follow through.

So why do men fear commitment? Because once we get over the fear of failure we might get stuck with something that we no longer want and cannot get out of it. The masculine trap is what we fear. And we lose ability to influence the situation or have control over it once the decision is made. Sadly, you can always change things afterwards.

These fears are really nothing more than testosterone talking. "Test head." Men are blessed with this powerful force called "creation" and we can create and re-create anything when we feel stuck or trapped with. While the masculine energy likes to run, or hide, it simply doesn't understand, let alone honor its most powerful element, **creation and recreation.** No matter what decision you make, things might change, your job is to decide, follow through and see your decision manifest.

Sometimes that means letting things play out and trusting the process, and sometimes it requires some influential muscle.

Our deepest fear is that having it all will feel so incredibly amazing, that we will have to admit we are powerful beyond measure and it freaking scares us! The question is why does it scare us?

Because once you admit your power, you now have to be responsible for it. Which means there is no one else to blame, no back door, no lying to yourself. That is the way of the responsible man. One that trusts himself. Not trusting yourself is a set up for failure.

100% responsibility means you are the only problem in your life. You are the reason you succeed or not. That nothing and no one has chosen the life you have right now. For some this is interpreted as "pressure" and for others it's "freedom." I am the latter!

For the Lionheart men who experience their feminine energy, making decisions will be hard. You may loop in your head, doubt, avoid deciding or need approval and validation from others. **This is your clue to go with your gut and align a competent strategy to your decision.**

For the Alpha Men who predominately experience masculine energy, they need to check with their hearts. They usually leave this out of the process and end up suffering later.

Creative Decisions:

Even the most Alpha Males have feminine qualities, like creativity. The most successful CEO's are creative, but they never acknowledge it as feminine energy, but it is.

Sit with this for a second.

- » Take away a man's ability to see.
- » Take away a man's ability to hear.
- » What's left?

To FEEL his way through it.

Feeling through it is NOT a matter of right and wrong, or good or bad, it's just a feeling. You can choose what is in alignment with you. If you refuse to feel it, you're not listening to source energy or your higher power. That part of you is the ONLY part that has your deepest interests at heart.

BE HEART PRACTICAL IN YOUR DECISION-MAKING PROCESS. COMBINE YOUR MIND AND HEART.

This is where to live, where your gut, higher power, GOD, and sources speak through you, as you. Everything else is mental masturbation. My analyst and scientific friends would argue this with me, yet most of them don't live in their body or soul anyways; so, what do I care?

Be Heart Practical and Trust

This was a hard shift for me because it requires trust, giving up being in control of my destiny, ego, and my will. Once you start down the path of trusting your decisions, you will have to face the reality that you alone are responsible for what happens. Men will do more to avoid failing than to live from their core. Trust becomes more imminent the closer you get to making consistent decisions and realizing, you have always been responsible anyways.

If you decide and trust it, the moment things head south; you will trust yourself to correct it. If you decide without trust, the moment things head south; you will feel helpless and incapable of correcting or re-routing the situation. You'll panic.

Decisions Shift Mindset

On a cellular level here is what happens when you decide:

Every cell in your body knows what every other cell is doing, all the time. If you insert a pin into your ear the cells in your feet react and know what is going on. When you decide with emotional intensity, the cells in your body react and align in the direction of your decision.

When you decide to cut something off in your life, you activate emotional intensity throughout your body, and act on it. Sometimes it is fear based. When your child is in a burning house, you decide, instantly, to save the child. Again, fear based. When a pretty woman calls and makes it clear she wants sex, you decide and act on it. This is pleasure based. When you decide to lose weight, your body and mind follow through for you. The stronger it is to start, the more powerfully you finish and complete the decision to a result.

What most men are doing is dabbling, trying, hoping, acting like they are going for it, but there is a part of them that is hesitant or holding back. Hence indecision. You cannot mentally claim decisiveness without engaging all of you. If we break man down to a 3 part being, body, mind and spirit/heart, making a decision with 1 part of you, while the rest is in a state of whatever!

A decision informs the cells in your body to respond accordingly. Your energy responds to your decisions. Your mind will shift in the direction of your decisions. Source, higher power, or heart, whichever you connect with, will guide you along and fuel you. A prime and overused example is when you buy a car. Once you purchase that car you see it everywhere. Your mind follows your decision and direction. The mind needs direction and clarity, and if you do not provide it direction it will remain scattered.

It's no different than when we worry about something going wrong. If you focus on it, a flurry of "wrongful" thoughts storm your mind, emotions of worry permeate your body, and you start to feel anxiety. Your heart rate increases, blood pressure, tension in your body and it changes how you breathe. Even the sound of your voice changes. Your body will begin to re-position itself to fit the energy you are experiencing, which drives your behavior or actions.

This energy can be felt up to 8 feet away. You create your own bubble within minutes, called "worry". This becomes your brand in that moment, the energy you give off is your brand, and how you represent yourself.

When you decide to make a comeback and gain or regain your million-dollar fortress; as an example, your thoughts flurry in that direction, as well as negative ones, emotions begin to generate, and millions of ideas start zapping through your electrical system. This can happen in minutes. These decisions cause shifts in your cellular body, your vibrations, and frequencies. You start to build momentum towards the decisions manifesting the results you want.

Decisions Are Constant

Every moment you are faced with a decision, some are simple, and some need to be radical. Radical meaning a quick, powerful act to move your body and mind in a direction opposite of how you may be feeling in that moment. This gives you power to shift yourself in any given moment. With fierceness and courage, you will need to decide to disrupt things. There are some decisions that cannot be made lightly or casually. Like throwing in the towel when your talent is getting beat up in the ring. There is nothing too casual about it, its instant.

There have been mornings when I struggled to get out of bed. No matter how powerful and inspired I am by my vision, my body was exhausted. If I came off from long nights with family, business matters, and last-minute emails to clients, I literally rip off the sheets, jump out of bed and scream, "whip it on, I'm ready." Suddenly my heavy eye lids are light, my heart rushing and energy lighting up every cell in my body. I brush my teeth, drank a liter of water, and hit the computer to knock out my day. Decisions shift your reality, it's how you can integrate a challenging day or moment to act, all the while honoring yourself.

Your comeback is a series of constant decisions. When you are connected to your why, decisions are made easily. When I am faced with a decision and I am connected to my why, my decision-making response naturally occurs. There isn't much to think about, I may have to strategize the implementation of my decision, but not the actual decision.

Stay current with your reality. Know what you can do and cannot do, where you are and where you want to be. It's a daily habit to know your reality so you can make decisions. Don't dabble with your life and NOT know the reality of where you are.

Indecision Kills Testosterone

As men, we were raised to help, be the hero, fix things, and just do it. Decisiveness is a major characteristic of masculinity. When we are unsure, uncertain, or loop in our minds about what decision to make, it drains us. It causes us to shrink or waiver. It is also the best opportunity to sit with the feeling of uncertainty and listen. Is there something here to learn? Is there something you might not see? Is there an unanswered question about something?

I always ask those 3 questions when I am feeling uncertain. It is in this state that your mind has no idea how to act. The mind does not like uncertainty. You see, when you ask most men a question, they go into their mind, unlock the files with all the answers and then respond. When you are uncertain you draw a blank or "don't know." Masculine energy runs from this; not knowing this causes men to beat themselves up, or worse, become nonchalant and say, "I'm just not going to worry about this." Both deactivate your potent masculine power, your testosterone.

The authentic answer cannot come from your mind. Your mind is filled with every memory of your life, a bit of knowledge you have learned, and things you don't even know are there. The authentic truth you are looking for is in the space of uncertainty, a black hole if you will. Sitting with this powerful hole of apparent nothingness is the source of new insights and answers. The truth for you will be pure and unconditioned responses. You won't find yourself saying things to look good, to get the right answer, or to get the answer you want to hear. No, instead, you will find the answer that is true to honor your path.

I often ask women in my talks, "how many have met a man who says and does all the "right things," but you just weren't feeling it?" Invariably, every woman raises their hand. This is what I am referring. It is not about having the "right answers," it's about speaking from your balls, the depth of your authentic feelings. Sitting in the hole of the unknown is where you gain access to the authentic part of you that knows.

If you stay in the state of indecision, you are chopping away at your balls and testosterone levels, unless you are willing to focus inward, ask questions, and get to know this deep place. The authentic answers will come, and the most powerful decisions will come from those answers. This is when you become unstoppable.

PRACTICE:

Start to notice where you make decisions from. Notice I asked, "where?" This is a geography question. Is it your head? If so, is it your upper head or lower head? Your heart? Your body? Or your emotions?

Regardless of the type of decision, notice where you are making it from. This helps you accomplish several things. One, you will notice a pattern. When you make compulsive decisions, you may notice you are trying to multitask or tell yourself you don't care and do it anyways. Two, you will notice the impact your lower head and feelings have on why you treat others the way you do. Three, you will notice that when your mind has control, you struggle to make a decision. Four, you may find you make many decisions from one place and thus, your life and business are a reflection of that one place.

This gives you the power to engage and start to make decisions like a pro, like Tony Larussa and CEO's. Your decisions are always WHY and VISION dependent. If you want to maintain integrity.

The Transition

As you continue reading this book, I must give you a heads up. The rest is a plan. Not just any plan, but a pathway to create a new direction, a new experience, and step into the next level of yourself.

If you read this through the eyes of your past, or try to use your mind, the same mind that got you in a tough time, NOTHING I say will work. In fact, nothing you do will work. Life is not a mind game, you cannot move chess pieces around, and fiddle or manipulate things to obtain results.

You cannot push, force, will-power your way to your next level. That won't work and you may risk dragging your past with you. I am offering you the chance to be free and do what man does best, create, procreate, build, and experience liberation.

This is your challenge. This is why you are here with me right now.

To fully accept this challenge, you must surrender your mind and your story. You must be present and deeply listen to answer the workbook experience in the remaining chapters. The harder you try to figure this out, the less likely you will be able to at all. I am speaking to you on a level you may never have been spoken to before.

Will you accept this challenge?

We'll see!

Man's Greatest Gift & Greatest Denial

Name a time growing up; when your parents showed you *how to listen to your heart*, in order to know what to do?

If you are a rare person who had parents like this, did you learn the strategy or continue doing it?

Paul Pearsall was an extraordinary psychologist and for a few years he went through a struggle of some sorts. A very successful and happily married man suddenly began crying for no apparent reason. He was experiencing frequent pain, but his doctor's all agreed that "it's all in his head." How funny is it to tell a shrink that his problem is in his head?

Dr. Pearsall was having insights about his body that science could not understand. The doctors told him it was all made up in his mind. Finally, after a meditation it was clear that he was to go back to the doctor and ask for an MRI. The doctors initially refused telling him he was fine, once again. Paul was explicit in asking for an MRI of his heart and pelvis. Paul sensed something was off.

Sure enough, he had cancer. It had been there since the days his tears began. The cancer was in both his heart and pelvis. The outcome was not good, but, while Paul is a pioneer in heart energy, he began to dedicate his energy and focus on only listening to his heart energy. He stayed closed to it, listened deeply and followed its intuition. While undergoing radiation the technician came out and said, "I cannot believe it, we are using the lowest dose, and your body is responding with limited side effects."

Paul was so anchored in his heart and love that the radiation was not impacting him. It was killing the cancer without destroying the rest of him. It was not long after this he was clear from cancer. His doctors still cannot figure it out. Paul calls this energy, L-heart energy. A heart monitor can detect heart rhythms and if you take those monitors and hold them 8 feet away from a beating heart, they can still be detected. There is profound energy that comes from your heart. The heart according to Paul, "can heal itself and carry the wisdom we need."

A study with a human heart and saliva cells proves this power. Scientists can take saliva cells from your mouth and place it in a petri dish and then place the petri dish 8 feet away in another room and the heart and saliva cells are still connected. If you place the heart under stress, the saliva cells react to the stress. The same is true for kids, when their mom is feeling off, kids react, even when their mother is not around.

You cannot have one part of your life that is fine, and think it's not affecting the rest. There is no such thing as compartmentalization.

Have you heard the phrase, "everything is connected?" Of course, but saying it and believing it are not the same. Every aspect of your life is the extension of your heart.

Every answer you are searching for is within. Every solution, every idea that is anchored to your destiny, is in your heart. The question is, *where are you*? The greatest gift is your heart, it is the source of certainty, fierce love, power, peace, empathy, and courage. It even provides you insight a few seconds ahead of actual events. Women love you for this part, and if you stop hiding it and operate from it, you will get everything you want.

Social media jib jabbers a lot about following purpose, heart, and getting in line with your destiny, but rarely do they give succinct advice or stories that men can utilize.

Until now, your greatest gifts have likely been your skills, knowledge, mind or willpower. Maybe some character trait or you are just lucky. Either way, the person you learned to be and the strategy you employed, may not work now. Not at your next level, let alone for a comeback.

The heart of a man is the core of his power. Rarely is it operating in its full capacity. Clearly, I am not talking about the heart beating, but the message and information it has for you.

The HeartMath Institute did a study about heart signals and messages to the brain. They took a group of people to do a study of roulette. These people played roulette wearing heart monitors, to detect heart rhythms when someone won or lost.

The second round detected that 3 seconds before the ball stopped on either red or black, the heart sent messages to the brain that were consistent with the emotions of winning or losing. This demonstrated the heart new just before the event occurred. That is remarkable. If only the heart could do this for the lottery.

YOUR HEART KNOWS. IT FEARS NOT THE UNKNOWN.
TRUST IT!

Yet, most of them did not sense the signals from the heart at all, they were not aware that their heart was communicating with their brains. Or that information is sent every moment from the heart. They were taken over by their own brain and willpower.

Your next level must be lead with your heart and your willpower, balls, testosterone, desire to achieve, and mind must align with your heart. Brother, that is serious fire power. This is what it looks like to be unstoppable. This is how you become unshakable; it's pure destiny and winning consistently.

Why? Because the heart knows. When you align it with willpower and the power of your mind, it's the ultimate fuel to manifest heart desire. You must risk opening up and staying open no matter what. If you do this, nothing will shake you up. You will have access to unlimited courage and love.

Consider your heart's desire before you act. Especially for the rest of this book. If you don't agree, you can always go back to the way you lived before. I can assure you I am setting you up for the best way to shift your operating system.

Let's roll!

Chapter 13 Notes: How PRO's MAKE EPIC DECISIONS:

» 90% of our decision are made unconsciously.

» Indecisiveness is a decision. You have decided to not decide which creates a power loss.

» Decision making is simple. We often confuse it with too many other factors. The goal of a decision is once you decide, you can follow through to ensure it's the right one.

» If you don't trust yourself, you may find yourself wanting more information. Thus, creating analysis paralysis.

» The best decisions are made from a state of mind called, "this is who I am." Rather than make decisions for someone else or because of someone else.

» Decisions are not emotions, they are an act.
» To avoid decisions because you don't trust the result, weakens are masculinity and causes men to become more controlling.
» Practice heart practical decision making.
» When you decide every cell in your body shifts accordingly to your decision. You create a magnetic force field and the elements of success align with you.
» Decisions are constant. Successful people make decisions daily.
» Indecisiveness kills testosterone. Forcing, pushing or pulling is not decisions making, its manipulation.
» Your heart usually knows that answer. Your job is to listen.

END OF CHAPTER 13 NOTES.

I am with you brother. You got this. Decisiveness triumphs confidence and competence.

Let's move on to chapter 14.

The Comeback Man with a Plan!

Chapter 14

RECRUIT MOMENTUM

Flight 247 to London is about to take off. The plane weighs 40,000 lbs. There are 430 passengers on this plan adding 2,000 lbs. of weight plus luggage. The total weight is 42,000 lbs. of mass.

Do you think this plane needs some serious momentum to lift off the ground?

YEP! When you make a comeback, and feel the weight of the path, you might feel like this plane taking off again. Either way, it doesn't matter. Success, failure, comeback or growth, every businessman or entrepreneur needs momentum to gain traction towards a goal. It's not necessary to wait for momentum to occur, it is something you can create.

Whether your vision is big or not, or if it should be bigger or not, is not as relevant as how much momentum you have. The key is to know yourself. If the vision is so big you cannot gain momentum around it to start, then you have a vision that is too big. If you have momentum when you think of your vision and plan for it, then you're on the right path.

A client of mine, Alan, wrote a book on sex, love and conscious relationships. Before he finished it, he called to discuss whether he should build a huge marketing plan or wait and see if posting it on Facebook would suffice. Perhaps, if it does succeed, then he will really try and market it.

In order to answer this, let's return to the plane example. I have 42,000 lbs. I need to get off the ground, should I wait and see if we can do it? Or just plan for it to lift off the ground?

Alan's book is as dead as these passengers if he doesn't have momentum before it is released. The average book sells less than 5,000 copies. Best sellers sell 10,000 copies and New York Times up to 30,000 per book. They didn't do that by taking a, "let's see how it does" attitude. I told Alan that if he was concerned about getting his hopes up, building momentum, and not getting the results, then he was questioning the power of his book. There is a time to test ideas and processes. You don't test momentum, you build it.

I engage with social media often, it's disgusting to see how much "just do it, go for it, and hustle, until you get it" that is out there. Without momentum the "doing it" is hard because it lacks any real power behind it. The next time you fly, tell the pilot to, "just do it" and watch what happens. The very first thing is the jets fire up and build momentum, release the brake, and wham! The plane leaps to the finish line.

I often ask business owners about the momentum they have in their business, and where in their business do you have momentum? They often try to tell me that so and so is interested in working with them, or they hired a new team member, or they feel good things are happening and last month they got some new referrals.

That's not momentum; momentum is when you're gaining traction by completing productive action steps. 200 people who like your post, is not real momentum, until they are converting down your pipeline. Feeling good and getting a dopamine high may feel like momentum, but it's not sustainable, nor productive if results are not being produced. A pilot feeling like his plane is awesome is not as momentous as accelerating at 185 knots and taking off.

Don't confuse elements of momentum for momentum. Massive progress with velocity can be seen and felt. It shows up in financial terms as well as your own physiology. However, feeling like good things are happening, are elements of momentum, but not momentum. Don't get stuck in the reality of "great things are happening" with no metrics for results to be accounted for.

DO NOT CONFUSE MOVEMENT WITH PROGRESS, BUSY WITH PRODUCTIVITY, AND FEELINGS WITH MOMENTUM.

A plane creates momentum and moves forward, it gains traction and lifts. It produces a result. A busy flight attendant doesn't produce results for the customers. They irritate customers and feel like things are moving along, but that doesn't mean progress is happening. Nor is being busy without measurable results productive.

Results don't lie, they are a clear indicator of how well you show up and what you are committed to.

The Function of Momentum

Energy is the precursor to comebacks and the only failure is the loss of energy. When a man is moving towards his goal and a setback occurs, it is really nothing more than energy loss. Once energy loss occurs emotionally, it feels like momentum has been lost. When you are making a comeback, it requires more energy; you are the airplane ready for takeoff.

MOMENTUM IS THE FORCE BEHIND YOUR ABILITY.

Momentum requires you to create three things, two of which can be done quickly, while the third requires consistent action.

1. The accumulation of energy.
2. The movement or expression of your energy.
3. The focus of both extended over time/concentration.

Accumulation of Energy

To accumulate energy requires you to experience your truest feelings about what you want to manifest. As you focus on the energy of "why" you want to manifest, you will naturally pick up an energetic charge. As you sit with this emotional charge it builds. In the beginning it might feel like pressure or tension, that is fine. At first dopamine creates a high, but the longer you sit with it, the more the energy alchemizes with source energy, which is sustainable. Dopamine or excitement is not sustainable energy.

As that energy builds in your body, it directs your mind, thought process, and begins to fixate on energy and begins seeking it out, until it is achieved. That is number one.

Movement or Expression of Energy

Number two is a natural response to number one. For example, when you build sexual energy to have an orgasm and then stop, how do you feel? Irritated, frustrated, or let down that you were not able to express those feelings or experience them.

While it is too easy for men to live in their head, the real power comes from the expression of it. You can tell a woman you love her verbally, but without expression or "throwing your body into it, it's just a word. If the energy only comes through your voice, it is short lived.

What is the value of experiencing happiness if it is not expressed? Or any emotion for that matter. Men too often reserve their feelings and rarely express the feelings behind their deepest purpose. This level of momentum is incredible, it will build anything you have been dreaming about. A man that is truly free has full access to experience his feelings and can express them at will any given moment. The movement of energy from the internal charge to the expression of it, means you are free. Men love freedom, we are wired for it.

Focus Extended Over Time

As you continue to practice these two components, your momentum will grow. It's easy to think that when things (outside of you) are working, that you have momentum. External happenings only add to your momentum. If you are not actively creating momentum then things working well outside of you are short-lived.

In the beginning of practicing this, you may feel like you are going to combust with power and energy. That is a great thing! As you practice, it will become a state of flow. This is where you are naturally expressing your energy and no longer holding back on what matters to you. There is freedom here, to be at ease with what you are creating.

The most effective way to generate energy is breathing and having a connection with your most dominant emotions. For me its passion, power, love, joy, and adventure. Those are dominant emotions for me that I want to experience in this momentum process. As I feel them in my body I breathe into them to expand the charge. I continue this process for as long as I want, it is what fuels me. It will fuel you. The deeper you go into it, the more powerful you become.

THE DEEPER YOU GO INTO IT THE MORE POWERFUL YOU BECOME.

It might seem odd at first, but my clients fall in love with it and they see the results. Let me offer a parallel so you can relate on some level, or even see you are doing this in minor ways already. When you are sexually charged your heart rate and breathing goes up, right? You are focused on the energy you are experiencing. You can sustain that energy for minutes or perhaps hours, it varies from man to man.

This process of building momentum is like having sex, with a different purpose. We accumulate energy through sexual feelings, we think about them and build tension and passion. It is through the action of sex that we express those feelings. Then right before men orgasm they stop breathing, they combust, then fall asleep, and lose their energy. We want to avoid bi-polar energy and have a constant flow.

This process of momentum continues to build ongoing, it puts you in the flow. Just like with success, we want a continuous flow of momentum, not a one-night stand. It's a practice and most men understand this parallel.

Momentum as an Agent of Change

One of the most remarkable times in my life was when I delivered my daughter Tristin at the hospital. A few hours after, while she was resting with her mom, I burst out in tears. I was so happy and overwhelmed, but scared at the same time. "What if I had dropped her?" It was a significant moment in my life.

The next day on our way home, it happened again. I had to pull the car over and cry. My heart was raw and cracked open, but I felt amazing. I was on fire and full of momentum. Mainly because I was free to feel everything. This continued for the next two months. I felt like I had the entire world behind me and in a way, I did.

That feeling never wore off. A while later I flew to Sedona, Arizona to speak. It was the first time in seven years that I felt fearless. I used to hate public speaking, yet I kept doing it because I knew it was a calling despite my fear of it. I spent the first 10 minutes talking to the group about delivering my daughter. Over 200 people were crying in joy. I was given a standing ovation. When my talk ended, I generated $60,000 in sales for my coaching business. When people came up afterwards, they didn't mention a word about the business strategies I presented or spending $5,000 each on coaching with me. What they mentioned was how I felt and who I was. That is when it occurred to me how powerless words are if there isn't a man behind them willing to express them with his deepest feelings. It was then I really learned the value of touching and impacting others. Everything I felt about the story I shared, I had felt intensely for months. I was focused on them and I expressed them without holding back. That is when I wrote out this process for other men to duplicate in any area of their lives, about anything that matters to them. Its time tested!

That momentum carried me through a barrier called, "fear of public speaking."

Practice It

It is important to call up the feelings behind your goals, this way you can accumulate energy. This is the first component. Write out your most dominate feelings for life and business.

1.
2.
3.
4.
5.

If you need help generating these feelings, just think of a time when you last experienced them. Perhaps at a party, at the movies or with your kids. This will help you recall those feelings.

As you accumulate the energy, feel them in your body. Eyes closed, breathe life into those emotions. Sit with this as long as you can, or at least until it's impossible not to smile or move your body into an expression of that feeling.

Each day sit with this as your practice and sit longer each time you practice by going deeper and deeper. Let the core of your truest and deepest purpose be revealed.

As a side note, if you are not moving, or feel like moving or allowing the energy to come through, you are holding on to tight. To live in a state of flow, start with letting these emotions flow out of you during this process.

As you extend this practice over time you will have momentum to make your comeback, shift a situation or change a circumstance. There is a gestation period. There is no end result here. This is life. If you stop this process because your world did not change, then I assure you your world will not change. Emotions are life. You must feel them until you are inspired to express them.

The degree to which you can experience the dominant feelings in your body will be the exact degree you can achieve fulfillment. Hence this guy who just received a check for $10,000,000 while sitting on the couch says, "it's a good day." There is no embodiment of the experience and no expression of it. His experience is limited to a few abstract feelings, rather than a life experience that lifts him up. He is not fulfilled.

Silent Killers

There are silent killers to be avoided in building momentum. Those killers are small things that creep up on men while they are grinding out the work day. Having awareness of these killers can help you maintain momentum.

Your Energy

As the CEO of your campaign, your energy level means everything. This is why self-care, especially during this phase, is vital. You should do everything you can to protect and preserve your energy during the momentum phase. This could mean walking away from your computer in the middle of the day just to rest. This also means setting up your day to hit the gym, nap, and feed your body. Cut out the porn, the alcohol, TV, killing time with friends and anything that is not aligned with your future.

Small Wins Matter

If you are the achiever type, you may naturally expect to consistently and quickly win big. Experiencing small wins through your day and week are vital. It recharges your momentum. For example, during an arduous marketing campaign where sales take months to occur, it challenges your energy levels to keep moving forward, without any short-term rewards. It's important to celebrate small wins and build a culture of success. However, it's tough for men; we like rewards.

Non-Reaction

Throughout this process, try and keep your reactions to a minimum. Learn to let them go. If you are reactive, you may find your comeback process to be more of a rollercoaster than a smooth ride. If you're reacting you are simply in a pattern that does not serve you. There is no reason to activate the past. Just let it go.

Laugh at Frustration

Suddenly, at 3 am, I found myself laughing hysterically. My Siberian Husky began howling at my laughter. What else could I do that would empower me during a frustrating experience? I was so close to launching my comeback and yet, it felt so far away.

Three weeks went by quickly. The launch occurred, 92 leads came in and $10,000 in sales. I'm still laughing!

Maintain Clarity

When you find you are overwhelmed or unsure, step back and get clear about what you want and why you want it. Those are the two most important aspects because they are the driving force for all your decisions. I have found this to be a challenge for me. I move quickly in the pursuit of what I want and the faster I go, the easier it is to lose clarity. I have enormous capacity and can take on a lot of goals. I also have enormous emotional capacity. I experience a wide range of emotions during my day, therefore, maintaining clarity and perspective is top priority for me.

Daily Practice

I am not a morning person, not even for sex, unless it's a fishing trip or skiing with my daughter, I am not up for morning activities. So, I arrange my day around having activation mornings. These can include yoga, walks in nature with my husky, playing with my kids, reading, or sitting in a coffee shop like I am right now as I write this chapter.

My mind and body becomes more active around 10 am. I start my actual workday at 11 am and finish around 2pm. Then I hit the gym and come back for a few more hours, but that is only to wrap up meetings, handle issues and finish a project like a book, recording, or a video.

I have a practice to keep me turned on; most of the time that practice is just with me and does not consists of a phone or computer. It is designed to fill me up and create a hunger to get on with my business. This way I head into business mode with momentum, instead of just half-asleep.

Honor your vibe and care for your vibe. It's the essence of who you are. As you do that you may find your energy is stronger than any fear or challenge you come up against. This is how you get on top of anything.

Chapter 14 Notes: Recruit Momentum

- Do not confuse movement with progress. Just because things feel like they are moving forward, does not mean measurable progress has been made.
- Acting busy is often a great way to cover up the reality that you're not producing anything.
- You may be feeling excited, but is that really momentum? Check in with this day to day.
- Momentum starts with an accumulation of energy.
- Momentum continues to build when you express your energy.
- Momentum is sustained when you focus on accumulation of energy and expression of energy.

» Momentum is an agent of change.

» You will experience the most success due to your most dominant feeling.

» Small wins matter. Don't discount them.

» Laugh frustration away.

END OF CHAPTER 14 NOTES.

I am with you brother. You got this. Go build massive momentum.

Let's move on to chapter 15.

Chapter 15

GAIN ACCESS TO NOUNS

You need support to sustain your momentum. Support is like adding extra beams to your house for structural soundness. By aligning yourself with the right **people, places and things** you can feel supported. Having access to nouns, is like building an ecosystem around yourself. And you must learn to 'ask for help.'

What type of support is most important to you?

» Is accessing other people's strengths, knowledge, and resources important?

» Is accessing places that have resources, opportunities, or potential clients important?

» Is accessing things that have the tools, systems, or platforms so you can succeed important?

» Is accessing support at home, through family, friends or partners needed?

» Is accessing the courage or strength important?

It is critical to gain access to the right elements of this section. By focusing on what type of support you need right now to continue momentum and propel you forward. Only focus your energy on the requirement right here and now, and build one beam at a time. Not all the elements are required right now.

Let's break each one down, so you can begin to inquire about which ones are missing and necessary for you right now. Choose only the ones that are necessary at this time.

People: If you look at the vision of your comeback, what types of strengths and skills are missing that you can acquire through others? For my comeback there were a few people necessary for it. My accountant, my mentor, my partner's support with family and our house, a social media expert and a Facebook ad professional.

These were all skills and strengths I needed to support my vision. During my comeback, I also knew I had less funds available. So, I was able to find a Facebook ad professional to work on a percentage of sales basis. I enrolled my accountant in lowering his fees in the interim for managing my money. Ray, my mentor, was willing to take a percentage of profit on the backend. Later, he decided to work with me because he loved what I was up to. Those skills cost me very little to make my comeback.

Even if you are low on funds, there is always a way, but you have to access people to get your vision moving. I am not a fan of self-made anything because any self-made person had to enroll someone else to either buy, loan, purchase, lease, and believe in their vision. Especially their customers.

Places: Where does your vision exist? That is an interesting question, naturally it exists inside of you, but where are the customers, clients, money, and resources to support your vision? Think in entrepreneurial terms, where does what I want exist so I can tap into a well? I know each month thousands of doctors, who are a niche market for me, attend relicensing seminars. I can speak at any of those events and instantly get in front of my market. I know social media, groups' form around certain disease and ailment topics. I can position myself and my message there. Anything you want lives somewhere, someone else has or has a space of people you can gain access to. Your job is to find and join them to gain access.

Things: What are the things or elements that are required for you to succeed? In my early days, my cell phone was my ATM machine. It was all I had and all I needed to make 100 phone calls per day. That turned my life around. The one thing that was missing was "marketing leads." I remember, to this day, sitting in the back of my Ford F-150, wondering how I was going to find leads. A few minutes later, I looked up to find a loud voice on the street corner. He was on a pay phone. That is when I laid eyes on millions of potential dollars, a phone book. This phone book had thousands of names and phone numbers. Then with my cell phone and courage, add a dash of "no freaking clue how to sell," and I knew something great was going to happen. It was also listening to an hour of power music, doing my morning affirmations and looking in my mirror and stating them out loud. Those were the things I needed to take on to make my comeback and several hundred phone calls later, I had new clients!

Things can also range from software, CRM, books, tools, resources and money, which are required. Only that which is required for you right now, some things may be required later. If you think a website is required, unless your business is only online, it may not be required. There was a day when people started a business and somehow thought business cards were necessary, but they are not. I only invest money on things that are necessary at this moment and can create a return. Short term and long term. If you are pressed for money, focus on return only things, then later you can invest in more long term things.

True Story: No Money Down Access

One of my first real estate deals manifested when I had no money. I took one of the infamous courses in "No Money Down" real estate. And yes, it works, only because I maintained my commitment to it working. The strategy itself is simple; find an owner of a home who wants to finance the property. I began searching for houses, in order for me to do that, I needed to access the courage to call people, find a listing of some sort where homes are advertised, and to talk with the right person to make a deal.

After two months, I had many great conversations and yet, no homeowner wanted to sell no money down. I called several agents and told them my plan and they laughed. They laughed and said, "I have not seen that work, nor do I think it will." Clearly what they were trying to say was, they were not the person for me. If they were not enrolled in my vision, then they are not the person for me. However, I did make sure I sent them a postcard in front of my new, "no money down" home when I did find the one.

Finally, a go-getter type agent Lisa in Delmar, California said she would be more than willing to help me. She too said she had not seen any on the market like I was looking for, however, she wasn't looking for them anyways.

Every week she sent me listings and ideas and even made some phone calls on my behalf. Each morning I spent two hours making calls, until I got what I wanted. There were many times when waking up was a challenge, but I did it anyways. There were a few times when I got discouraged from many no responses. After 3-months I started to wonder if I was crazy and wouldn't find what I was looking for. I dismissed those thoughts and reminded myself that anything I wanted was possible.

One Friday morning, Lisa sent me an email titled, "you won't believe it!" The owner of an Oceanside condo just listed his home for $179K with 92% owner financing. The owner would even give a $2,000 credit for new carpet.

We had an offer in by noon that day. I had no idea where I was going to get the money for the 8% down and costs, but I came up with $12,000 from a family member, to be paid back upon the sale of the home. I even negotiated the $2,000 credit be paid in cash, so I could make repairs and pocket the rest; which is exactly what I did.

My first home took 5 months to create by accessing people, places, and things. Resources are the answer, always. I had no idea how to be a landlord, but I didn't need to know until I had to become one, right? There is no point in wasting time educating myself about being a landlord if I had no rental. So, learning to become one was not a part of my sequence to success yet. I rented the property to 3 different people over 2 years, made some cash, then sold it for $249,000.

Mathew was a client of mine and was a medical biller for a long list of doctors. He basically did all the insurance billings and filings for doctors. It is a very time consuming and arduous process negotiating and collecting payments from insurance companies. Matthew got paid a percentage of the money he collected on behalf of his clients.

When Matthew called me, he had many goals that were not being accomplished. His biggest issue was he didn't have enough time or money. His time was largely spent taking care of his clients and the money came and went, his income is at the beck and call of insurance payouts. The larger invoices usually took longer to pay, since they would be stalled by reviews and audits. This is another way of insurance companies saying we don't have the money to pay out, so delay until the insurance company can.

Matthew was fabulous at accessing resources for his clients, but not for himself. If he turned his focus on accessing for himself, he could literally invent the time and money out of his current situation.

Think about this, we all have 24 hours in a day and Matthew has potential money sitting in his client's unpaid invoices. What can he do to access time and money, while taking care of his clients?

As it turns out, Matthew has a high collections rate. Among the best in the industry and collects high dollar amount on top of informing his doctors when they are not using the right insurance codes to access more money. He literally makes his clients' money that they would not have made without him.

I suggested he determine who his top 10 clients are, and plan to make them even more money. Then asked them to switch from their in-house billing to his company. By doing that he could hire more people to deal with the low income generating clients and save his own time. When he ran the numbers he realized he could increase his monthly income by over $7,200 and approximately 12 hours per week back of time.

I also suggested Matthew use those same numbers and promote himself to pick up 5 more top clients, while asking his current top ten list for referrals to their colleagues. 45 days later he picked up 3 new clients who billed over $100,000 per month, adding an extra $15,000 monthly to his income. He picked up 7 new referrals adding another $6,500 to his month revenue. When he called to tell me, he was excited.

"Now what Coach Carl?" He asked.

"First let's acknowledge that you accessed wealth, people, and resources to better yourself and your clients and their patients. It was right in front of you the entire time and you had the guts to present your results and ask for more.

Now, here is what's next, hire a staff member and unload at least 15 hours per week of work on him or her. Then delegate. Matthew agreed, and a year later has 2 staff members and is taking home well over $500,000, while keeping an overhead under $125,000. That is dynamite!

Have you ever heard the phrase, "whatever it takes?" I ran a multimillion-dollar business from home, while taking care of my daughter. On the third week, I got a heavy dose of parenting and a low dose of sleep. My wife at the time had a seminar to do and she needed to leave for 3 hours. I was happy to stay home and play Mom & Dad and then came the "I am hungry cry." I warmed up the breast milk we had frozen in the freezer. Tristin, my daughter wanted nothing to do with it, she screamed when I placed the bottle in her mouth.

I tried putting her in a different position, but that didn't work either. I talked to her and then sang for her and that didn't work. I rocked her in a chair and kept putting the bottle in her mouth to drink. That made it worse. I was ready to cry myself, she didn't want anything, but Mom's milk. It was something I could not offer her; I had run out of options.

Or did I?

The back of my mind said, "okay Coach Carl, you're the guy who teaches access, start accessing something." As soon as I said that, a thought came to me to grab her mom's pajama top and put it on. This way she could smell mom and probably some breast milk that leaked on it. As soon as I put it on, her crying settled down. "Thank God," I said. I tried the bottle again as she rejected it by closing her mouth. Tristin looked up as if to say, "good job Dad, but it's not working."

I decided to cut a hole in the shirt and slipped the bottle under my shirt and the nipple on the bottle through the hole. I cradled Tristin to put her mouth on the nipple, so she would feel like she was drinking right from Mom's fountain of food and BAM, she took it perfectly.

Whew! I was in a panic. I can remember texting my other half to get home, "I can't do this!" and 5 minutes later Tristin was still drinking, and Mom came home. As soon as she heard her mom, she spit out the bottle and cried again. This was too funny, but at least I had five minutes of fame.

WHATEVER IT TAKES IS NOT A CONCEPT, IT'S A REALITY TO LIVE.

Access resources and do not stop until she drinks! Whichever example I have given you or can give you, I believe you get the point. Access is a dance and you have to keep shifting and dancing until you get it. Sometimes it's a quick dance and sometimes you have to battle with dancing for long periods of times. You are never without resources, you may think you lack the resources, but there is no lack of resources, not this day and age.

There are a lack of resourceful people and states of mind. People who are not opening doors, seeking opportunities or looking for ways to make connections are acting unresourceful. People who feel disempowered, think there is no way they can fund their business or refuse to see the world as an unlimited resource center have unresourceful mindsets.

Looking for resources, opportunities or people to support you are not a matter of what to do. It's a matter of setting your mind to access the resources. Resources are everywhere, but an un-resourceful mind will rarely see it. The un-resourceful mind seeks to find opportunities, but they are usually limited as the mind searching for it is.

Un-resourceful vs. Resourceful Men

When you failed, why did you fail?

If you asked any of the people who recently ran for President, they might all say something like this;

» I didn't have enough votes.

» The media favored Trump.

» I didn't have enough money to campaign.

» The voting booths miss counted votes.

» The Electoral College needs to be eliminated.

» America is angry and wanted an angry person.

» I wasn't a good debater.

» I didn't relate to a certain ethnic group.

What do you notice about all these possible responses?

They are all a lack of resources coupled with ZERO responsibility. Trump spent the least money to win the primary and the Presidency in comparison to anyone else. He is a man who can access more resources, people, places, and things than anyone. He also accessed more emotional resources than anyone else running. He was the master enrollment man. I am not talking politics here, but as a person, a businessman and entrepreneur he was far more engaging than anyone. He got votes from people who liked him and hated him.

Nearly every failure is a result of lacking some type of resource.

Let's review the un-resourceful responses from above.

From Un-resourceful to Resourceful

- I didn't have enough votes, to, **I could have been more influential and enrolling. I could access people's emotions, hearts, and shown them the value I could provide.**
- The media favored Trump, to, **I could have accessed better media time, coverage, and given the media powerful reasons to listen to me. I could have challenged Trump to a live debate, just the two of us and leveraged his media time.**
- I didn't have enough money to campaign, to **I could have enrolled more people to donate money. I could have used my own money.**
- The voting booths missed votes, to, **I could have demanded better voting booths and programs before I ran, so I wouldn't lose on a technicality.**
- The Electoral College needs to be eliminated, to, **if I enrolled people powerfully enough, the Electoral College would have been in my favor.**
- America is angry and wanted an angry person, to, **if I had listened to people and met them where they were, I could have been a better leader for them. I could have approached through understanding.**
- I wasn't a good debater, to, **I didn't access the language, message, or ability to inspire others; I could have practiced better and hired the right people to bring out my greatness.**
- I didn't relate to a certain ethnic group, to, **I could have created more passion and equality in my talks and discovered what they wanted before I spoke to them.**

Do you notice how my responses are from a responsible point of view? A state of resourcefulness that I could have accessed more inside of me, rather than blame something else, or someone else. At this level, the resources available are endless. Acquiring people's votes through inspiration, influence, meeting their needs, and relating to them are inner resources called emotions. In the example of politics, most are so darn diplomatic and unemotional that it's hard to feel alive when listening to them. However,, Trump and Sanders are very emotionally enrolling and bold. They reached more people and created a movement above and beyond anyone else. I am not talking politics here, but resourcefulness of man and enrollment.

AS A REMINDER, YOUR COMEBACK IS POSSIBLE. IT CAN BE DONE. YOU ARE FARTHER AHEAD THAN MOST WHO HAVE FAILED OR SUFFERED A LOSS OF ANY KIND.

Emotional Resources

What I am about to share with you is one of the most powerful things that aids in you becoming more resourceful. Most men are one-dimensional and we operate to achieve maximum capacity, freedom and fullness, but without the ability to experience all ranges of emotions, we cannot be free to experience life.

The one-dimensional man, experiences about 5 emotions or so, such are, anger, insecurity, fear, excitement and happiness. That is a limited life experience. As man grows internally, he will experience more joy, gratitude, thankfulness, love, to varying degrees as well as guilt and regret.

However, there are hundreds of emotional experiences to experience. Your capacity to handle life, success, wealth, family, and more is in direct proportion to how well you experience your own emotional depth. The moment men are overwhelmed or challenged by fear; we shut down or hold back.

This limits our view of the world and we can only focus on a few things at once or throughout the day. Men also don't like distractions or getting pulled off track once we start something. The point A to point B is our path and yet, we miss the experience of the journey in-between.

It limits our view of women, money, and family. For most men those three things are about protecting, providing, and procreating, but this is primarily social conditioning and biology.

The multi-dimensional man experiences fear, but channels it into being grounded and coming from power, using it for fuel. The multi-dimensional man experiences 15-20 emotions and alchemizes them for the betterment of himself, his family, his business and the planet. He realizes the respect he has for himself, impacts everything and everyone around him.

The multi-dimensional man has full access too internal resources that he can flow through his day. He can manage his sales and marketing, work with clients, make money, be present with his kids throughout the day. He can also bang headboards all night with his wife, take care of his body, respect his emotions and nutrition needs. He can also be conscious to lead with love and do the dishes and paint his daughter's nails. He can cry when he needs to. This man kicks butt in all that he does. The one-dimensional man wants to, but struggles with time, energy and willingness to connect with his wife in a profound and romantic way, while taking care of business and the rest.

You have unlimited power to experience anything you want through your feelings. Accessing those feelings gives you the freedom to express and embrace life as you choose to. Avoiding them, hinders your life experience.

Be that which does that! This one principle has made a significant difference **for** my clients **and for me**. You can summon courage as needed, when you need it. You can summon love, when you need it. You can summon passion or power, when you need it. If you start to view yourself as an unlimited generation machine, you will realize you can create anything. Most men get stuck on "how," rather than feeling the feelings.

As you learn to engage your emotional strength, you realize whenever you are stuck, you are just unclear about the emotion or why behind your actions. Knowing what to do is the easy part, even when you don't think you know what to do, drop into your why and feel what needs to occur, then act.

Chapter 15 Notes: Gain Access to NOUNS

» Resources for your comeback are available in massive abundance.

» Access people and their strengths so you can utilize them for your comeback.

» Access already existing tools, platforms, and programs to support you.

» Successful people create access to the top, rather than reinventing alone.

» Always be on the lookout for people, places and things.

» Yes, you can create something with NO money. Plenty of people have what you want, align with them and make deals with them.

» Whatever it takes is not a concept, it's a way of living. Which one is it for you?

» There are no lack of resources, only resourceful and unresourceful states of mind.

» Emotions are our biggest resource.

END OF CHAPTER 15 NOTES.

I am with you brother. You got this. You are more resourceful than you know.

Let's move on to chapter 16.

Chapter 16

ENROLLMENT- YOUR UNYIELDING, UNWAVERING, AND UNSHAKABLE COMMITMENT

Enrollment is often used in place of the word selling. There are similarities, but by principle it is a higher-level conversation. There are two types of enrollment you will learn in this chapter. Enrollment starts with you being 100% engaged and committed into your vision, so you are empowered to share it. The second is how to enroll others into their vision so they want to buy your product or service. In other words, how do you get what you want, in a powerful way?

Every day the best of the best, from a CEO to a small company owner, spend their time enrolling others into their vision. If you look at any political candidate, promoter, even some of the highly transparent authors, like Gary Vaynerchuk, are 100% enrolled in their vision. In order for them to succeed they must live in the realm of enrollment of other people through enthusiasm and inspiration. Throughout this book I have shared with you specifics about living at the expression of your power. They penetrate the world with their heart and guts and choose courage to take on what really matters. Now, through enrollment you can create a conversation that truly moves people into inspired action.

All throughout history, the people who enroll others into their vision are the most successful, but those who cannot enroll others are passed up, forgotten and rest in the status quo.

You have a goal, a vision or dream and in order for that to become realized, someone else needs to be enrolled for it to succeed. That means someone needs to believe 100% in what you do. This way they will value who you are or what you bring to the table.

A child is a master enroller, they are very good at creating stories, persuasion, and getting parents to do what they want them to. Although they have limited learned skills, they are very good at connecting to people and getting them to act on their behalf. When you first looked at your own child, you were 100% enrolled and in love with them, no matter what. Children are natural enrollers because they don't have to say or do anything, who they are is precious, lovable, and amazing. This is the ultimate form of enrollment -- when who you are speaks loudly enough that you have grabbed people's attention. You have that ability too, it just may not be activated.

Al Torredo is a high school biology teacher, I would not expect you to know him, but he won the Teacher of the Year award for 7 straight years. Al was a wrestling coach and a burly beast of a man, yet as soft and sensitive as they come. My first day in his class he walked into the room with a huge stick and slammed it on everyone's desks until we moved our bags off the table and were 100% present. I remember watching his stick go up and moving my bags in midair, before it landed, thrusting the table up in midair. He enrolled us from the first day in this class, your attention matters. If you want to succeed in this class, pay attention was his enrollment message.

After he had our attention, he pointed to the ceiling and offered us a quote to succeed in his class. I still remember it today, ***"from ignorance***

to enlightenment, this is how you learn." That class was by far the most fun, enjoyable and I learned more from him than any other teachers. His tests were 100-200 questions each and we were always prepared for them. Rather than teach us about ocean biology from a book, he took us to the ocean. He had a passion for what lives under the sea, and though I could have cared less about the subject, I was suddenly hooked. I too wanted to see what lies at the bottom of the ocean with thirst for enlightenment. His intense curiosity made me curious about what really lives under the sea. His passion was contagious and I was sold.

There are key parts to enrollment and I will break each of them down below.

The Context:

Your Vision:

The big picture plays a significant role in how enrolling you are. It also plays a role in how well others are enrolled into your vision so they can support you, align with you, work for you, or become a customer or client with your company. If your big picture is to become a janitor, buy a home, and have 2 kids, then naturally find a woman that has a similar vision and is enrolled and trusts your vision. It is unlikely this man will attract a high-profile female lawyer who despises the Becky home-Ecky lifestyle.

Everyone is enrolling others into something, to believe in them, to date them, to hang out with them, to watch Sunday football with them or to marry them. You have been enrolling others your entire life, and like Grant Cardone says, "sell or be sold to."

Knowing what you want is one thing, enrolling yourself is the first step. To do that, you must be 100% clear on your vision and sold on yourself first. People can only believe to the level that you believe. Your conviction, your certainty sells.

The Science of Enrollment

Think of communication as the transfer of vision from one person to another, until the other person feels it. How we communicate consciously to another person is through words, pictures and gestures. How we communicate unconsciously to another person is through **vibration, a feeling.**

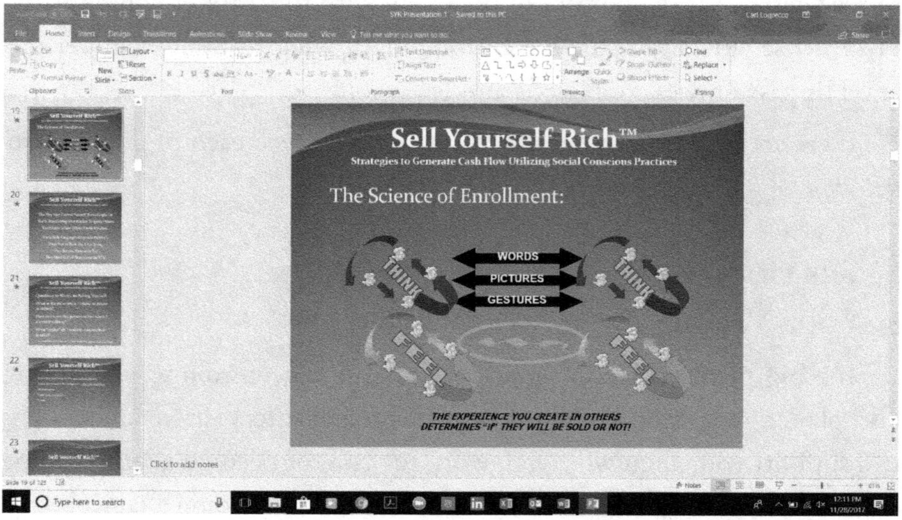

While most of us spend way too much time on words, and saying things right, we forget the fundamental science that energy is what impacts people the most. Your energy is always speaking to people, telling them the truth and it will land more powerfully than anything you can say. As I mentioned before, you have to be sold first so that what you say is a congruent reflection of your vibration. Otherwise, you run the risk of manipulation, convincing and trying to push yourself onto someone else.

As a simple test, ask a woman you know how many times a man has said and done all the right things for her on a date, but something didn't feel right? I can promise you the answers will surprise you. Women operate from the vibration more easily than men do. Potency is you're your vision and expression of your vision are in alignment.

Years ago, I was giving a seminar in Atlanta, Georgia and I invited a woman on stage and asked her if she wants to become a millionaire. She said, "yes," but shook her head NO at the same time. Her vision was clear, but the rest of her did not believe what she was saying. She was not 100% enrolled in her own vision, but so desperately wanted to be. I decided to make this a lesson for her to change her life. I asked the crowd to raise their hands if they believed her. Several raised their hands and some clapped. They didn't even see it themselves. I asked the crowd, "who did not believe her?" A handful of people raised their hands. I asked the video man to rewind and play her responses on the power point screen.

Maybe we're surprised at how easily they get hooked. I tested the audience again by asking them, after watching this recording, "do you still believe her?" The same amount said yes. They even re-affirmed how passionate she was. I then played the video back, but this time I muted her words and asked, "now do you believe her?"

The audience was stunned; they saw her head finally move back and forth in a NO position, while she was talking. Some even noticed that her energy started to shrink in watching her. Even Lucia, the woman I invited up to the stage said, "oh my God." While she may have said the right things, her vibration was saying the opposite.

Many raised their hands and someone stood up and said, "there was nothing behind it, but words, and she seemed hesitant." Conversely, those who clapped and cheered, wanted her to become a millionaire, but after talking with them they didn't fully believe it enough to bet on her. They too were not fully enrolled.

Her headshaking was an unconscious movement. She wouldn't have been able see or feel it, which is why most men say what they want, and the claim to feel it or see it, but what is underneath keeps them back. Or they claim they have no fear, while stating their goals, and yet their body is stiff, motionless, and has no passion scorching through it. That's fraud. You cannot feel one thing, while saying another. It won't work.

Until this shift happens and she is 100% sold on her, she will continue to say things that she really does not believe. Sadly, she will continue working hard to make her millions, but to no avail. This is true for many, men love to get excited about things and convince themselves of something, but if they really listen to the vibe it often isn't adding up.

The viability of your manhood, your vision and legacy, depends on the consistent enrollment of your own vision. In other words, you must be 100% enrolled every day because if there is any % of you not enrolled, then you can only manifest to the level in which you are enrolled. Anything less than 100% and you are leaving the fullness of life and business experience on the table.

If you're vision is so clear that you can communicate it to ten people and have all ten people get it; then you are unstoppable, unshakable, and unyielding in the pursuit of getting what you want.

Your Vision

Your vision is about what you stand for. For your comeback to succeed, you must be willing to take a stand for yourself and how you want to show up. Your vision is why people will want to work with you, love you, and be friends with you. A man without one, spins around hoping to hit the mark. A man with one, always finds a way until he realizes he is the way.

This vision should consist of a few key elements:

1. **You must believe it** in your very core you must believe in it. In fact, you must have several supportive beliefs to back up your vision so that it moves you forward.
2. **Your ability to live it.** The sustainability of your vision is in your habits of daily living and business. Your habits are the demonstration of your vision. Your vision is to be lived every day. Not something you turn on or off like a light switch.
3. **Others must believe in it:** The ongoing sustainability of your vision is that your friends, family and colleagues believe in it and

want to see it succeed. Your ability to enroll others into your vision, means your vision is supported.

Full Engagement

Let's expand on this. Fully engaged in it, means you are demonstrating your vision. In your conversations, that way you approach life, people, your wife and family. It is not some random task or something you will get around to, or even schedule it so you can get to it. It is the color of your skin and you cannot turn it on or off. That should not be confused with feeling good about it or excited about it. Imagine, writing a book like the one you are reading. There were times during the editing I was not feeling excited, but I was fully engaged. For men, when we don't feel excited about something we often don't see that it's not a requirement to live the vision.

I often use a boxing analogy, during a fight, the boxer is 100% engaged. Every muscle and ounce of mental focus is 100% ready to duck, dodge, punch and jab with full intensity. Even when a boxer is tired, they are fully engaged. They may at times be on the defense, offense, or even losing side of the punches, but they stay engaged, most of the time.

You can tell when a boxer disengages or is shaken up by watching his actions. Even when a boxer is close to hitting the canvas, he may still engage by grabbing onto his opponent to survive and revive his energy, but he himself has not disengaged from his vision. He didn't stop striving for the vision, even if in that moment the vision feels farther away. No boxer would survive partially engaged, let alone dare show up in the ring.

For men, this concept is easy to understand, but it also scares them. To be fully unleashed and engaged, means feeling the fullness of your power and trusting to let it go. Engagement means, you are connected to your vision and stay in the process regardless of the results that may or may not happen.

To engage is more than just physically showing up, although, you need to take one step forward and engage the space you wish to experience.

You also need to engage your emotions, your vision and be 100% willing to share from your depths so others want to engage in your vision with you. As I mentioned, a person can only be enrolled to the level in which you are, this is true for engagement. Others can only engage in your vision, passion, and love to the level you are.

IF YOU WANT OTHERS TO ENGAGE MORE, BE ENGAGING. IF YOU WANT OTHERS TO RESPOND MORE, BE RESPPONSIVE. IF YOU WANT OTHERS TO SAY YES MORE, BE A YES MAN.

Blake is a powerful man; he is a healer and a doctor. Blake vision was to create a wellness center that helped patients without the use of drugs or surgery. He was clear about what he wanted to create. As I listened to Blake talk about his frustrations and his worry there was disconnection. I could feel his passion for his vision. His words were vibrant and sincere, but it still wasn't adding up in my mind. Between what he said and what was happening there was a gap.

Blake is an introverted kind of guy and calm in his approach to everything. Rather than expect him to be someone he is not, he needed more potent energy behind his vision. It needed to speak with a loudness that woke people up. He is in the business of healing and most people who need it are not fully awake. We were onto something with this approach. Blake wanted more people to say yes, to engage his services, but was not a yes man, and took 4 weeks to say yes to my coaching. He waits too long to respond and delays things, is it hard to believe people are not showing up differently than he does?

I asked Blake if he felt there was room to fully engage into this vision, to bring it into his body so that when he walked into a room, his church, or his office or when he jumped on the train to the city, people could feel this man was on a mission. Stuart felt there was a lot of room for improvement.

It's one thing to have the vision and clarity, it's another to bring it out in the expression of what you do. Until you can feel you "own it."

It was time for Stuart to charge his vision in his own body. I will use a sexual example for this, since most men can connect to it. When you are attracted to a woman and are pursuing your raw instinct, your desire for sex can be felt in your body. Hormones release, your brain gets excited, and your nervous system carries out a wave of sexual energy. You are engaged and every cell in your body is alive and charged up. Your vision is the same with your body, when you charge it up you are engaged and now embodied in your vision. You may not have sexual energy as your context or vision is different, but the relationship between your vision and body is the same.

This charge needed to occur because Blake was simply missing a couple of steps between vision and manifestation. Then again, who taught this to us growing up? This challenge is not exclusive to Blake. He began the process of charging up his vision. The best way to do that is meditation and vivid visualization. While this occurs, you will find a spark or two, but the real magic does not happen until you focus for 18 seconds. Focus on that vision so your mind attracts more thoughts, more images, and your body responds to the feelings associated to it and you create a charge.

The beautiful thing is you know how to do this already. If you ever listen to music, while thinking about your day or something important to you, you have created the charge in your body. If you have ever fantasized about anything, and all kids do this by the way, then you already know how. You just need to practice for 18 seconds as many times as you can so the vision creates a life in you. You will know when you have arrived because the vision causes you to fully engage and the energy will be strong enough to explode or express the vision. When you feel you are going to erupt, you have succeeded and are ready to manifest it. Until then, it is just a vision, no matter how powerful, valuable, or important it is to you. Without charging your energy, nothing can manifest. From idea or vision, to actuality, requires energy and a spark to combust it, which is science. The art of enrollment comes later during the expression of your vision and your ability to deliver your vision.

Stand and Deliver

Stuart was not ready to stand and deliver. I often use this analogy; let's pretend for a moment you are on national TV. Are you ready to enroll me into your vision so your phone rings off the hook?

Most would say no, some would need practice, but very few would stand and deliver their message in the moment they were asked. The final piece to enrollment, once you are fully enrolled into your own vision is your ability to stand and deliver it in any situation. It should be as easy and natural as breathing and it is here that results manifest.

At one of my workshops I had a surprise visit from Oprah, yep, Oprah. A handsome and wonderful black man named Henry, disguised in a dress with toilet paper roles in his bra looking just like Oprah. Well, at least a funny version of her. Henry came out of the back of the room and sat on his couch and interviewed my clients. It gave them the chance to stand and deliver on the spot.

Pervious to calling my fake Oprah to the front of the room, I took a poll in the audience. I asked them a few questions…

1. How many of you are ready to stand and deliver your message?
2. How many of you are not ready?
3. If I brought Oprah to the front of this room, who would stand and deliver?

After a few hours of training I wouldn't expect the first question to yield a high response. About 80% of the room did not raise their hands. To the second question, most were not ready. They had their excuses. Some didn't feel ready, some needed more time and some were just flat out nervous. When I asked the final question, 3 people raised their hands.

By the end of the three-day workshop, I polled them again. Everyone had their hand raised and some of them were rushing to the front of the room as Henry, A.K.A. Oprah, was coming back on the final day to interview them again.

This is where most men falter, it is not just an enrollment in business, but rather, enrollment is everything. Sexually you want to turn your partner on, you are enrolling her with romance, attention, talking, and so on. When you want to have your kids do chores or homework, you are enrolling them into wanting to do it, versus yelling or forcing them to. Enrollment is all the time and you have to participate in the expression of your vision. Participating is the expression or demonstration of your purpose in communication and presence and so is standing and delivering.

When you want a relationship, you must deliver who you say you are and what you want. The expression of what you stand for is where you get the results you want. Not in the vision of it alone.

You may recall earlier in this book when I shared with you that public speaking was an area of difficulty for me. I used to vomit twenty minutes before I took the stage. Yet, the only way through it was to follow the same steps to clarifying my vision, engaging fully in it, so much so, that I could be driving down the road thinking about giving a seminar and words would come out of my mouth. My daughter often says, “Dad, who are you giving a seminar to now?” That is how intense I feel it. Regardless of the fear and vomit, I have a choice to stand and deliver and when I let go of that energy, through the expression of it, people get it.

The “bring it” attitude is what stand and deliver is about, there are no steps to it. Just like there are no steps to sitting in a chair or typing, you just do. You may fall out of the chair or hit the keys inaccurately, but that does not mean you are not bringing it. Even the best athletes bring the juice and they don’t succeed every time. Basketball players don’t shoot 100% and baseball hitters don’t get a hit 70% of the time. They just have to stand and deliver 30% of the time.

Who You Are Speaks

You have a vibe and it speaks to others whether you are speaking or not. This is the part of you that shows up in a room before you enter. It is the part of you that can leave people speechless, awed, or attracted and interested in wanting to know you. Your vibe can be felt.

This is a critical part that most men don't pay attention to. What makes up this vibe? Basically, everything that is inside of you or goes inside of you. It is made up of thoughts, feelings, habits, nutrition, and how well you treat yourself. How well you treat yourself, determines how well your purpose shows up in your life and business.

If five men walk into a room, you can feel which one is on a mission and which ones are not. You can feel their energy and since it's an unconscious energy, people may or may not realize it and have reactions and responses to you.

From this point on I would recommend you be incredibly conscious of your energy. Three seconds before you meet a friend, your energy has already spoken. Three seconds before you answer your phone, your energy has already spoken. As you walk away from a friend or wife or child, your energy is speaking and leaving them with an impression; hopefully one that uplifts them.

LET ALL THOSE YOU CONNECT WITH FEEL BETTER OFF KNOWING YOU THAN NOT. YOUR ENERGY SPEAKS BEFORE YOU ENTER AND IS FELT LONG AFTER YOU LEAVE.

Notice that people may respond to your energy before you say and do a thing. Your energy influences people. I remember a time when I was married and I walked in the front door and took off my shoes and my wife was reacting to me as if I had a bad day. When she asked me how my day was I said, "fine." Which in the female mind is a lie, but your energy does not lie. Having sensed something was already wrong, my "fine" answer just confirmed her senses and she was already defensive. An argument started before I had said a word.

She was responding to my energy. I had no chance with words, unless I admitted or spoke about the energy I carried home. This is also true in reverse. I often love to surprise people. When I would come home through the back door in attempts to surprise her with something special, she knew it was a good day. My energy lit her up upon my arrival, in fact, she would frequently tell me she knew something was up before I had arrived. You have felt this energy before; I am just asking you to live from this place, so you are in more control of your comeback.

How often do you take credit for how powerful your energy is?

How often do you take responsibility for the impact of your energy when it's off?

Write about these questions, don't try to answer them, but rather bring them into your awareness and get curious about it. Energy is not a right or wrong or yes or no answer. You have to explore and see it for yourself to understand it, more than just mentally thinking, "I get it."

Chapter 16 Notes: Enrollment- Your Unyielding, Unwavering, and Unshakable Commitment

» Enrollment is about inspiring others to support you vision.

» Successful people are about enrolling others into their vision. The more you have enrolled, the more likely you will succeed.

» Enrollment happens from one person to another through a vibration. Not just words, gestures and pictures.

» Mental and verbal masturbation don't work. People must feel what you are saying.

» For others to become enrolled, invest in you, YOU first must believe in you, be living what you say, and communicate in a way that inspires others.

» Whatever you want from others, you need to bring that energy to them. If you want others to engage more, become more engaging.

» Your results happen when you are willing to stand and deliver.

» Who you are speaks volumes. Your energy shows up before you arrive in the room. What energy are you sending before you arrive?

» People respond to your energy more than your words.

» Are you giving yourself enough credit for how powerfully you show up?

END OF CHAPTER 16 NOTES.

I am with you brother. You got this. Your energy is magnetic.

Let's move on to chapter 17.

Chapter 17

CONTENTS FOR ENROLLMENT: SELL YOURSELF RICH

Once you learn the bigger context for enrollment, the how to's are now important. Earlier in this book I showed you a chart about living from the inside out. It starts with why, then what, and finally how. When I work with business clients they always want to know what to do and how. If you deviate from your WHY, knowing what to do will be a "figuring it out" struggle. If I stand for peace, I can think of many things to do about a hostile co-worker or employee or spouse. However, if I want to have peace, I may not know what to do or how to get it and there is a difference. One is operating from "having peace," the latter is operating to "get peace". Ghandi never could have changed the course of history if he wasn't standing in peace. Can you imagine, a non-peaceful person attempting to create peace? It wouldn't work.

Operate from having what you want. Remember, any goal you want is nothing more than a *feeling* you think you don't have, but you do have access to and if you start with that feeling you will manifest that reality.

A client of mine named Victor, was faced with a similar situation. His wife had passed away and left him with 4 kids. That is a hard task for a man to take on, especially if he was unprepared for it. It's not an easy transition for anyone.

He needed to come up with $18,000 to stay in his home and pay the bills. He knew his why. It was to be an amazing dad and up-level his game, so his children would be proud of him and feel safe. When he called me, the first question I asked was, "what is right in front of you, that if you followed through you could knock out this goal?"

He said, "my action plan that I have not followed through on."

Usually the how-to's are nearby, if not already in front of you. If he didn't have a plan, he could have put one together in an hour and been off and running making money. In less than 90 days Victor had generated $23,000 and in 3 months he generated a total of $60,000, much of which was in new client contracts.

Victor used the same method I am going to show you, this method has also been modified to fit this book. This is my sales process for my business and how I sell $15,000 to $50,000 deals, from $1,000 to my name to $140,000 then to $2.8 million. I have modified it since there are no specific sales to be made here, but your enrollment of you and all those who you need to support you in making your comeback. It can be used with kids, family, friends, business and business deals.

Here are the steps to mastering enrollment:

½ PRE-QUAL

1. Where is the person on the timeline of deciding to enroll?

You cannot afford to spend time with just anyone, life is too short and your comeback is top priority. There is a gentle approach to pre-qualifying people who will add to your vision. Any failure on your part to spend time, energy or money on people who won't support your vision, only gives rise to a roadblock on your journey.

I am not suggesting you answer your phone and say, "what specifically do you want?" Who talks like that!? Yet, I do want you to be clear in all communications and not waste any time getting to clarity or purpose in any conversation. You are here, you called, now ask why in a gentle tone.

Before I spend time, invest energy or resources I want to know if the opportunity in front of me fits my vision. This gives me a choice, I can pursue my vision with this person or I can write it off as a no. I want to quickly decipher what the contexts of all interactions are, that way I can live at choice, instead of waiting to find out. It is honoring and respecting your time and it commands greatness for you.

Everyone you want to enroll has a timeline. Some are ready right now, some need clarification and some are simply not ready. My goal is to find out where in the timeline anyone I am talking with is, that way I know the current reality and what to do about it.

RAPPORT

Rapport is very easy to do and very easy to mess up. Your only intention here is to make the other person feel safe. Create a space of non-defensiveness. People have preconceived ideas about what might happen during your meeting. They may have a fear of being sold, rejected or think they know what you are going to do and say.

Bring down all their defenses, whether they are seen or unseen, felt or unfelt. Then create IMMEDIATE commonality. Their needs to be a connection to your past or your future. Given you are on a comeback mission, be sure to align with those who are aligned with your future, NOT your past. People like people who have a common past and/or a common future.

If you are asking for money, love, happiness or forgiveness, you are asking for some level of vulnerability. Might it be helpful to have some solid ground first?

Make a list of rapport questions that produce the intention of rapport:

1.

2.

3.

*Avoid senseless questions like, "how is the weather today?" Rather, always ask in a new sales or business meeting question that creates commonality, a bond or a shared perspective. Shared perspectives are the most powerful; as they say, "I see what you see." So therefore, we might be a like.

Be a person of value, rather than chit chat or simply share information, be a person that connects and adds value. In one of my men's programs, Rarity, the first hour hundreds of men have breakfast together and talk. The following two hours I curate a wealth of information around men's health, finance, technology and futuristic support.

One day, I noticed a group of men seemed to have formulated relationships with each other, yet when they came into the meeting room they were scattered in the theater auditorium. Most had 2-3 seats in-between the next guy. I started my talk off with a curveball.

I began calling men up to the front of the room and asked them who they met this morning? What did you learn about the men that you met?

Most of the responses I got are typical and yet predictable.

"Uh, I met John, he's cool, and he is an architect and seemed excited about it and likes to fish."

That tells me they know what each other does, but it doesn't demonstrate any commonality or give me a sense of who they are. There are many men who are in the profession of architecture and likes to fish, but who are they?

A client of mine was in the audience and I brought him up. Dean and I had worked together years ago. I asked Dean, "who did you meet? What did you learn about him?"

"I met Scott, Radcliff, and Jensen. Scott is a compassionate guy who is all about changing the way we think about food, he grew up in an unhealthy family and wants to see people take better care of themselves. I was blown away with his ability and insights and he is a food consultant for the school system."

Do you see the difference? When Dean shared his experience of building rapport with the group, we all became connected to Scott. Scott is now a person of value, and we can relate to Scott.

When you are done building rapport or letting people get to know you; if they can stand in front of a group of strangers and talk about your value and who you are, you have generated the rapport needed for the next step.

Be transparent, and let people see who you are so you can see who they are.

DISENGAGE (EXCUSES AND OBJECTIONS)

I know what type of excuses or objections I am going to get. You know when you ask your wife to build a workshop in the garage, she may object and say, "paying off the credit card is more important."

It's better to know how to relate and handle these objections as you enter an enrollment conversation. I know in my business I will get 3 major excuses or objections. People will say, "I need to think about it, I don't have the money and I want to talk it over." Given this, I take those objection conversations away from them in the beginning as to not waste any energy going further. It also creates the opportunity to give them resources and an assignment to do before I spend time selling or engaging further. This way when they come back ready we can roll, if they don't follow back up with me, then I was right for not spending time with them.

If I am talking with my child and I ask them to do their homework, I may get a combination of objections like, "I am tired" or "I did it already," or "My teacher is stupid." Rather than argue back and forth, it is better to have a response beforehand to disable the objection. As you get good at this, they are less likely to come up at all.

It is important to discover where they are on the timeline of potential.

No Objections Objections/Concerns Open Minded

This is a visual for you to keep in mind as you speak with people. It gives you insight into where a person's state of mind may be.

Write out the top 3 objections you get and how to solve them prior to:

1.

2.

3.

Here is an example: I know I will get the objection of I need to think about it, so beforehand I will speak like this…

"Name, the best way I can help you is to know how soon you want to make this change?" If you are someone who likes to think things over and uses that to delay deciding, then it would be best to research me online or read one of my books before you engage in a coaching conversation with me."

Two things will happen here, the first is they will say, "I am here because I feel ready. Or two, they are not ready and want to do more research now." Either way I win. I am most likely to get the sale, and most likely not waste my time with someone who is going to already delay the decision after spending 30 minutes or more together.

"Thinking about it," is really a lack of decisiveness on this person's part. They might use their spouse as an example, that they need to talk with a spouse. But they knew that coming into this conversation and should have been prepared. People also fear making the wrong decision; I want to put them into decision-making mode before we get too deep into the enrollment conversation.

DISCOVER THEIR READINESS & WHY

It is also important to understand that people will only be as ready as you are. If you are not fully ready it is hard for anyone else to engage you. I always ask about readiness and why now. I want to know if this person, who is engaging me, is just talking 'about' it or is ready to be in action about it. ***How soon were you looking to do something?***

Whenever someone says they want to do something, I usually ask why? It reveals their motivation or pain that is causing them to search for my product or service. It tells me how decided they are to buy. Interested people rarely get results or change because interested is a scape for deciding to do something. It's merely safe but produces no results. Thinkers, waiters, delayers, and mental masturbators are undecided people.

People's decision-making muscles are weak. They think they will buy if the price is right. "If the price is right, then I will buy." This is poor man's thinking. If you decide you want something, then you go out and find the product or service at the price you want, you do not let the price dictate whether you decide or not. You let it dictate whether you buy from that person or not. I do not let the menu dictate what I want, I decide. This is what I am looking for here. If you do this, you will find more people say yes than no because they have now revealed they are in a YES state of mind. It may not be a YES to buying from you, but it's a yes that they are moving forward with or without me.

When a person reveals their why, it tells me if I want to spend time with them, hire them, date them, befriend them or offer my products or services. I want them to take a minute or two and enroll me in their inspiration and motivation so I can be inspired to invest my life energy with them. I want to offer them my product or services. If there is no inspiration, then I have a no. If there is, I'm in. If I am not sure I will ask for more information and say not now and revisit later.

DISCOVERY QUESTIONS

Once rapport is established and they feel comfortable, start asking deeper questions. I want to know about people's fears, challenges, pain, commitment, what is stopping them and most of all WHY do they want what they say they want!

This can be used with anyone and opening people up is the path of powerful men. In any situation to help those unveil what lies underneath, makes you an asset in their lives. You are not replaceable. In a business context, it creates loyalty and people will spend more money with you.

I am also savvy to the fact that some people might answer from their head. When I hear someone say, "I am fine" despite the fact they are not hitting their goals – I know they are not fine. I want people to be emotionally engaged with me, it's the most powerful way to be a man of enrollment so others will act on their commitments.

This is why rapport is so important because you won't have powerful relationships if you don't have solid rapport. It will just be a play on words with little authenticity.

My goal here is to get them in the EXPERIENCE of their responses.

As you discover people's motivation, commitments and listen to their why, they should be experiencing these on an emotional level. They should be enrolled in their own answers. When someone tells me they want to make one million dollars and I cannot feel it, they don't believe it and neither do I. A goal without emotion is a wish; which is why the next step is about engaging the problem so you two can create a pathway to transformation, resolution, or a purchase.

Make a list of discovery questions that can elicit responses to the 3 main categories below:

» Motivation

» Commitment to change

» Reason WHY they really want it

1.

2.

3.

Example: Why change this now? How long have you wanted this to change? How committed are you to having what you want?

DEFINE THE NEED

Underneath every problem is a need for something. What is this person's biggest need? I want to identify one because if I can solve this one, then I have an opportunity to solve it and make an offer.

Needs are always connected to emotions. The main needs each person has in any enrollment conversation are:

» The need to feel safe, secure or have certainty that something will work for them.

» The need to feel connected and belong.

» The need to feel important and significant.

» The need to feel loved and appreciated.

Be aware that they may give NON-emotional answers to their needs. Your job is to listen to what is underneath. When I listen for someone's needs, they will often tell me a practical or emotional need. A client of mine named Zeek, always shared that he wanted "accountability."

What is underneath his need is support, guidance, trust, and certainty that someone is there for him. I want to speak on this as well because some may not know.

Some clients will tell me they don't feel important. This is the emotional need. What they are not saying is having a partner who values them, creates confidence and collaboration is needed.

Your job is to define both. You want the practical and the emotional because it speaks to what they ask for and provides deeper meaning.

If you put an alarm in your home, the practical action is to secure your family and because you have been robbed before. The emotion is to feel safe and sleep at night or have peace of mind. That is what I am probing for and going to offer. If I do not get to this, then I really don't know how to position myself during the offer or enrollment phase.

Make a list of questions that aid in eliciting the primary need (both emotional & practical).

1.
2.
3.

ENGAGE THE PROBLEM

Problems allow connections and enrollment to become a more powerful process. Part of having a vision to chase is also having a challenge to overcome. During an enrollment conversation, identifying and engaging a challenge opens up new doorways. Without it, no major goal or vision can be obtained. The value of who you can be for this person or offer them won't be seen as significant.

Braxton is an award-winning restauranteur and recently sold a hotel-restaurant in Mexico. Braxton is near retirement and thinking of moving to Mexico permanently. When he called me, he said, "I don't know why I am doing this." He shared that he is at the age where he doesn't need the stress of starting another restaurant and is questioning why. After about an hour working with me, he offered me the typical responses, "send me some information about you and I will get back to you."

I engaged that problem a little more, even though I wasn't sure what was going on. He called me and wanted guidance about his next move. I told him there was something that is not being addressed. "What is your real concern? Is there a fear present?" He fought to answer the question for a few more minutes and then said, "I guess I am in transition. I am shedding this identity of being a recognized restaurant owner and now I feel like a nobody. Yet, I have everything I want. If I can just do a 3-year run and build something amazing, leave it to my team or sell it, that would make me happy."

I responded by saying, "now you know why you are doing it, you don't know how to be anyone else, (retired) and you're jumping back in the game for one last hurrah. It's better than feeling like a nobody."

He said, "yes, that is right. I am not sure I can figure this out on my own." Braxton then said, "forget the information, I want to start coaching." I didn't have to ask him, he offered. In fact, I didn't get to finish the rest of the enrollment conversation with him, we leapt from there to my fees and scheduling dates to start.

We're human beings. We don't change things when we are happy, instead we wait until we are desperate or disgusted by something, someone, or ourselves. Usually in that order, sadly. The revelation of these challenges provides people the space to decide and break through it. Just as I have done throughout this book, you can now do for anyone in any situation.

Engaging the problem means practicing feeling what it's like to be the person in front of you, your customer, your client, your spouse or child. As you have learned to be in your body, you now have the power to experience what others experience.

This gives you unlimited power to feel what they feel, see, and hear. It is authenticity at its fullest. The most money, success, and empowerment you will ever experience, rests in how well you can engage your own problems and others, then lead to victory!

In other words, you MESH with them and BECOME them. I have done this with a homeless person named Ricky. He said, after a few minutes of talking with him, "you didn't want something from me, you just cared to listen." It is almost like a mystical game, becoming them for a few moments without an agenda. You will find that everyone wins in this conversation.

The ultimate outcome of engaging the problem is so the person is enrolled in making a decision to change, shift, or move through it, rather than be held captive. No one can change what they are not willing to experience. If you are not experiencing what you want to change, you cannot change a non-experience. The emotions we suppress around a problem, creates momentum for the change to occur. When you watch others, and check in with yourself, you may notice right before a decision is made, there is some sort of emotional spark and build up prior to the decision. For example, if a man is not feeling like having sex, he rarely seeks it out. The feeling of it shows up, the buildup of the sexual energy causes him to decide quicker than without feeling sexual energy. Whether the emotion is positive or negative is irrelevant.

When you move people in to action by solving a problem, your value becomes non-negotiable.

Make a list of questions you can use to engage a problem or challenge.

1.

2.

3.

Example: John, can you tell me what it is like not knowing what to do? And what would happen if this doesn't change? And what is the impact of this issue on you? Family? Finances? Have them describe the feelings associated to this, until you feel it as well.

VISION TO ACTION

Would it be odd to stop talking after the previous step and exit the conversation? It sure would. Now is where you bring the rollercoaster back to the top. Having guided someone in an enrollment conversation, you want to leave them stepping into their future. As you learned to lead yourself and step into your own vision, you now get to do this for others.

Now is the time to build them up and help them lead themselves into their vision. To set a new tone of what is possible. That calls them into this vision, so they will act and experience what they want.

I remember a time when Ali from Colorado, called me about his business and personal life. He was in disarray and overwhelmed with decisions he was facing and a fear of making the wrong one. He was barely surviving in his business and wanted to buy a home as well. In his mind, this would be a powerful step forward to having a wife and family. As a side note, it's interesting to see how men think, "if I get this, then I can have that." And "if this goes well, then everything else will also." Although common, it is also admitting that your vision is too small to have it all. Having a more aligned vision is the breakthrough here.

I asked Ali some "engage the problem" questions and he was able to get clear and let the emotional charge around it out. At that point, I could proceed to the vision to action step. I asked him to share his vision so that it would inspire me and anyone else he was listening to.

This went on for over an hour and something clicked for Ali. He ultimately realized he was chasing linear steps and that one day when he had, x, y and z in place, then he was worthy enough to have a wife and family and could care for them. However, the truth was he just wanted to feel unstoppable. He lacked the feeling of being unstoppable and the momentum to carry through on his decision. It was not about self-worth or even fear.

His vision was "t*o be an unstoppable man of action and create financial prosperity.*" By the time he was done, my bones were aching to go do it for him, that is how enrolled I was. I wanted it for me just as much as he wanted it. That is how you get someone enrolled into their vision, and you don't have to sell anything to them. If you do this right, they will sell themselves for you.

PEOPLE WILL SELL THEMVSELVES ON
WHAT THEY WANT FOR YOU.

I want Ali to create a new vision, a goal that he is excited and passionate about, one he will take a stand for. Until then, can I really help him? If it were a retail client, this approach is also applicable. If a woman comes into my cosmetics store and is unhappy with her eyes. I do want to know if she has an occasion she is preparing for or if this in general is a concern for her. I want to know how she would rather feel. How do you want to feel when you see your eyes in the mirror? I want her to share what she wants to have more than anything; then I can align a product or service to support her.

Make a list of questions that you can use to help someone get enrolled into their vision.

1.
2.
3.

Example: What do you want more than anything? What is your big vision? How do you see yourself accomplishing this goal? Describe what it would feel like if you had accomplished this already.

DECLARE ACTION STEPS

The final step is the ultimate admission of declaring that you own your decision and nothing will stop you. A declaration is a statement starting with **I am**, **I will, or I have.** If the declaration is stated in the present, the statement will be empowering.

When someone is in their vision, it's the best time to move them forward. The way to do that is to have them take a stand and state their declaration out loud. They need to hear it and feel it for themselves and declare it to you and others. This way a public statement is engrained. You can tell yourself all day you are going to do something, and then let yourself off the hook, but when you speak publicly, it takes your statement to a different level.

When the vision is strong enough, the action comes naturally. When the vision is just talk with a bit of passion, action stops people from moving forward and excuses set in.

We want people to take ownership of their decisions. What we are asking is for a decision without the fear and pressure of deciding. When I work with clients, I want them to feel solid, taking actions to solve their problems. If you are a coach, an inspector, plumber, etc. this still applies. Here is an example, "Mr. Jones, all your pipes are clogged, I know this bothers you, but are you willing to give up three days of your time so my team can have full access to your house and fix these pipes for you?"

It is not just about getting a YES, it is about having the other person state what they are willing to do. For example, "Mr. Jones, I have laid out the plan to solve your problems, what would you like to do about this?"

Here are some examples:

"I will show up and create financial prosperity."

"I have decided 100% to kick butt on my vision starting right now."

These are both solid examples of declarations. As you can see, they start with the present moment and demonstrate action and commitment to next steps and a future.

Make a list of questions you can use to support someone in creating their own declarative action statement.

1.

2.

3.

When people make a declaration, they own it. When they say it, it means everything.

The most powerful men I know ask for what they want. They also charge any fee they want. Even their products are priced well. Their beliefs about themselves, their products, and their service is so strong that others buy from them.

The enrollment process takes the sale out of the equation. Your focus is on the betterment of the other person and facilitating a decision. Often the potential new customer or client will decide and ask to buy, or at the very least, inquire about it. Building value leads to this kind of action. In contrast, selling raises red flags.

The difference is, this process is asking clients to move forward, rather than asking to pay us. There is no force or pressure in this process. After you have demonstrated value, it is time to ask for the next step. Ask the person for their next best step.

"Ms. Jones, it's clear we can meet your goals and needs. I have a sense you want to move forward, what is the next step for you right now?"

Give the power to the client and let them decide their next step and they will choose to do business with you.

ASK FOR IT

The reason wealthy and successful people get what they want is they ask for what they want. They are determined and powerful in their ability to ask for what they want. They have no fear of the responses or reactions of others; they are prepared for any response.

Asking is how you call people into action. This entire process is set up for the customer and client to win. Asking is the next step for them to have what they want. Asking is a sign of power and confidence, not greed.

Asking consists of two factors; *how you ask and how connected you are when you ask.* Your energy should be clear, decided and neutral. There is no doubt in your voice, or sketchy energy. It's as simple as, "how would you like to invest?" Create a list of ways to ask for what you want for any situation. I have found that any time I have created value, made an impact or touched someone, asking became natural. Anytime I felt I didn't have an impact, asking became a challenge.

This is not a step to hold back on.

It's easy to confuse "asking for something" with being pushy, greedy, or sounding like a salesman. On the other end of the spectrum, NOT asking for what you want is weak and lacks commitment to your own value. It also sells the other person short of having what they want. Imagine, having the best experience ever on a blind date, then you walk away without asking for a second date? Not only do you not get what you want, neither does she. Enrollment is the same way.

Felling pushy is not an "asking" issue, it's an issue about "how you show up." If you show up as someone who is trying to get something from someone, then it won't matter how you ask. The truth will be felt in your energy. Enrollment is not about something you do to someone, it's about something you do for someone.

The powerful part about asking is it draws the line and the other person can choose to accept it or deny it. If you are operating out of value, you will experience more YES answers than not. If you truly created value and someone says NO, they will be glad. You either helped them or they are not ready to receive the value you provide.

Remember, in your comeback you have to be a fierce lover of providing value, the money will come in avalanches. That means create so much value that supports your customers and clients that they decide to choose you. Convincing or manipulation is not required. If I am committed to creating value, showing concern and commitment to another and they don't want anything to do with me, I move on! Do not stop being who you are because of the choices others make. Do not hold back in the asking, step forward and ask. This is where the fun is you get to move forward and so does the customer or client.

What are all the ways in which you can ask for money? Ask for a sale?

1.

2.

3.

3.

5.

Example: "My fee is $15,000, which credit card would you prefer to use." *Notice I did not use a question mark at the end. It wasn't a question!*

Chapter 17 Notes: Contents for Enrollment: Sell Yourself Rich

» You're on a mission. Only spend time with those that are in alignment with your mission.

» ½ step. Pre-qualify everyone.

» Build stronger rapport. This way you can guide and lead people for the better, and to fulfill your mission.

» Learn to disengage the objections and excuses of others before they come up.

» Discover the readiness of others before proceeding into a sales conversation. Invest where things can become fruitful for both people.

» Remember, most people's decision making muscles are weak.

» Always be ready to discover what motivates, inspires and causes other people pain.

» In order to help people the most, determine the primary need that must be fulfilled.

» Needs are always connected to emotions. Your role is to listen for the unspoken emotion.

» Be courageous enough to engage in the wounds of others.

» By connecting people's vision to action, you can move them along to the next steps. To success, and to purchase your product or service.

» If you ask the right questions, people will sell themselves for you.

» Always leave people making some type of declarative action step.

» Powerful men ask for what they want.

END OF CHAPTER 17 NOTES.

I am with you brother. You got this. Ask for what you want.

Let's move on to chapter 18.

Chapter 18

MILLION DOLLAR JOINT VENTURE PROCESS

If you have a product or service and you want to grow your wealth, there are many other businesses or people who can promote your product or service for you. A simple example of this is when I wrote my first book and had 12 authors promote my book to their database of customers and followers. They did this for free and in return I gave them some of the proceeds of my book. They all agreed to promote my book via email and within one-hour, my book was on the top ten best sellers list on Amazon.

There is a way to get ahead, to get to prosperity faster than you can imagine. Kenny Chesney, a famous country singer, used this approach. Rather than spend years and a lot of money hoping to get to the top, he formed joint ventures with other singers. For his concerts, Kenny invited other well-known performers to appear and sing at his concerts.

This drew even bigger attention to Chesney, it led to bigger crowds. He rose to the top of the charts in a couple of years, he became #1 out of nowhere. Rather than compete with other singers, he aligned with them. They got to perform, he got their audience. It's a win-win.

The airlines do partnerships with other companies and you may not even know they are in a partnership. When you book an airplane reservation online, you are asked if you need the following.

» A rental car

» A hotel

» Theater or amusement park tickets

Have you ever noticed that? Each of these companies have formed partnerships with airlines to get their company included in the sale of airline tickets. If you purchase a rental car, while purchasing an airline ticket, that airline gets a credit for it. Since you are the customer of the airlines, and it's a brand new customer for the car rental company, they share profits. On top of profit-sharing, the car rental company also gets free marketing in front of millions of people who purchase airline tickets.

This is how you get ahead, you don't need Southwest airlines to market you. You just need the right businesses, entrepreneurs or people promoting you to your market that you don't have now.

Partnerships Are The Future

Starting over requires energy and partnerships provide extra energy and channels for your comeback. Partnerships are about collaboration, synergy, and joint efforts that allow both parties to win. If of course, they are utilized correctly. Keep the greed factor out of the equation.

The advantages of your comeback are epic. Here is a brief review of them:

1. **Partnerships.** You get to co-brand with accomplished and successful businesses and/or entrepreneurs who already have a following and establishment. Instead of spending years creating a foundation, you can now be associated with one and generate brand awareness, leads, reputation and sales.
2. **Pathways.** By having an already existing company or entrepreneur promote your product or service, you get an instant sales and marketing channel. It gets in front of thousands of potential customers, with no upfront fee and generates new leads and sales.
3. **Value.** It's a value add to other companies and entrepreneurs. Many businesses have clients with issues they cannot solve. An account-

ing firm will have clients who are grossly disorganized when they send in their books each month. That firm could benefit from your organization and leadership skills. By partnering with them, you get referred to their clients, and the accounting firm gets organized finances from their clients. Any company you can partner with has customers or clients who have problems you can solve, in return, you are adding value to the partnership.

4. **Fast growth.** If your product gets promoted by 50 partners, your business will grow quickly. If you want to launch a book and have 50 authors who have 10,000 email addresses each, they can promote your book to 500,000 people in a month. It would take you years, if at all, to generate that many emails and contacts.
5. **Sustainable results.** With partnerships, you can generate results with a single-hit or as ongoing marketing and promotion campaigns. A client of mine, John Robinson, has collected 800 species of birds on a CD, called Birds of Paradise. He sells the CD on a profit-sharing basis at Costco, Best Buy and other retail stores. John has sold over 2,000 CDs and generated nearly $200,000 in revenue. This is short term and long-term cash flow.

When I consulted with authors of *The Secret,* about launching their book, we created a list of joint venture partners. To generate as many book sales as possible, we needed to market the book on a big scale. In a few months, we rounded up hundreds of joint venture partners. They each committed to marketing their book on a specific day. For 3 months we had 200 partners sending out emails to their database. The total number of emails were close to 600,000.

We sold 20,000 books. Even before all the partners had sent their emails, we had reached the New York Times Best Seller list. This was the first book of many we launched. We could have spent two years trying to sell that many books.

Book or Product Joint Venture

If you have a product or book and you want to accelerate your comeback here is the strategy you can follow.

1. Create a list of all businesses and entrepreneurs who have a database of clients or customers that might have a need for your product or service. This way you can contact them for a joint venture.
2. Decide on a joint venture profit plan ahead of time. The partner will want to be paid on the profit of promoting you. Up to 50% of the cost of the product is the highest I would offer. As long as you break even, who cares? On the back end you can offer that customer more product or service to purchase and you keep 100% of that money. Always share some of the profit to get a lead, new sales and the chance to make even more sales.
3. Contact the potential partner via phone or email and enroll them in a joint venture. Let them know you would like them to become part of your launch.
4. Offer the partner your terms and ask for a date when they can promote you.
5. You may need to negotiate profits and dates. They may ask you if you are willing to promote them in return. The answer is always yes, but, if you are just starting out and are not able to accommodate reciprocation, then offer more profits. Don't be greedy. This is not a one-shot deal, but an overall strategy, don't burn the potential relationship.
6. Put together a mini contract and demonstrate how sales are tracked. Using an email list or a merchant account with an affiliate ID is more than enough.
7. Provide your partner with the marketing materials to use. If they are promoting you, then provide the information they will send to their list. The link that their customers or email list click on is specifically for that partner; no one else uses it.

8. Once sales are in, make sure you pay your partner with documentation of all sales.
9. Reciprocate if that is in your agreement.
10. Duplicate this process with as many partners as you want.

You can launch this with as many partners as you want or with a specific number per month, like 2-3 partners. Either way, it is a long-term and awesome strategy costing nothing upfront.

The Business Awareness Partner

In the past, when business would launch a product or service or have a grand opening, they would do the typical marketing. Fliers, radio, TV, Chamber of Commerce, and so on. Although these are great strategies, what is often better is having other businesses promote you. This strategy gives your partner massive credibility and places your business in front of all their customers.

I did a joint venture with Subway once. Subway has thousands of customers each month. Since I was printing brochure cards and business cards that I would have to hand out or hire someone to, what if Subway handed them out for me with each sandwich?

I offered the owner of Subway the opportunity to put an ad on the back of my brochures and he wouldn't have to pay anything. All I asked of him was to pass them out or place them in the bag of each customer and he agreed.

10 days later, Eugene called me and said, "do you have more cards, we're out?"

Product Placement Joint Venture

A client of mine named Brian and his wife Olivia, were business owners. Brian owned rental properties and laundromats and Olivia created homemade purses and handbags. She didn't know how to get these into the market without spending money on advertising. Her focus was to sell what she had and keep making more.

This joint venture was a slam dunk. I can rattle off thousands of businesses that sell purses and handbags, and a thousand more businesses that women visit and purchase from that do not sell purses and handbags.

I advised her to make a list of all the women visited businesses in her area. At the time she lived in North Carolina. She made a list of 100 businesses. I advised her to call or visit these businesses and ask if they were open to a joint venture and many of them said yes.

Here was the deal we made, Brian and Olivia created a spreadsheet with her product inventory. They allocated a certain number of handbags and purses to be sold at each store that said yes. Along with the price of the bag and the partners profit. If a hand bag costs $30.00 to buy, and $10 to make, there is $20 net profit to work with. A $10 dollar profit to each person is a great deal. It doesn't seem like a lot of profit, does it?

Olivia had 37 stores who offered to place her purses and handbags and she gave them 5 products each. That is 185 products to be sold worth $5,500.00. Minus the cost to make them is $1,850 for a net profit of $3,650. With a 50-50 split, the business and Olivia each walk away with $1,825 per month in sales. Olivia accomplished this by making phone calls from home and stopping by the stores.

Six months later she was earning $5,200- $7,400 per month in profit. At some point she couldn't keep making the handbags and purses herself. It cost her nothing in marketing or advertising. She didn't have to do customer service or sell. She made handbags and found partners to sell them for her.

You can do this with any product because there is always an outlet or channel to tap into where your market already visits. Your job is to list those places and create joint venture partners who want to make extra money offering a product they don't have, while you get to leverage someone else's business for profit. It's a win-win.

Big Brand Joint Venture

Here is the tag along with a big brand joint venture, or big branding. Imagine if a major bank offered your financial app after the completion of opening a new bank account? Or if every book bought at a bookstore offered a pair of reading glasses or bookmark as part of the sale. I am not referring to having a stand with your products next to the register, but working your products into each sale.

In other words, I want to become the secondary purchase people make at big brand stores or with high end entrepreneurs. If each sale they make automatically adds your product to the receipt for a secondary purchase, you get free marketing and sales. For example, if I sell candles and you have a candleholder product, those two go together. I could very easily include your product to be purchased by my customers when they buy my product. Imagine a visitor arrives at my website to buy candles and at check-out they enter their credit card and purchase. On the very next page I include your offer for specialty candle holders. If the customer then decides to buy one, I keep 50% of the revenue and send you 50% of the revenue. It cost you nothing to do this. No time or energy, and you make sales. In fact, you get to promote your product through my company and all its customers. It's a smart and easy revenue for you. Even if your cost is $25 per candleholder and you are making $10 per sale on a $35 sale. Once you do this with multiple companies and are generating a few hundred dollars a day, you're in the money, i fact, it's primarily passive income to you.

Or you can spend most of the first year of your comeback and build up enough visitors to your website and do it yourself, but that is not acceleration. Leverage is king on your comeback.

Joint Venture Mindset

The possibility for partnerships are everywhere. Those who can leverage other's databases to grow their businesses faster and generate capital quicker. Your mindset around this is important. The joint venture process I outlined above is simple. Anyone can do that, but not everything sees the multitude of joint ventures available to them.

Think of a mutual beneficial relationship, both parties benefit and utilize one another's strengths. When the two come together and promote each other for profits on the backend, everyone wins, or everyone walks away with mutual opportunities. I want you thinking about a few things, so you can see where joint ventures may exist for you already.

Who is your primary market and what businesses already have them as clients? If you're walking down the street and notice there is a line outside of a video game store, that just happens to have your target market, start thinking about how you can leverage that video game store for your benefit. If your target market is the millennial market or even 40-year-old virgins, you have a chance to tap into what someone else already created.

If you offer an online backup storage program, then there is a perfect opportunity for a joint venture. If you sell kids shoes, that may also be an opportunity. Even if you are a dentist that may be a good fit. Kids eat sugar, while playing video games, right?

Make the connection between your market and who already has your market, then you can begin to discover if your product is a fit for a joint venture promotion. Instagram does this very well, followers with large lists, share posts or offers from other people that sell a product. Entrepreneurs with large email lists do this as well. You have probably received emails from people promoting someone else's work, success, or products. That is a joint venture using email marketing.

It is important to make a list of all the businesses on and offline that may have your market's attention. Make this list as big as you can and as you begin to contact businesses on the list, one will for sure say yes. In fact, many are already doing joint ventures and surprisingly, many don't know joint ventures exist at all.

Make the commitment to reach out to them every day. Start with the businesses that are savvier or marketing conscious because they are most likely to say yes. You also want to ensure your product or service is a match for your partners business. Meaning their customers have a need and the business does not fulfill that need. Unless you have already existing connections to big brands, avoid them for now; that is a dream down the road.

If you sell a cleaning product and you want to joint venture with a dry cleaner, this can work if the dry cleaners don't have competing products. If you sell maid services, you can partner with handymen, construction workers, and plumbers, if they do not provide any of those services or have other partners already. What you offer needs to fill a void or a problem the customer has that the business does not already solve.

Do not try to convince a joint venture partner that your product or service is better. No one is going to promote their competition. Make sure your product or service *benefits* your partner, that it is an add on and does not compete or take away from their business. You want to fill a void or solve a problem with their customers, not create a new one for your partner.

Once you make that list you need to act on it. Remember, all you are asking for is a mutually beneficial relationship. If you can generate ten new partners in the next month or even 100 over the next year, the impact will be significant.

Chapter 18 Notes: Million Dollar Joint Venture Process

» Partnerships are the future.

» Partnerships allow you to cobrand with already successful businesses.

» Partnership provide a pathway that can accelerate your success.

» You can use partnerships to promote your book or product to already existing customers, rather than create your own.

- » Always create mutual terms and conditions with your partners.
- » Remember, always give up a percentage of profits in return for free marketing.
- » If a partner promotes my services for free, and I generate $10,000 from that, I am happy to give up $5,000 for it. It cost me nothing.
- » The joint venture mindset is important. It is about a win-win relationship.
- » Joint ventures are about solving problems and adding value to other companies.
- » You can do joint ventures with anyone.
- » On your first joint venture make sure you do it with someone who already knows how.
- » Always look for ways to add value to other businesses.

END OF CHAPTER 18 NOTES.

I am with you brother. You got this. Go forth and conquer.

Let's move on to chapter 19.

Chapter 19

SETBACK, NOW FORWARD

As much as men love to figure out life, to live in the "now," there is always a mystery to it. Bumps in the road, setbacks, successes, and failures are unavoidable. What you make of it is what really matters. Some men get stronger when they are knocked down, some don't. You get to choose to be the man you know yourself to be and no one can take that away from you.

To fully engage in all you do, with all you are, is what will make the difference in your comeback. It is not the end for you when the setback happened and it's not the end for you when you comeback from it all. Life continues to evolve and grow. The men that are accomplished, on purpose, and satisfied with it all are those who stay fully engaged in the process.

You are not alone; one of the most profound things I discovered in my life was that I wasn't alone. Even though I spent a lot of time working and less time at parties, I always felt like something was taking care of me, that something was watching out for me. The evidence of that was surreal. A new and approved credit card would show up exactly when I needed it. Someone would call me or walk into me at the store with the answer I was searching for. Something would happen that appeared random only to discover later that it was set up perfectly for me to win. I was always one phone call away from a friend or colleague willing to offer support.

Be The Difference

The critical difference for me, when I decided a comeback was in order, was to reach out and implement everything I shared with you in previous chapters.

I began calling my resources, I started with committing to a vision. I meditated every day and listened for my why. Each day it percolated within me, until I could no longer hold back and pursued my dreams relentlessly.

As part of that I made phone calls to very important people in my life; my closest friends asking for their support. Once my vision was clear to me and I was enrolled, asking for support became a simple must and needless to stay my friends and colleagues were thrilled.

My closest friend Meeks said, "what the hell have you been waiting for?"

I then put an action plan together, mainly the integration of each assignment in this book. It was my daily study and routine. I stayed the course and locked on. I knew nothing was going to stop me and a newly found level of relaxing into the process came over me.

In my calendar was sixty minutes per day of focus on my plan, followed up with 90 minutes or radical action on my plan. In the back of my mind I kept hearing this voice, "You could have done this all along." Although it was true. At any given moment in time I could have rebuilt anything I wanted to, but I didn't. I needed to go through the pain and suffering of a setback and an epic failure, to deepen my identity.

Accountability is key, only weak men dislike accountability. I was to report to each of my closest friends, by 5pm every Friday. If it didn't follow up and complete my commitment, I had to pay each of them $1,000.00.

I didn't miss one action item so they received no money from me. This is where the magic happens. How committed are you to your comeback? If you're willing to go for it, then you are willing to put things on the line.

Most men believe in themselves, to a point. A $1,000.00 accountability fee will stop many men. Whether you have the money or not, isn't relevant. That money represents how well you take on challenges or how well you honor them.

Be the man who honors his commitments. Plain and simple, those who do get results. Those who don't, end up wishing, hoping and praying for results and that won't cut it. In fact, it hurts even more to not honor things. Albeit safer and more comforting, but comfort is what the doctor gives you before you die. It's not a place to live!

COMFORT IS WHAT THE DOCTOR GIVES YOU BEFORE YOU DIE ITS NOT A PLACE TO LIVE.

Accountability destroys comfort at first, but then it becomes the norm. It is through accountability that true production occurs. Then you will realize with accountability, you step into your greatness and that becomes your new daily experience.

You At The Center

You are the center of your universe, you are resourceful enough to make anything happen. You have unlimited resources, some are easy to tap into, but some are more challenging. Recently, a friend of mine called me to borrow $500, I laughed at him because I was expecting him to ask for $5,000, which I happily would have paid.

Before giving him the money I challenged him. I challenged him about why he is in the position of needing money. He gave me tons of excuses and reasons, but I was asking what within him created this situation. When he could not answer, I reminded him that no amount of money would break this pattern. I also asked him why he would ask me for $500 when he needs $8,000? He said he was afraid to ask, which gave me insight into why he is not doing well financially. The courage and willingness to ask for what you need is often why men don't take advantage of the resources, let alone see them. Fear of asking will cause the mind to avoid looking for resources at all.

You know the phrase, "don't be that guy?" I would love to tell you not to be, if I could prove telling you that it works, but, I cannot. Be willing to have the courage to tap into those resources, it's your universe and those resources exist for you and your path. Not tapping into this vast resource is basically telling the universe not to conspire on your behalf.

Think of your comeback like your baby, you want to protect, nurture, and give it your fullest attention. You will be faced with new decisions frequently, decisions about who to spend time with, how to invest your time, and if you have set the steps to your comeback in the right order. It will be a series of yes and no decisions. Your only role is to acquire the assets needed for your comeback in this moment so don't be foolish. Just because you may need a lot and some assets don't work out, it does not mean you cannot continue acquiring what you need.

List those assets out on paper is critical, as is the sequence of the list you are acquiring. This way you have the right assets at the right time. Remember, getting stuck on one asset or acquiring it, does not mean you cannot keep moving forward. They may not come to you in the exact order you have listed, but as long as you keep pursuing them you will get them.

This mentality also refers to people, you need to surround yourself with those who can support your vision and are willing to check-in about your vision. You only need to demonstrate confidence and decisiveness to fully get the resources you need.

An Extra Edge:

I remember my first office manager Tamura, she was unique. The first time I was introduced to her was over the phone through a client and she peaked my interest. She was amazing and handled my life and business well. One day she told me, "the universe will help you." I laughed and said, "when did you become a hippie?" Later she revealed to me how intuitive and psychic she was, and I laughed again.

Today Tamura is a well-known intuitive medical woman and is no joke. Years later, she was only showing up to work because she loved me and was also hiding out, afraid to take the leap to go out on her own. A few days later someone called my office hoping to speak with her. He was a CEO of a wellness center in Australia. He heard her participate in a conference call with me and loved her energy.

Six months later, Tamura was in Australia, in love with a new man, and up and running in her new business with the CEO who asked her to be a partner.

"Conspiring with the universe." I never really relied or trusted anything to do it for me, however, aligning myself and having faith, turned out to be the best way to empower myself.

Everything is a vibration, when you focus on what you want and generate feelings for it, those feelings are experienced as a vibe. The universe works through vibration, thoughts and feelings are all vibrations. You can easily detect this when someone is glowing or smiling, and you say, "that person has good vibes." What you are experiencing is that person's thoughts and feelings magnified to a high degree, so much so, you can experience that person's energy.

If you are not finding the resources you need, it is often because your vibration is scarce. If you feel like you "have to find money," or "nothing good is happening" is a sign you are resisting the available money and good things from happening. Also, you can only meet and attract the people who are similar to your vibe. If you want an investor to invest into your future business when your vibe is, "I need this to save my ass," you may not be the most attractive to an authentic investor, but you will be attractive to an investor who is greedy, wants to save you and negotiate you down as well. Do you see how that works?

You do not need to analyze this, just feel into it and trust. If you want filet mignon and the universe keeps giving you beef tacos, it is not the universe that got it wrong. To lock in on this point, take a minute answer the following questions yes or no.

1. Have you ever experienced a day in your life without gravity?
2. Have you ever experiences a day in your life where the earth stopped rotating?
3. Have you ever experienced a day in your life where the sun did not shine?
4. Have the oceans that make up most of our planet, ever been still all at the same time?
5. Has the moon not orbited around the earth?
6. Did the law of lift suddenly fail and every plane failed to take off?
7. Did the law of speed, momentum, and velocity cease to exist ever in your life?

The universe my friend, always works and it has never failed. It cannot fail as it was not created by man, only man is subject to failure.

Now the analytical or skeptics reading this might say, "what about hurricanes? Isn't that a failure?" Hurricanes are not an operational law of the universe. One might argue that he has not seen the sun in 5 days, its been overcast and rainy, it didn't come out?" No knucklehead, the sun is out, just because you cannot see it does not mean the sun suddenly stopped existing.

Let's be clear, the universe is always seeking to meet your aspirations. The only damn reason these laws exist and constantly work is so you can have the life you want. Can you imagine if the universe woke up tomorrow, like some men do, and said, "I don't feel like gravity today, the hell with it?"

You would have bought this book in California and by the time you were done with it, you would be in Tokyo somewhere, if not Pluto. Wake up brother. Thinking the universe doesn't have your back or that you are going through life alone is what's keeping things hard for you.

The universe is also very funny, it sends the perfect woman to your life at the worst time and during your best times; you cannot seem to find a date. Why? Just to keep you humble and honest.

I used to race Dune Buggies with my brother. The dunes were amazing, and I found it especially remarkable I could ride one dune after another, but still, no dune was the same. You had to ebb and flow with what mother nature presented you.

We rode in the hot dunes for hours and stopped only to let the buggies rest and avoid over heating them. Then we would ride back over the same dunes to get back to camp. This time my big brother looked at me and said, "You're up, take us home."

As we rode the dunes, heading back was like a jigsaw puzzle written in Chinese. Nothing looked familiar, it was like someone changed the dunes and didn't tell us. I miscalculated half the slopes, then bottomed out in a hole, called a witch eye. Then later, as one thing led to another, I drove up a hill only to discover a cliff at the top. Suddenly I was in midair. When we landed my brother wasn't pleased. I was sure he was about to yell at me.

He said, "welcome to Mother Nature, she changes hour by hour. The wind comes through and blows the sand, reshaping the mountains. Never, ever disrespect Mother Nature, you won't win. If you respect her, you can flow with her and let her guide you, instead of becoming pompous about what a great driver you are."

Chapter 19 Notes: Setback, Now Forward

» You're not alone. Many have experienced the same setback and failures as you have. Join forces with those who have made their comeback.

» Be the difference you want to make in the world.

» This is not about finding comfort. Comfort is what the doctor gives you before you die. It's not a place to live.

- Protect your comeback like a baby. Do not allow any distraction, temptations or fear based people in your space.
- The universe always has your back. Conspire with it.
- The universe is always seeking to meet your needs.
- Always be respectful of the process.

END OF CHAPTER 19 NOTES.

Chapter 20

IT'S TIME TO ACT

Now that you have reached this far in the book it is time to stand and deliver greatness, it's time to act.

I have found that 90 minutes per day of radical action, produces far better results, productivity and momentum than grinding for hours a day. I wrote this book in one month at about 90 minutes per day. There were days when I did blocks of time, but it was always between one and two hours. I have never found locking myself up in a hotel for a weekend produced more.

The most powerful CEO's spend 90 minutes per day, day in and day out in radical productivity mode. Are there times when they may need to spend more time in a day? Absolutely! That is a given, but I do not believe that leads to long term results, nor have I seen anyone sustain grinding days for long periods of time. I despise Instagram pictures that constantly promote hustle and grinding. Even a body builder doesn't grind hours a day! A gymnast and boxer may spend 8-12 hours per day grinding, but that is for a specific event, coupled with 4 weeks or more of rest after the event.

Life and business is a nonstop journey, they require an ebb and flow. There are times of struggle, but the struggle is *in* you and it *is* you. Unlike a boxer, who may struggle in rounds 2, 6 and 10, he cannot walk away and regroup. He has to stay in the grind and fight his way through. There are times in life where you may have to do this too, but that is not day in and day out experiences. If for some reason that is the case, you may want to check in and ask yourself if you really love what you are doing.

In the past half-century, the rule of success was graduate high school and get a job, better yet go to college, earn a degree then get a job, with benefits and fill up your 401K plan. If you do then you can have a family and a house and once you can work until 55, pay off your debt and retire rich!

That lie was shattered in the first decade of the 21st century and now, we have gone to the opposite end of the spectrum. People can exit the rat race, build wealth faster and make a masterpiece out of their life.

Someone intelligent once said to me, "we have created such a busy world, yet we are still unproductive. We have created better ways to communicate, yet have less intimacy and human connection. We have more roads, but we still don't' get where we want to go on time. We have more access to information, and yet we're no more enlightened today then we were a decade ago." I couldn't agree more.

Action without purpose is stressful and action just to look busy is a cover-up. We keep employees at work all day, even after they've accomplished their goals. A few years ago, a VP of a medical clinic called to discuss his customer service team. He mentioned they didn't understand why they had to stay at work if their productivity was high and they finished their roles and responsibilities for the day. His view was because the company was paying them to be present.

I told him he was wrong and I went on to explain he was paying them to produce – and they are. If you pay them to be present, you are paying to babysit them. People who have accomplished something should be sent home. How awesome is it that his team can produce results in less than 8 hours? He could become the leader in his industry and have more people wanting to work for him if he changed how he thought about productivity and accomplishment.

Two years later he was voted the best clinic to work for and best customer service in San Diego.

You must not fool yourself on this journey, not ever! You can lie to yourself to feel better, but if you speak the truth regardless of how it feels, you gain control over yourself and get on top of the situation. Be the man willing to feel short-term discomfort and trade that in for long-term freedom. Most men avoid short-term pain and so, rarely feel free.

Ignorance is not a value. Some men like to inflate their illusions, so they don't have to feel the pain, mainly to avoid reality. I am asking you to take that reality on regardless of how it may feel, because once you feel reality, the pain and fear begins to break down. Fear likes to hide, but reality likes to be seen. Once it is seen, fear dissolves and loves magnifies. You win!

I am all about you winning, but that can only be done living in reality.

Chapter 20 Notes: It's Time to Act

» 90 minutes per day of radical action is what is required for your comeback.

» Do no fool yourself on this journey. It is a journey. There is no destination.

» Do not confuse knowledge with application. You may know it, but until you act, knowledge is not the answer.

» It is time for you to be all about winning.

END OF CHAPTER 20 NOTES.

I am with you brother. Now is your time.

Let's move on to chapter 21.

Chapter 21

PUT IT ON THE LINE!

JAMES WAS 22 YEARS OLD and had been dreaming of building a $1 million-dollar company. While discussing how I could help him meet his goals, I made it clear that it is only through commitment that one can achieve anything significant.

Men talk a big game, but when it comes time to put it on the line, feelings can change. If they do change in a way that causes you to hold back from your commitment, we have a challenge to deal with in order for the one million to become realized. If you win the challenge, you're closer to the $1 million. If you deny it and still try, you may fail. I won't sugar coat it, you may say you're committed and the moment difficulty comes up, if you fade away, it's a lie. Through and through.

There is a standard to be set and to adhere to, men must have a code to live by or flip flop through life.

Would you hesitate? Would you hold back when it came time to put it on the line? Or would you declare what you want anywhere, anytime?

I told James I needed to feel his commitment and he needed to hear it. Can you imagine standing on the table at a restaurant stating to everyone, "I will become a seven-figure income earner in the next 18 months?"

Guess what? James did just that. I wish you could have seen the look on people's face.

People whispered, "Is he on drugs?" "why do I care?" "who is this guy?" The truth is, it does not matter what they had to say. Most people are asleep and have no clue that while in a restaurant that others around them have dreams, destinies, and a purpose to live -- all of which does not stop while eating food. I eat to feed my dreams, not mess around with fillers.

This declaration makes it real, James put it on the line and that is power! Unabashed, unyielding, and unwavering commitment to his goal and I was inspired by him. When he sat back down I said, "let's get to work," With that, I was **enrolled.**

What does put it on the line mean?

1. ***You need to buy into your commitment, either in your statement to others or financially.*** Your skin must be in the game. You can't let yourself off the hook to get what you want.
2. ***You need to make clear to others what you are up to.*** Those around you can support your new comeback vision. The more of the right people you have enrolled in your vision, the more successful you will become. The more people you have committed to *seeing* you successful, the more you will become successful.
3. ***Speak and act with complete knowingness that what you want will happen.*** Hold this idea so strongly that you believe fully that what you want is exactly what will happen. As you grow stronger with this idea it becomes an embodiment. Nothing will shake you from this, absolutely nothing.

I remember a time when I put it all on the line. A client of mine, who became my wife, made a major mistake at my expense. During a weekend of huge financial success, a best-selling book launch and getting engaged, she crushed me when I had everything on the line. It was the weekend of June 2007, my daughter was nearly 1 year old, and I was high on life. We were in Los Angeles doing a 2-day seminar with about 300 people. We had just launched a New York Time Best Seller and it was selling like hot cakes.

I led the entire 2-day weekend generating over $550,000 in sales. The day after this event I held a millionaire coaches training with millionaire coaches for 3 days. During our weekend, we had several hundreds of people attend a book party in a fancy restaurant. I was asked by her assistant to give a toast and a prayer. I had announced after the prayer that she and I were getting married and my love for her and her work. I unloaded my heart and how much I loved the kids and what we were creating together.

I introduced her to the stage and she thanks her family, staff and public relations team. She spoke for about 15 minutes and I remember standing in the middle of the group, at a table watching. I was so happy for her.

Then the moment came. "and most of all I want to thank.... MYSELF for all my hard work." The group laughed, she laughed, and even I laughed as I thought it was a joke. Then she said, "let's eat."

I stood in the middle of the room shrinking on the inside; I could feel my heartbeat and this crushing feeling coming over me. Meanwhile, the group knew who I was, and people began to turn their heads at me. What could I do? If I broke down, it wouldn't look good, if I leave like I am upset, that would create a drama. Or I could carry on like nothing had happened and people think I was just faking it.

I was the elephant in the room. I turned around to the standing table behind me and noticed I was the only one at the table and that wasn't odd! After I said "Hi" to a few people and acknowledged how fun tonight was, I escaped gracefully to the bathroom. She (for contract reasons, I cannot say her name) stopped me before I reached the door of the men's room. She said, "are you okay, what is wrong?" As if she didn't know. She knew first-hand what happened.

The next day she said, "I feel bad." Yet she did not apologize. Our life was fast paced, the next day her and my daughter left for another speaking engagement. A few hours later, a bouquet of flowers arrived with a card apologizing for it.

The last thing a guy wants are flowers! This was not the first time, but I put it all on the line and got crushed for it publicly.

I share this with you because if I was sitting on the sidelines and not being thanked, then that would be a wakeup call that I have to get my ass off the sidelines.

I realized that because I put it on the line, I had won in so many ways.

RISK

The hardest thing in my life was never being in the game. Winning, losing, failing, being rejected or feeling unworthy was not difficult. It was sitting on the sidelines, watching the very game I wanted to play, get played by everyone else, but me. Watching others succeed, while I was stuck in my own stuff, was far more difficult than the game itself.

Until you get back in the game, things may seem incredibly challenging at first. Putting it on the line seems risky. Conversely, when you are fully in the game and doing well, not putting it on the line may seem risky. Risk is always seen from a place of where you are now. If you have $10,000 in the bank, spending all that on marketing seems risky, but, if you have $100,000 in the bank spending 10% of that seems easy.

Whatever your financial situation is, the potential challenges and your emotions around it are still the same. You just *feel* better if you lose $10,000 and have $90,000 left. You are getting what you want and honoring your word is what is most important.

The ultimate risk may not be financial. I believe the biggest risk we face is the ***emotions*** around what we want. Men invest too much into their emotions when taking the leap than we do in risking our emotions for love, intimacy, and romance. The risk is you don't want to feel something that you think will be uncomfortable.

Your emotional investment, whether it's positive or negative is equivalent to what you get back. The more you invest in your emotional self, the more you get back. This is full engagement as we discussed earlier in this book. With each emotional investment, you get a release and experience freedom. Here you can get what you want in return for your willingness to keep yourself big. Holding back your emotion is playing small, in fact, it sends the message as the brand who represents himself that you are unable to handle your own emotions.

Without emotions, you are as good as dead, but with emotions, you never die. No one ever has been so badly hurt from putting their emotions on the line and owning them. I can tell you that liberation as a man, requires you put it on the line, because your life experience is all that matters. You cannot experience life fully without putting your emotions and intentions on the line.

Chapter 22

YOUR INVITATION TO JOIN ME

www.CarlLogrecco.com

Every month a group of dynamic men, entrepreneurs and fathers, meet with me at my home or throughout California. Our goal is simple, to architect a masterful comeback.

It's for men only. We tackle the 3 most important things about modern men. "How we solve problems, how we relate to ourselves as modern men and how we approach the world."

Times have changed, the rules for men have changed and a new framework for men to embody power, purpose, and productivity, while maintaining freedom is in order. I have built such a framework for these men and each month we tackle the framework and integrate it into our lives.

We focus on 4 main areas of our lives as men.

Our Body: Bio hacking and bio masculine engineering, unleashes unlimited power and passion in our bodies so we can manifest our purpose, on demand.

Our Purpose: Cracking the Heart Code is a top ten life experience and for men that help them discover, reveal and take ownership of their purpose. I have a protocol called **Accessing the Divine Masculine**

Matrix. It's a series of experiences combined with 5 questions that your mind cannot answer, only your heart can. In two and half days, men discover their purpose and begin building their life around it.

Our Business: The Automated Man is a business process designed to set up men to FUND and FUEL their lifestyle through financial profits. By utilizing this framework, men can leverage their time, create more profits and become highly productive, *without sacrificing and grinding their way in a hamster wheel.*

Our Legacy: Mastering the Art & Science of Love, Sensuality and Fatherhood. Men discover a framework to enjoy more freedom, appreciation and respect with the feminine energy and their children.

I invite you to go to my website, www.CarlLogrecco.com and reserve a 30 minute conversation with me.

During this time together we will discuss:

1. What caused your setback?
2. Where are you stuck?
3. What is your new vision?
4. What is the best comeback plan?

The call is free. If you are willing to have an open conversation, to look at reality, then I can help. If you want to resurrect your passion, love life or relationships, there is a plan for that.

If you want to start, restart or grow your business there is a plan for that.

If you want more money, wealth or financial freedom, there is a plan for that.

There is a plan for anything, as long as you can be real with me. I can show you how to architect your masterful comeback.

Give yourself the chance, book the time with me at

www.CarlLogrecco.com

I look forward to seeing you soon. Thank you for giving me a chance to guide you along this journey through Setback, Now Forward.

All the best,

Coach Carl

CPSIA information can be obtained
at www.ICGtesting.com
Printed in the USA
LVHW04s0727180918
590464LV00005B/5/P

9 781628 655414